GLOBALISATION

Anthropology, Culture and Society

Series Editors:
Professor Thomas Hylland Eriksen, University of Oslo
Dr Katy Gardner, University of Sussex
Dr Jon P. Mitchell, University of Sussex

RECENT TITLES

GLOBALISATION

Studies in Anthropology

Edited by
THOMAS HYLLAND ERIKSEN

Pluto Press
LONDON • STERLING, VIRGINIA

First published 2003
by PLUTO PRESS
345 Archway Road, London N6 5AA
and 22883 Quicksilver Drive,
Sterling, VA 20166–2012, USA

www.plutobooks.com

British Library Cataloguing in Publication Data
A catalogue record for this book is available from
the British Library

ISBN 0 7453 2060 0 hardback
ISBN 0 7453 2059 7 paperback

Library of Congress Cataloging in Publication Data
Globalisation : studies in anthropology / edited by Thomas Hylland
Eriksen.
       p. cm. — (Anthropology, culture, and society)
Includes bibliographical references.
   ISBN 0–7453–2060–0 (hbk) — ISBN 0–7453–2059–7 (pbk)
   1. Anthropology. 2. Globalization. 3. Law and anthropology. I.
Eriksen, Thomas Hylland. II. Series.
   GN27 .G56 2003
   301—dc21

                                                    2003007062

10   9   8   7   6   5   4   3   2   1

Designed and produced for Pluto Press by
Chase Publishing Services, Fortescue, Sidmouth EX10 9QG
Typeset from disk by Stanford DTP Services, Towcester
Printed and bound in the European Union
by Antony Rowe, Chippenham and Eastbourne, England

CONTENTS

ACKNOWLEDGEMENTS

Most of the chapters that make up this book are based on papers presented at the workshop 'Transnational Flows: Methodological and epistemological issues', Oslo, 6–7 June 2001. The workshop was organised by the research project Transnational Flows of Substances and Concepts, which is directed by Marianne E. Lien and supported financially by the Norwegian Research Council in the period 2001–04.

Chapter 2 is adapted from the introduction to a book edited by Ulf Hannerz. Published only in Swedish (and entitled *Flera fält i ett*) the book showcases the breadth and scope of current transnational multi-sited research at the Department of Social Anthropology at Stockholm University. The references to Hannerz's Stockholm colleagues generally refer to chapters in the book, and offer an insight into some of the accomplishments made, and some of the methodological problems encountered, in this pioneering research environment.

1 INTRODUCTION

Thomas Hylland Eriksen

Although the term 'globalisation' has been common in anthropology and neighbouring disciplines only since around 1990, it has spawned an impressive range of books, journal articles and academic conferences. In the mid-1990s, it actually seemed more difficult to find a major sociology or social anthropology conference that did *not* feature the word prominently in its programme, than to find one that did.

In spite of the flurry of interdisciplinary activity around the term 'globalisation', the need for new studies will not go away until the phenomena they describe disappear. Moreover, there still remains necessary work to be done on the conceptual and methodological basis of globalisation studies. As can only be expected of a research field that has grown too fast, globalisation studies have yet to be connected properly to the disciplines and intellectual traditions they have sprung from. In the case of social anthropology, there has been a tendency to emphasise the *newness* of globalisation studies. The obligatory contrast to Malinowski's fieldwork is perhaps drawn, some remarks are made about the interconnectedness of everything, the hybridity of cultural identities and the irrelevance of what we may perhaps call the 'quadruple S' (synchronous single-society study) – but rarely do we see a sustained attempt to show the continuities between current research on globally embedded networks and mainstream twentieth-century anthropology.

Perhaps for the sake of argument, it can be tempting to highlight and pick on statements and positions that are as far removed from one's own as possible. This approach, perhaps underpinned by selected quotations, may offer striking and convincing contrasts between contemporary work and functionalism or structural-functionalism in Britain, and some of the dominant post-Boas schools in the USA, such as culture-and-personality and Geertzian hermeneutics. However, closer examination more often than not reveals that many of the problems grappled with today (flows, ambiguities, relativity of boundaries, etc.) were by no means foreign to earlier

1

generations of anthropologists. The contrasts are not spurious, but they need not be exaggerated.

The approach of this book does not, in other words, consist in advertising the newness of globalisation research. Rather, I will devote most of this introduction to arguing that the new empirical domains belong, in important ways, to the mainstream of anthropological research. Of course, we do not wish to argue that nothing has changed. The contemporary world is one of global embeddedness, ubiquitous rights movements and reflexive identity politics, universal capitalism and globally integrated financial markets, transnational families, biotechnology and urbanisation; in a word, it is in substantial ways different from the world in which twentieth-century anthropology developed. It is a trivial fact that this must be reflected in research agendas. The question that we find it pertinent to raise concerns the implications of shifts in empirical concerns for theory and methodology. In order to begin to answer it, I now turn to an attempt to anchor studies of transnational processes to the mainstream in twentieth-century anthropology, showing eventually at which crucial junctions the present must depart from the past.

ANTHROPOLOGICAL LINEAGES

If the word is recent, the concerns that animate research on globalisation, or transnational flows, are not. The affinity between globalisation and early twentieth-century diffusionism is sometimes remarked upon (e.g. Barnard, 2000: 168), thus placing one of the latest fads in academia firmly in a lineage few are eager to see themselves as part of. The shortcomings of classic diffusionism – speculation about a patchily known past, poor contextualisation – can nevertheless easily be overcome in studies of contemporary transnational flows, provided the methodology is sound.

A less common, but hardly less relevant parallel can be drawn to evolutionism. Since studies of globalisation always engage with some notion of modernity and some notion of its spreading out from a centre to peripheries, they seem to share fundamental assumptions with the cultural evolutionists of Victorian anthropology. The appropriation of Western modes of production and consumption, Western rights concepts and notions of personhood, appears inevitable and irreversible, though with important local contextualisations and variations. Studies of transnational flows that move in the opposite direction, which lead to the 'orientalisation of the West', to use one of Marshall McLuhan's sphinx-like phrases, are few and far between, and it may be tempting to conclude, Fukuyama-like, that the reason is, simply, that non-Westerners cannot compete with the persuasive power and institutional strengths of Western culture in its many guises. Whether Western or not, empirical work on globalisation does little to counter claims that this body of research largely deals with the dissemination and recontextualisation of, and resistance to, modernity. This is not tantamount to admitting that globalisation is Westernisation. Anthropology's strength lies, among other things, in making the world a more complex place and revealing the nooks and crannies of seemingly straightforward, linear historical change. The original critique of unilinear evolutionism thus still holds good, and is echoed in several of the chapters in this book. The assumption that globalisation has something to do with modernity or modernities, on the other hand, is not challenged.

The two most obvious lineages for globalisation studies, then – diffusionism and cultural evolutionism – were for most of the twentieth-century among the least fashionable theoretical frameworks in anthropology. To these sources of dubious merit we may add that globalisation studies have received important inspiration from general sociological theory (e.g. Castells, 1996; Giddens, 1990), macrohistory (e.g. Wallerstein, 1974) and media studies (e.g. McLuhan, 1964). A consideration of these historical contexts for the field makes it easy to understand why globalisation studies have been regarded as something of a stepchild in anthropology by some prominent practitioners of the discipline, not to say an embarrassment. The scope as well as the substance of globalisation seems to represent everything that a good social anthropologist should be wary of: grand comparisons often underpinned by flimsy evidence, whimsical and eclectic methodologies, a fondness for sweeping generalisations and, hovering in the background, the spectre of evolutionism. Admittedly, the most blatant generalisations usually come from non-anthropologists, but guilt by association is never far away in an era when Bauman, Beck, Castells and Giddens are second only to Bourdieu in the pantheon of social theory. Quite unlike what the advocates of globalisation research claim, the trend, viewed in this perspective, seems to be anything but avant-garde. Fundamental achievements of twentieth-century anthropology – the primacy of the local, the sophistication of field methods and the unanimous rejection of evolutionism – seem to have been momentarily forgotten by the many anthropologists keen to understand linkages and connections in the modern world.

With these sometimes fully justified objections or prejudices in mind, it is a task of paramount importance to show that globalisation studies not only matter empirically, but also that there is no necessary contradiction between twentieth-century anthropological methodology and studies of transnational flows. I shall now proceed to show that the continuity between classic anthropology and the anthropology of globalisation is much more pronounced than commonly assumed, both by its defenders and by its detractors. First of all, however, we need to get rid of the word itself.

TRANSNATIONAL FLOWS

If the rapid ascent of the term 'globalisation' has been something of a *succès de scandale*, making it a password in some milieux and a four-letter word in others, the explanation is partly that it is a promiscuous and unfaithful word engaging in a bewildering variety of relationships, most of which would be better off using more accurate concepts. If economic globalisation refers to the increasing transnational character of production, marketing and transactions, and cultural globalisation refers to the increasing irrelevance of distance (see Giddens, 1990, on disembedding mechanisms), then the recent widespread and often uncritical use of the word has give it misleading connotations. First, although there are doubtless aspects of social organisation and symbolic universes in virtually every society that conform with these notions of globalisation – statehood and citizenship, monetary economies, modern mass media and so on – their actual realisation is always local and embedded in locally constituted life-worlds and power relations. Second, the term globalisation obfuscates the concrete and bounded nature of many of the flows of exchange and communication that turn the world simultaneously into a larger and a smaller place. *Commoditisation* is often seen as a typical aspect of globalisation – politics are commoditised in identity politics; social relations are commoditised through the (IMF and World Bank-aided) global spread of market logic, and globalisation is often seen as a function of neo-liberalism. Although it is true that the term rose to fame in the same period – the 1990s – as neo-liberalism became the hegemonic world ideology, globalisation is of course much older, more diverse and ideologically more ambiguous than this view would allow.

Partly because of its strong ideological connotations, most of the contributors to this book find it relevant to talk of their empirical material in terms of *transnational flows* rather than globalisation. Whether it is ideas or substances that flow, or both, they have origins and destinations, and the flows are instigated by people. The ideational and institutional framework of the flows may be 'placeless' or global in principle (the Internet is, and so are the Universal Declaration of Human Rights, the dominance of Microsoft software and the global salmon market), but their instantiation necessarily involves situated agents and delineated social contexts. This way of re-focusing of the research object is typical of anthro-pological reconceptualisations of grand theories and, in this case, it responds to the methodological problems associated with diffu-sionism and evolutionism. Instead of *assuming* the existence of global processes, the contributors to this book follow their informants and their cultural production wherever they go. When Marianne Lien writes about the connections between Finnmark fisheries and Japanese business, it is not because that relationship is of intrinsic interest, but because this entanglement has become an important part of the local. And when Karen Fog Olwig describes the creation of place among migrants from Nevis in far-flung places in the USA and Europe, it is not necessarily because she is interested in movement as such, but because she is committed to a long-term ethnographic project dealing with Nevisians, whose social worlds cannot be physically encircled by the shores of Nevis itself. Christian Krohn-Hansen, similarly, discovered that in order to complete his ethnographic endeavour in the Dominican Republic he would have to do fieldwork in New York City. Quite clearly, the 'non-places' famously described by Augé (1995), are saturated with symbolic meanings to the people who engage with them, although their 'objective' meaning may be opaque because they mean different things to different people (see Hannerz's chapter). If we consider Appadurai's (1996) proposed fields of significance – ethnoscapes, technoscapes, ideoscapes and so on – it is also clear that they are only brought into being in so far as people invest them with content, that they are only activated through social processes.

The point may seem trivial, yet it is easily overlooked if one sees 'the global' as a kind of Hegelian world spirit looming above and beyond human lives. The global only exists to the extent that it is being created through ongoing social life.

The fact that social worlds engage with wider systems is, of course, not new; it is not even a new concern for anthropology. Notwith-standing the orthodoxies of late Victorian anthropology, post-Malinowskian anthropology has also long engaged with the relationship between local communities and the outside world. The abhorrence of large-scale systems, change, mixing and modernity ascribed, in clichéd narratives of intellectual pasts, to mid-twentieth-century anthropology, is counteracted by a no less pronounced interest in the same phenomena. There has been a continuous, if sometimes unfashionable, interest in the articulation of the local with large-scale systems, including capitalism, individualism and the state. This is not to say that all criticism of earlier insularity is misplaced, only that it should not be exaggerated.

METHODOLOGICAL PEERS

To put it differently: quests for symbolic power and professional identity sometimes tempt academics to caricature the positions taken by their predecessors, so that their own contribution may shine with an exceptionally brilliant glow of originality and sophistication. Let us resist that temptation here.

Malinowski himself, the founding father of the single-sited community fieldwork and the synchronic analysis, made his reputation on a study of mobility, translocal connections and what we might today call the identity politics of the *kula* (Malinowski, 1984/1922). Moreover, Mr Structural-Functionalism himself expressed a concern that the units studied in social anthropology were about to dissolve into larger and fuzzier systems, making them difficult to handle methodologically (Radcliffe-Brown, 1952: 193). The third 'founding father' of modern anthropology, Boas, remained sympathetic to diffusionism until his death, judging the study of diffusion as complementary to his historical particularist study of single cultures. However, of all the twentieth-century *Gründers*, it was especially Mauss who made historical change and cultural diffusion an integral part of his intellectual programme. In *The Gift* (Mauss, 1954/1924), Mauss explores both the historical origins of exchange regimes and their geographical distribution (especially in the Pacific region), and, in the final chapter, he laments the currently weak position of exchange as total social phenomenon in modern France.

This is not to deny that the single-society synchronic study was the standard form of anthropological inquiry for decades. Yet its shortcomings have been known, but were accepted as a trade-off for its advantages. Sometimes spoken of as the trade-off between depth and breadth, the contrast between time-intensive, slow and concentrated village fieldwork and the more breathless, fragmented and dispersed urban or translocal fieldwork should nevertheless not be overstated. One of the classic *Gemeinschaft* studies of American sociology was a study of a street-corner gang in a US city (Whyte, 1943) and, conversely, many of the classic studies of North American Indians were characterised by limited access to informants, resultant patchy knowledge of their culture and social organisation, and even the enforced dislocation of the informant group (onto reservations).

Amit (2000: 5) takes Hastrup to task for a seeming self-contradiction, namely that the latter had first emphasised the continued need for in-depth fieldwork (Hastrup and Hervik, 1994), and then, a few years later (Hastrup and Olwig, 1997), argued that there was no longer a one-to-one relationship between place and cultural production. However, in the context of the present book, we must stress the need to accept both views simultaneously. The fact that the field of inquiry is not a physical place can never be an excuse for not doing long-term fieldwork. Engagement with the field varies – in modern complex societies, it may be difficult to follow informants around in different contexts, and many simply do not have a lot of spare time on their hands. Yet this problem can be partly compensated for through the improved availability of other sources in complex societies; and besides, limited access to informants is probably also more widespread in traditional locality-based fieldwork than is commonly assumed.

As noted above, problems concerning origins and the subsequent distribution and recontextualisation of phenomena were far from unfamiliar to early twentieth-century anthropologists, nor were issues relating to change and systemic interconnectedness. It can still be said that such issues tended not to be at the forefront in a discipline dominated by questions concerning cultural integration (in the USA) and social integration (in Britain). However, several of the mid-twentieth-century anthropological traditions following, or reacting against, earlier efforts took on methodological problems closely related to the ones that are raised in studies of transnational processes.

First, urban anthropology and network studies developed sophisticated understandings of social complexity and methods for studying weakly incorporated social systems. The Chicago School of the interwar years and the Manchester School of the early postwar years were particularly important in this regard (cf. Hannerz, 1980: chapters 2 and 4). A collective volume confidently entitled *The Craft of Social Anthropology* (Epstein, 1967), published in the twilight years of the Manchester School, describes a number of methodological strategies developed in the context of African urbanisation – sociometrics, extended case method, systems analysis – which have attained extreme importance in studies of unbounded (but not unregulated) flows.

Second, systems theory proper, as witnessed in the work of Bateson (1972), Rappaport (1968), human ecologists and a wide range of non-anthropologists, has for decades offered robust methods for studying the parameters that regulate certain kinds of flows. While it would be unwise to use techniques devised for measuring energy exchange in studies of people and their cultural production, some of the general methodological guidelines of systems theory, such as the need to 'follow the loops' of repetitive interaction and redundancy in information, should be useful in studies of transnationalism as well.

Third, the strains of anthropological Marxism that were concerned with political economy placed the mutual interdependence of societies at the forefront of the agenda. Lacking the mainstream's search for cultural authenticity and social cohesion, syncretic books by Wolf (1982), Worsley (1984) and others instead emphasised flows, connections and – more so than recent studies of transnationalism – power discrepancies that needed to be understood in a global framework. Emphasising the necessity to understand higher systemic levels than those usually described by anthropologists, this line of neo-Marxism also added historical depth to the understanding of global interconnectedness. Sidney Mintz's (1985) study of sugar, to mention one outstanding example, splendidly weaves together present and past, global and local, insider's and outsider's perspectives in a coherent, powerful analysis of the role of one colonial commodity in recent world history.

SOME SUBSTANTIAL CONCERNS

There is a strained relationship between transnational studies or globalisation studies in anthropology and cultural anthropology proper, seen as the comparative study of symbolic universes and cultural specificity. Both Sahlins (1994) and Geertz (1994) have spoken ironically about the disenchanted world of global communication, intimating that, when all is said and done, the study object proper to anthropology is bounded and local. Many younger American anthropologists who have felt straitjacketed by their peers' demand for coherence and boundedness, have ended up writing *against* culture. All of the sources of inspiration for transnational studies mentioned so far in this introduction, moreover, seem to belong to the sociological camp in anthropology. All this apparently makes it possible to bracket or even obliterate culture or symbolic meaning as a primary research focus. Studies of identity politics or the politics of culture, for example, tend to concentrate on the externalising social manipulation and appropriation of cultural symbols and identity markers, rather than exploring the life-world meanings of them. Yet the importance of actual cultural differences is not necessarily neglected in such work; one need only think of Kapferer's (1988) comparative study of the Sri Lankan and Australian nationalisms, where cultural differences play a central part. Hannerz's seminal *Cultural Complexity* (1992), moreover, pays particular attention to the production of meaning in transnational contexts. Many other examples could have been mentioned, not least from recent American anthropology.

The contributions to this book do not bracket or leave culture out, but claim cultural process (culture as a verb rather than a noun, in the sense of Street, 1991) as one of their main subjects. Although some dimensions of culture tend to be taken for granted in all studies of modernity – think of the glib ways in which anthropologists used to talk about 'Western culture' as a single, taken-for-granted entity, while they were at pains to present all the differentiating nuances and details of their chosen non-Western culture – there is a deep concern with the interpretation of symbolic universes and description of their substantial content throughout this book. Even if the very term trans*national* (rather than say, trans*local*) indicates that central dimensions of modernity are taken for granted, several of the chapters (most notably, perhaps, Nustad's and Abram's) offer fine-grained cultural accounts of some aspects of contemporary bureaucratic management. Others, such as Melhuus and Howell, take great pains to elaborate symbolic meanings embedded in a cultural universe that is just as much 'their own' as 'that of others', while Lund, herself an American anthropologist of Norwegian descent living for many years in Norway, tries to make sense of a transatlantic practice involving Norwegians and Norwegian-Americans, which initially caught her interest because it seemed so puzzling. Although none of this involves 'otherness' in the old sense, the ensuing analyses cannot be accused of not taking culture seriously, and in spite of dealing with the culture of 'home', they are in every way far removed from contrived depictions of, say, New York stockbrokers 'as if' they were a Papuan tribe.

Several of the classic staples of anthropological research are amply covered in the chapters that make up this book.

Identity and Community

Four of the chapters shed new light on problems relating to these core concepts in socal anthropology, indicating both continuity with past efforts and the need for new approaches in the fast-moving contemporary world.

Olwig, who has studied Caribbean diasporas for many years, discusses the concept 'global places' in the context of research in the Caribbean and on Caribbean migration. Her chapter shows the importance of discussing spatial identities in their actual concrete settings rather than in relation to the categories and concepts that have become dominant in the global discourse about place. Whether in the small island of Nevis or in a big Western city, her informants relate to places in ambiguous and complex ways, which cannot be subsumed under categories such as 'transnationalism' or 'diaspora'. Varying emphases on family networks, Caribbean places and the spatial significance of personal experiences among her informants are shown to transcend such general concepts, probably, she remarks, because her fieldwork has concentrated on intimate, 'primary' relationships.

Christian Krohn-Hansen, in a complex argument involving the fall of the Berlin Wall, the meanings of race and Caribbean history, argues that an improved anthropology of the present crucially depends on an improved anthropology of the past, making a strong case for better historical research in the discipline. This is not least because, as he puts it, in our world of global flows, the human interest in genealogies (and blood, and place, and soil, and roots) remains tremendous.

Marianne Lien, whose research concerns food and transnationalism, discusses the significance of the term 'marginality' in her contribution. The fishing community of Båtsfjord, northern Norway, is commonly seen as a marginal place – small, isolated, remote from every centre – and yet its marginality is shown to be negotiable. Partly it is a notion constructed by the political centre and reproduced locally as a self-fulfilling prophecy denying Båtsfjord its place in global networks; partly it is contingent on Båtsfjord's alleged lack of inclusion in wider networks of communication and exchange. Through several concomitant processes (a new airport, revival of trade with Russians of the Kola peninsula, local attempts at re-fashioning local identity, globalisation of the fish market), the community's marginality is shown to be shifting and context-dependent. However, Lien also shows that the impact of various 'globalising' processes varies because of variations in local agency, thereby making a case for ethnography in globalisation studies.

Sarah Lund presents an intriguing ethnographic case in her chapter: the physical transfer of Norwegian-inspired buildings from the US Midwest to a site in western Norway, as a form of commemoration. Migration from Norway to the Midwest was massive in the nineteenth century, and these acts of reciprocity are interpreted as a way of creating a transatlantic locality. More pertinently, the chapter indicates the importance of historical depth in studies of transnational flows. Without an understanding of family ties, Scandinavian Lutheranism in the Midwest and the cultural importance of community, both in Norway and among Scandinavian-Americans, this expensive and labour-intensive movement would have been difficult to understand.

Institutional and Informal Politics

The subdiscipline of political anthropology used the relationship between the normative, institutional level and the level of strategic action virtually as its constitutive tension. In Abram's and Nustad's chapters, we see the tension being played out in the context of auditing, in western Europe and South Africa, respectively.

Knut Nustad begins his chapter by presenting a useful distinction between a global system and reflexive awareness of globality, detailing the latter as a tension between globalism (as a form of neo-liberalism) and globality (the cultural notion that we now live in an unbounded world). Attempting to 'cut globalisation down to size', he argues, using the IMF audit system as his main example, that although 'global actors' may exist, their reach through 'long networks' varies and is always confronted with resistance. There is no local/global duality – this would have presupposed an empirically incorrect dependence on the nation-state as the paradigm of social organisation – and what must be studied instead is how 'global actors' achieve their size through associating other actors and objects.

Abram's chapter discusses methodological issues associated with studying bureaucracies. She identifies two main approaches: one place-based and one policy-based; and two main kinds of data: informants' statements and actions, and documents. By presenting three very different examples from her own research on planning and bureacracy (two from Buckinghamshire, England and one from the Oslo region, Norway), she reveals how methodological choices affect the production of knowledge. She also shows that, paradoxically, it is often necessary to set aside constructs such as local and global when one is studying these phenomena, since the appropriate methodological level – whether one studies interaction or documents – is that of the network.

Kinship and Gender

Both Howell and Melhuus, who have formerly worked in South-East Asia and Latin America, respectively, engage with these classic issues in new empirical settings. Melhuus raises some important questions regarding the flow of fertilised human eggs and human sperm – an activity rarely included in globalisation studies, but clearly relevant for any discussion about boundaries, flows and transnationalism. Using Norwegian legislative practices as her main case, she shows ways in which the transnational circulation of bodily substances involves power discrepancies and tensions between boundedness and openness which closely resemble similar dimensions in economic, political and cultural flows. The obstacles confronted in attempts to redefine human substances as commodities moreover serve as a reminder that there are implicit rules regulating flows. Some things and ideas travel, while others don't.

Howell's chapter on the dissemination of children's rights is an original contribution to a classic issue in anthropology and global politics, namely the tension between universal pretentions and local realities. Exploring the history, development and attempted implementation of children's rights, she compares what can loosely be called 'new-style colonialism' (the more complex and less clear-cut globalising processes led by UN agencies and NGOs) with classic colonialism, showing the former to be informed by many of the same basic value orientations as the latter. Like Krohn-Hansen, she shows the importance of historical depth in globalisation studies – in this case adoption practices, notions of childhood, rights discourses and other relevant, historically contingent aspects of children's rights, connecting this historical perspective to a reading of both documents and social practices (like Abram). When Howell and Melhuus write about international conventions and legislation, regulating the adoption of children and the flow of reproductive material respectively, their work stands in a long anthropological tradition of relating cultural norms to the ongoing negotiations and 'hybrid actions' of social life.

Place

In his chapter, Hannerz turns the notion of multi-sited fieldwork inside out by showing that a single site in a complex society may be conceptualised as a multiple one. Since 'spaces' require agency and human interpretation in order to become 'places', it is clear that each 'space' may exist as various 'places' in so far as many agents invest it with different meanings. Hannerz presents a variety of research projects engaged in by his colleagues in Stockholm to indicate the generality of this 'multivocality of places', also pointing out that it requires great ethnographic sensitivity and thoroughness to comprehend the multidimensionality of an apparently single site. This point is also made forcefully in Lien's chapter.

Although Miller and Slater's chapter can be read largely as a strong defence of ethnographic work as an indispensable tool for understanding the contemporary world, it is also a valuable contribution to the understanding of place. The Internet is often seen as the virtual and global place *par excellence* but, as Miller and Slater show, it is both imbued with local meanings everywhere in the world and connected to pre-existing practices. Indeed, they argue, the 'dot com crisis' in 2000–01 was partly caused by a failure to understand the embeddedness of Internet use in everyday offline life.

In the Epilogue, Keith Hart moves in the opposite direction from usual with regard to scale and place, by asking what it would be like to study *world society* rather than transnational processes – in other words moving upwards rather than downwards in scale. Taking his cue from Immanuel Kant (among the classics) and Manuel Castells (among the contemporaries), Hart argues that global embeddedness is increasingly a fundamental characteristic of the sites we study, and that world history is therefore now a crucial discipline for anthropology. Hart also argues the case for a more relaxed attitude to methodological issues: long-term single-sited fieldwork is in many cases, and for different reasons, no longer feasible. In its place, he offers existential engagement. Given the fact that anthropologists have always used themselves as their most important 'tools of measurement' in their research, this requirement makes immediate sense, and yet it feels as if Hart has violated a taboo.

An implicit theme in all the chapters is continuity and community. During the last decades, strongly marked by critiques of the allegedly static and conservative views of culture and society dominating early to mid-twentieh-century anthropology, the general ability to describe and analyse movement, mixing and discontinuity has increased considerably. Change is no longer seen as a theoretical and methodological problem, but as an inherent property of social life. Some social theorists (e.g. Urry, 2000) have even proposed a sociology based on movement rather than society as the fundamental concept; and, in anthropology, Strathern (e.g. 1991) has been foremost among those arguing that the search for wholeness and integration is ultimately fruitless (cf. also Ardener, 1985, on the end of modernism in social anthropology, and Amit and Rapport, 2002, for a recent discussion). In this situation, it is not facetious to argue that the conceptual and methodological apparatuses required to handle change and disruption are developing at a healthy pace, but that there is at the same time a risk that the classic skills of anthropologists in describing continuity and community are being weakened. In the context of transnational flows, it is true that continuity and community can no longer be taken for granted, as axiomatic points of departure. This does not mean that they cannot be identified, but that they need to be accounted for. If we are to believe the most sweeping statements about the disembedding and deterritorialising effects of globalisation, then it may seem nothing short of miraculous that long-term multiplex relationships continue to exist, that traditional social practices and cultural notions remain doxic, and that social communities based on generalised reciprocity and shared cultural values continue to be reproduced. Conversely, as Appadurai (1996: 179ff.) points out, localities were never *sui generis* and always required sustained hard work to continue to exist. While no serious student of the social should be surprised by this, it is true that social and cultural continuity now need to be described in more accurate terms than before, and also display greater variation than is often assumed. For example, communities need not be localised in order to offer comparable ontological security, normative control and social constraints on individuals, as the proverbial village did. Since the community is no longer necessarily a spatial entity, however, its existence has to be demonstrated. Most of the chapters of this book indicate, sometimes in striking ways, the resilience and continued importance of *Gemeinschaft*-like social arrangements based on trust, social commitments and shared interpretations. The methodology required to produce knowledge about these communities, however, is more complex and in some ways more demanding (though, admittedly, in other ways less demanding) than the classic single-site synchronic fieldwork.

WHAT *IS* NEW?

In the foregoing I have relinquished intellectual one-upmanship and instead emphasised continuity between the methods and objectives of classic modernist anthropology and studies of transnational processes. Many of the same general problems are addressed, and the research methodology presented in this book does not represent a revolutionary departure from that of Malinowski or Evans-Pritchard. Yet it cannot, and should not, be denied that studies of transnational processes, be it Internet users in Trinidad, the sense of community among Caribbean migrants to North America or the flow of sperm and eggs across state borders, require a somewhat different conceptual apparatus and methodological toolbox than the kind of research typical of the discipline half a century ago. Some of this is well known. For example, much has been written about the need to see culture as a process rather than a thing, the inherent complexity and variation of cultural phenomena, and the problem of boundaries (for some of the most influential statements, see Clifford and Marcus, 1986; Hannerz, 1992; Strathern, 1991). The battle to escape the straitjacket of a reified concept of culture, along with its concomitant reified ideas of identity, seems to have been won for now, and besides, the processual notion of culture is not the exclusive property of globalisation studies (see e.g. Barth, 1989). The following points, elaborated at greater length in the chapters that follow, are neither more nor less than some regulative ideas that distinguish studies of transnational processes from – dare I use the term – traditional modernist anthropology.

First, studies of transnational processes rely on a greater diversity of materials than classic ethnography. Although participant observation is usually indispensable, written sources – often produced in the society in question (see Archetti, 1994) – can never be ignored. In a complex urban environment, questionnaire surveys and formal interviews also tend to be applied more frequently than in a local community. Studies of the Internet, to mention an example of growing interest, will always involve online research. The importance of historical material in this kind of research, moreover, in fact makes it necessary for very many anthropologists to become better historians – if for other reasons than those imagined by Evans-Pritchard (1962).

A second and related point is the tendency, in transnational research, to develop a different, less multiplex kind of relationship to most informants than that which is feasible in a physical locality. Although this does not necessarily lead to a trade-off between 'depth' and 'breadth', it is clearly less easy to share the lives of informants for extended periods when the field is multilocal or even non-local, than when one 'pitches one's tent in a savage village'. Even when the number of informants is limited, as in Hannerz's recent research on foreign correspondents (Hannerz, 1996; forthcoming), this kind of informant is far less available than the villager of the classic monograph.

Third, research on transnational processes often involves multi-sited fieldwork but, as noted above, it may also involve multi-levelled single-site fieldwork, and this could moreover mean different things, such as studying the same setting from the perspective of different social groups participating in it, or studying a site at several levels of abstraction from ongoing social process.

Fourth and finally, in order for the transnational flows to be fully understood, they must not only be contextualised historically and systemically, but they must also be explicitly articulated with processes at the macro level. Thus the critique of the likes of Wolf and Worsley, that anthropology needed a better grasp of the large-scale processes in order to make sense of the small-scale ones, meets massive resonance among students of transnational processes, which is evident in all the chapters of this book.

Like the study of identity politics, the study of transnational processes or globalisation is interdisciplinary, engaging academics from sociology, human geography, political science, cultural studies and many other disciplines. What anthropology has to bring to globalisation studies is the recognition that social and cultural worlds, which are constituted from diverse materials of various origins, are always expressed through meaningful relationships. Through its ethnographic depth, anthropology also has the authority and the ability to collapse a number of counterproductive dichotomies: the local and the global, the virtual and the real, the place-bound and the 'non-place', the universal and the particular. In real-life settings, such contrasts evaporate.

What this book has to offer to the craft of social anthropology amounts to cutting globalisation research down to size by reintegrating it into the methodological mainstream of anthropology. If the research presented in this book should prove uninteresting and bad, at least the verdict should not be made on the basis of weak methodology and poor empirical material. Seeing the anthropology of transnational processes as 'not really anthropology' should, hopefully, be a little bit more difficult after this book.

Thanks to Marianne Lien, Marit Melhuus and Knut Nustad for useful comments on the first draft.

REFERENCES

Amit, V. 2000. Introduction. In V. Amit (ed.) *Constructing the Field: Ethnographic Fieldwork in the Contemporary World*, pp. 1–18. London: Routledge.

Amit, V. and N. Rapport. 2002. *The Trouble with Community: Anthropological Reflections on Movement, Identity and Collectivity*. London: Pluto Press.

Appadurai, A. 1996. *Modernity at Large*. Minneapolis: Minnesota University Press.

Archetti, E. (ed.) 1994. *Exploring the Written: Anthropology and the Multiplicity of Writing*. Oslo: Scandinavian University Press.

Ardener, E. 1985. The end of modernism in social anthropology. In Joanna Overing (ed.) *Reason and Morality*, pp. 47–70. London: Tavistock.

Augé, M. 1995. *Non-Places: An Introduction to an Anthropology of Supermodernity*, trans. John Howe. London: Verso.

Barnard, A. 2000. *History and Theory in Anthropology*. Cambridge: Cambridge University Press.

Barth, F. 1989. The analysis of culture in complex societies, *Ethnos* 54(3–4): 120–42.

Bateson, G. 1972. *Steps to an Ecology of Mind*. New York: Bantam.

Castells, M. 1996. *The Rise of the Network Society*. Oxford: Blackwell.

Clifford, J. and G. Marcus (eds) 1986. *Writing Culture: The Poetics and Politics of Ethnography*. Berkeley: University of California Press.

Epstein, A.L. (ed.) 1967. *The Craft of Social Anthropology*. London: Tavistock.

Evans-Pritchard, E.E. 1962. Anthropology and history. In E.E. Evans-Pritchard, *Social Anthropology and Other Essays*. New York: Free Press.

Geertz, C. 1994. The uses of diversity. In R. Borofsky (ed.) *Assessing Cultural Anthropology*, pp. 454–65. New York: McGraw-Hill.

Giddens, A. 1990. *The Consequences of Modernity*. Cambridge: Polity Press.

Hannerz, U. 1980. *Exploring the City: Inquiries toward an Urban Anthropology*. New York: Columbia University Press.

—— 1992. *Cultural Complexity*. New York: Columbia University Press.

—— 1996. *Transnational Connections*. London: Routledge

Hannerz, U. forthcoming. *Foreign News*. Chicago: University of Chicago Press.

Hastrup, K. and P. Hervik. 1994. Introduction. In K. Hastrup and P. Hervik (eds) *Social Experience and Anthropological Knowledge*, pp. 1–14. London: Routledge.

Hastrup, K. and K.F. Olwig. 1997. Introduction. In K. Hastrup and K.F. Olwig (eds) *Siting Culture*, pp. 1–14. London: Routledge.

Kapferer, B. 1988. *Legends of People, Myths of States: Violence, Intolerance and Political Culture in Sri Lanka and Australia*. Washington, DC: Smithsonian Institution.

McLuhan, M. 1964. *Understanding Media*. New York: McGraw-Hill.

Malinowski, B. 1984/1922. *Argonauts of the Western Pacific*. Prospect Heights, IL: Waveland.

Mauss, M. 1954/1924. *The Gift*, trans. Ian Cunnison. London: Cohen & West.

Mintz, S. 1985. *Sweetness and Power: The Place of Sugar in Modern History*. New York: Viking.

Radcliffe-Brown, A.R. 1952. On social structure. In A.R. Radcliffe-Brown, *Structure and Function in Primitive Society*, pp. 188–204. London: Cohen & West.

Rappaport, R.A. 1968. *Pigs for the Ancestors: Ritual in the Ecology of a New Guinea People*. New Haven, CT: Yale University Press.

Sahlins, M. 1994. Goodbye to tristes tropes: ethnography in the context of modern world history. In R. Borofsky (ed.) *Assessing Cultural Anthropology*, pp. 377–94. New York: McGraw-Hill.

Strathern, M. 1991. *Partial Connections*. Savage, MD: Rowman & Littlefield.

Street, B. 1991. Culture as a verb: anthropological aspects of language and cultural process. In D. Graddol, L. Thompson and M. Byram (eds) *Language and Culture: Papers from the Annual Meeting of the British Association for Applied Linguistics, 1991*. Philadelphia: British Association for Applied Linguistics.

Urry, J. 2000. *Sociology beyond Societies: Mobilities for the Twenty-first Century*. London: Routledge.

Wallerstein, I. 1974. *The Modern World-System* , vol. 1. New York: Academic Press.

Whyte, W.F. 1943. *Street-corner Society: The Social Structure of an Italian Slum*. Chicago: University of Chicago Press.

Wolf, E. 1982. *Europe and the People without History*. Berkeley: University of California Press.

Worsley, P. 1984. *The Three Worlds: Culture and World Development*. London: Weidenfeld & Nicolson.

2 SEVERAL SITES IN ONE

Ulf Hannerz

When the evening comes, I sit down in front of our TV, switch to perhaps CNN or BBC World, and sometimes a familiar face turns up – hello Mike, hello Lyse! And the next morning, when I glance through the Stockholm morning papers, it feels nice to come upon some especially familiar signatures – hi Leif, Göran, Cordelia ...

What is all this? It is a result of a social anthropological study I have been involved with over the several years, of news-media foreign correspondents, their work and working conditions. Because of the study, some of the people whom I would otherwise only have known by their faces on screen, their radio voices or their writing I have also met personally, in many places around the world, such as in Jerusalem, Cape Town, Hong Kong or Tokyo. A little like the foreign correspondents themselves, I have moved in and out of various places, trying to obtain an idea of who they are and what happens before their reports about the state of the world reach us viewers, listeners and readers. But besides meeting the correspondents in various places, I have also tried to follow their reporting, read their memoirs and report books, and meet some of the international news editors at their home news stations, in order to get a picture of what happens as the work of foreign correspondents is compiled into a couple of pages, or into a few segments of a news programme.[1]

When I began as a social anthropologist in the 1960s, the possibility of working in this manner would hardly have been thinkable. I made my first field study in an Afro-American neighbourhood in Washington, DC, and even though I did not completely stay within the block which was my original focus, just about everything which became part of my 'field' was within walking distance: other neighbourhoods where friends of friends lived, churches, gathering places, some of the black ghetto's entertainment facilities. I moved primarily within the framework of those direct personal contacts which anthropologists usually call face-to-face relations, and in the tense social and political atmosphere which characterised relationships between black and white. I endeavoured not to deviate too much from the ordinary forms of conduct in black everyday life. In other words, I was engaged in a rather pure form of what is described as 'participant observation', without much use for formal interviews or other methods which might risk increasing the distance between myself, and my friends and neighbours. (Although, as a young, white foreigner, I was still enough of an outsider that I had a certain newsworthiness and entertainment value.)[2]

CLASSICAL FIELDWORK AND ITS LIMITS

'The field' has long been the symbolic centre of anthropology. It is there that knowledge is collected and experience built up. Fieldwork is the initiation rite of the professional anthropologist, and constitutes an important part of his or her symbolic capital. (The anthropologist who never does fieldwork is as much an oddity as a theoretical swimmer.) To do anthropological fieldwork in the middle of a large, Western city was still quite unorthodox in the 1960s. But in many ways, my research in Washington still resembled a classical field study, as far as its spatial concentration went. The established picture of a field is that of a locality. Bronislaw Malinowski, one of anthropology's founders, painted it in the introduction to *Argonauts of the Western Pacific* (1922), his famous book about life on the Melanesian Trobriand Islands: 'Imagine yourself suddenly set down surrounded by all your gear, alone on a tropical beach close to a native village ...' When the day began, Malinowski climbed out from under his mosquito net, saw life awaken in the village, took his morning promenade and saw his neighbours bathing and preparing food. As the sun climbed in the sky, he followed them in all their activities, nosed into arguments and scandals – and, as this was repeated month after month, he became himself a part of the villagers' everyday scenery. The basic premise is that it is possible to get a fairly complete picture of a way of life if one is in one place, with eyes and ears open, over a long period.

What kinds of social life and what forms of culture is this type of anthropological fieldwork best suited for? A way of life, probably, where the participant observer has most things pretty much within viewing and reaching distance, where face-to-face relationships completely dominate, where communication is oral, and where people do not move around so much that one loses track of them. Even in these days of mobile telephones and the Internet, it can be necessary to point out just how much human life this description is still relevant for: most people still spend their everyday lives within a narrow radius, and do a very large part of their communicating through face-to-face conversations.

But it was not long before anthropologists developed interests that took them beyond a purely local field. My Stockholm colleague Ulf

Björklund points out that not even Malinowski's study of the Trobriands was completely local: one of the main themes was the complicated ritualised chains of exchange, where shells were exchanged between partners on different Melanesian islands – in the so-called Kula ring. This tendency reflects a tension between the local focus of the traditional field study and anthropology's ambition of illuminating the entire breadth of human life. The well-known American anthropologist Clifford Geertz (1973: 22) once pointed out that anthropologists do not study villages, they study *in* villages – and from there, with this perspective, one may make sense of a multitude of the phenomena of human life. That certainly widens the horizons of the discipline. But the question quickly arises why one should only choose that vantage point, or if one does not understand some things best by going around them and looking at them from various perspectives, instead of standing still. The risk is perhaps also that the locally oriented perspective often returns to the same kinds of insights, with which one may in the end become a little impatient, no matter how true and important they may be.

And in a time of express trains, jet planes, long-distance commuting, the Internet, courses in intercultural communication, transnational companies, dozens of channels to zap between on cable TV, world conferences and rusty, overloaded refugee ships, it becomes particularly obvious that culture and people often are in motion, and that social structures are extended in space in such a way that from a local viewpoint, one can only get an incomplete picture of some types of activities. Social theorists in recent years have often commented on the changes in the world's spatial order. The British sociologist Anthony Giddens (for example, 1990: 18–19) points out that it is one of the characteristics of modernity that 'the local' is formed by distant influences and therefore, despite its tangible presence, it is a phantasmagoric entity. And the American historian of ideas Mark Poster (1990: 74) asks dramatically:

If I can speak directly or by electronic mail to a friend in Paris while sitting in California, if I can witness political and cultural events as they occur across the globe without leaving my home, if a database at a remote location contains my profile and informs government agencies which make decisions that affect my life without any knowledge on my part of these events, if I can shop in my home by using my TV or computer, then where am I and who am I?

Perhaps as an anthropologist one can choose, even under such circumstances, to hold on to a local viewpoint by identifying the phenomena that can really be studied in one place. This does not necessarily mean that one disregards the integration of local life into wider contexts, only that one clarifies for oneself and one's audience

how one handles the delimitation of one´s object of study, method-
ically and analytically. In my study of Afro-American
neighbourhood life in Washington, I tried, for example, to make
clear to what degree this life consisted of a collective adaptation to
the surrounding structures of American society, and to the Afro-
Americans' special place in these structures.[3] But what is clear is that
one cannot take the local field as 'given' any more. How localities
are constructed can in itself be seen as a problem.[4]

THE FIELD AS A NETWORK OF LOCALITIES

In recent years, a growing number of anthropologists have begun to
attempt to define their fields in ways other than as a geographical
locality. My study of foreign correspondents is one example of this,
as are other studies recently undertaken at the Department of Social
Anthropology at Stockholm University. The common denominator
of all these studies is that each of the researchers has collected their
materials from several different localities. The studies may therefore
be termed 'multi-local'. Yet in a way this term is inadequate, because
it really is not just a question of having several local fields. The point
is that these fields are also linked to each other in some kind of
cohesive structure. One could just as well say that each study
concerns *one* field, which consists of a network of localities – 'several
fields in one', in other words. What happens in one locality
influences what happens in the others, whether that is intended and
can be foreseen or not. This is why it becomes necessary, or at least
preferable, to combine several points of observation. It also means
that the field is not only *multi-local*, it is also *translocal*, in the sense
that it is necessary to clarify the nature of relations *between* localities.
Some people might claim that while the analytical entity is
translocal, the fieldwork is multi-local, quite simply because one is
always somewhere.

In international anthropology, the term 'multi-local' is now more
common than 'translocal', and when the history of multi-local
anthropology is written, it will be pointed out how the adoption of
this term happened fairly early in migration studies, where it became
clear that large groups of people lived their lives in two or several
places, distant from each other – perhaps with national borders,
continents and oceans in between. True, many studies of migrant
groups are conducted only in one locality, most often the one the
group has moved to. But in *Between Two Cultures* (1977), a book
where the contributors described various immigrant groups in Great
Britain – Italians, Chinese, Poles, Cypriots, Sikhs, Pakistanis, West
Indians and West Africans – the editor, James L. Watson, maintained

that it was a unique feature that all of the chapters drew on fieldwork at both ends of the migration stream. And in the years which have passed since Watson's book, this type of migration study has become increasingly common. This is probably partly due to the fact that the place which the migrant has left and the place where he has arrived have become more closely linked over time. When people can travel back and forth both regularly and frequently, when, in addition, they have close telephone contact and exchanges of commodities and services between places, and when they are in contact with friends and relatives in a similar situation in both places, it becomes all the less reasonable that the anthropologist examines only one of them.[5] Among the Stockholm researchers, Ulf Björklund has an early experience of such migration research – his study of Syrian Orthodox Christians in Sweden (Björklund, 1981) has its centre of gravity in a suburb of Södertälje, a town just south of Stockholm, but he also visited an important emigrant area in south-eastern Turkey, and it was in this study that he first became acquainted with the problematic of national diasporas.

Still, the term 'multi-local' was for some time not much in evidence within this kind of migration research which was, at least, bi-local. 'Multi-local field studies' has only been used as a term in international anthropology since the late 1980s, not least through a series of programmatic contributions by George Marcus (1986, 1989, 1995, Marcus and Fischer 1986: 91ff.), an influential and controversial thinker in several areas. It is still worth noticing that when Marcus began promulgating the idea of how combined field studies in several localities could illuminate wider social and cultural interrelations, he apparently had some difficulty finding professional anthropological studies which he could use as examples.

Social anthropologists at Stockholm University were at the forefront in establishing multi-local anthropology. They have probably produced a larger quantity of such studies than any other anthropology department in the world.[6] Christina Garsten described the organisation of the transnational computer company Apple in her doctoral dissertation *Apple World* (1994). Her study had three vantage points: the Swedish office in the Stockholm suburb of Kista, the international main office in Silicon Valley and the European main office in Paris. Garsten has more recently looked at other organisations, such as the employment agency Olsten, to explore the organisation of working life in general, and in particular the growing mobility which turns the offices of our time into places inhabited by nomads – workers are here one day, somewhere else tomorrow. Karin Norman started a local field study in a small town in central Sweden, but after a while found Albanian refugees from Kosovo moving in. And as she turned her attention to them, the project became multi-local, tracing the mobility of the group between Sweden and Kosovo as well as between several sites in Sweden. Eva Maria Hardtmann has studied various places and contexts where a movement for India's low castes – Dalits – develops its resistance against the caste system – not only in India, but also in England, as well as in a village outside Borås, Sweden. Ulf Björklund has moved from the Syrian to the Armenian diaspora; although the Armenians were among the first to spread around the world, ethnic and national diasporas have become ever more numerous over the years, making 'diaspora' a key idea in the contemporary world. One kind of religious diaspora, which, at the same time, has a national anchorage, is analysed in Eva Evers Rosander's research among the West African Mourids – on the Canary Islands, but also in their holy city in Senegal (and we learn that the Mourids are also conspicuous for example on the streets of New York). Annette Henning deals with a completely different type of multi-local field – with an internally ever-shifting network around the spread of solar energy, with a starting point in an office in Borlänge, Sweden, but with linkages, for example, to conferences all over Europe. 'Culture shock' has become one of our time's most widely used new concepts, and around minor conflicts and misunderstandings in everyday contact between cultures, a new profession has emerged: interculturalists. Tommy Dahlén has studied their work. Helena Wulff, on the other hand, has done research on an occupation – ballet – which has been around longer, and which from its beginnings moved across national borders between its various centres. Hasse Huss has followed the pathways of reggae, and through this gives an example of how a popular music genre is spread over the world, from Jamaica to London and Tokyo, among other places. And Galina Lindquist has described some of the types of localities which are meeting places within neo-shamanism, a contemporary subculture which forms its conceptual world from many sources, and builds networks across borders. An introduction to all of these research projects can be found in a book edited by the current author (Hannerz, 2001).

WHAT THE FIELD IS

The problems raised by the Stockholm researchers, as well as by the contributors to *this* book, concern methods, assumptions, approaches and experiences in fieldwork. Here I will identify some of the questions which the multi-local/translocal field studies actualise.

To begin with, we should consider the social forms these studies examine. Hardtmann studies a political movement, that of people resisting the caste system. Hardtmann herself points out that, for a long time, movements were not among the usual topics of anthropological research interest. Characteristics of a movement – a will to spread ideas and convert one's fellow human beings can also be found amongst Henning's solar energy enthusiasts (even if some of them now discover that the heritage of 1970s ecological activism can be a bit of a burden), among Evers Rosander's Mourids, among Dahlén's interculturalists and among Lindquist's neo-shamans and their apprentices. The prominence of movements in these multi-local studies may reflect, on the one hand, the fact that these are major organisational phenomena in our time and, on the other, their tendency to be so spatially extended indicates that they require field studies going beyond local areas.

Another category of multi-local studies relates to work and occupational life: Dahlén on interculturalists, Wulff on ballet dancers, Huss on the artists, producers and distributors of reggae, Henning on solar energy experts and Garsten on office life; and my study of foreign correspondents also belongs here. But between movement studies and occupational studies, one already finds overlap: it is clear that not all fields allow themselves to be identified with only one type.

Yet another category concerns ethnicity and nationality: Evers Rosander's and Hartmann's work again, Björklund's on Armenians, Karin Norman's on Kosovo-Albanian refugees – but are they primarily Albanians or primarily refugees? And then one might notice that two of the occupational studies are about forms of art, with dance in one case and music in the other – aesthetic and expressive phenomena often move through the world.

All except two of the research projects – Björklund's and Evers Rosander's – concern studies in Sweden (although Hardtmann only has a single Swedish Dalit in a corner of her field). The time is past when anthropologists concerned themselves only with exotic, non-Western material. On the other hand, none of the studies remains entirely within Sweden. In these cases, the translocal studies are also transnational: they apply to units that stretch across the borders between states. (The term 'nation', of course, is complicated – Björklund's study of the Armenian diaspora is simultaneously about crossing borders, and about a people who see themselves as a nation.)

Translocal and transnational are not synonyms. It is entirely possible to do a translocal study within one country. However, it is clear that the growing interest in translocal studies on the methodological level within anthropology has a connection with the intensified interest, also on the theoretical level, in transnational processes and structures, and in what might be described as 'globalisation'.[7] This latter term, let us note, is not used in anthropology in the same way that one often finds it in public debates and in everyday discourse, referring primarily to deregulated markets, or to world cultural homogenisation. What globalisation means in anthropology is rather an increasingly dense web of all kinds of communication and relationships across borders and between continents – and, as far as field research in some part of this web is concerned, it then also often makes sense to be mobile across borders. (One should remember that some parts of this web of relationships are new, such as the Internet, and some very old, such as the Armenian diaspora.)

How are the objects of study in these research projects actually defined and delimited? In some cases, one might say that they are about 'groups'. In other cases, however, the objects of study are so loosely organised, and so diffusely bounded, that the term is hardly applicable. Often a practical solution is to speak about a 'network' – a term that has already been used here, and which has a long history in anthropological thought, when it come to examining various types of chains and patterns of connected social relations.[8] Here we can see how networks are formed around, for example, complexes of notions and rituals, such as within neo-shamanism, or around a technique, such as solar energy, or around a struggle for equality, such as among Indian Dalits. The point of using the term 'network' is, not least, that it can encompass much internal diversity.

TO COMPOSE THE TRANSLOCAL FIELD

We may ask ourselves when a field should be called 'multi-local' or 'translocal' – how such a field is different from a local field. Karin Norman's work illuminates the issue. Her research in the town of Smedjebacken does not quite conform to the Malinowskian model of fieldwork: Smedjebacken was an often-changing environment, and the social realities were not such that everything was clearly connected and easily accessible. One might first think that public institutions such as the municipal office, the retirement home and the schools offered entrances to the single local field of Smedjebacken. But one could also consider Smedjebacken to be a multi-local field with various segments each consisting of its own collection of people.

One might also describe a study of a herding people as multi-local, where the anthropologist follows a group of individuals through various grazing areas. While the surroundings vary, and perhaps also the daily activities, this could still be considered a study which closely corresponds to the Malinowskian picture of local fieldwork. But we need not become preoccupied with the borderline cases. There are also many clear cases of translocal anthropology where the localities are separated by great distances from each other, perhaps many hours of air travel, and where the people in these localities do not move between them as entire groups.

How does the anthropologist piece together his field from such fragmented realities? In some cases, it may appear obvious, as in some migration studies. If we are interested in immigrants from the Turkish town of Kulu and its vicinity, who settled in the Stockholm suburb Rinkeby, it is reasonable to divide fieldwork between Kulu and Rinkeby. The field becomes naturally bi-local. The situation becomes more complex if one broadens the field to encompass emigration from Kulu, or immigrants in Rinkeby, in general. The question arises of how many places in the world should be dealt with apart from, respectively, Kulu and Rinkeby. Here we may distinguish between a potential field, which can be very large, and the real field which the anthropologists actually try to become acquainted with through their own research. We see the distinction in various ways throughout this chapter. For example, in principle Helena Wulff studies the world of transnational ballet, but in practice she focuses on four companies in four countries. Ulf Björklund works on a worldwide Armenian diaspora, but she explores this through specific sites: a number of places in the USA, Paris, Nicosia, Istanbul and Jerusalem.

Multi-local field studies inevitably involve choices, as the real field is carved out from the potential field. This may be done in various ways. One may make a selection of localities at the outset and then stick with it, or it may be advantageous, if not always possible, to be able to modify one's plans as one goes on to take into account what one has learned during the course of the study, and include new opportunities. There may be an element of improvisation here, of seizing the moment. Where Annette Henning finds herself, as a spider in the web, at Dalarna College's Centre for Solar Energy Research, she can hear talk about information meetings, study circles and conferences in many places, and perhaps on very short notice she makes a journey to a new site. In my own study of foreign correspondents, a number of places were added to the study because I had the opportunity to stop there in connection with some other journey – such as Tokyo and Hong Kong after conferences.

Anthropologists are generally more interested in documenting and understanding variation, rather than in identifying only what is typical and average. Variation can be studied between nations: Helena Wulff has chosen to study ballet companies in Sweden, England, Germany and the USA in order to discover national differences in what is still a tightly knit occupational world with common ideals and forms of expression. Another dimension can be organisational: of these four companies, two are state-supported, one belongs to the city of Frankfurt, and one functions as an independent enterprise in the cultural market, with its own inherent logic. And the dimension of centre and periphery also influences in the selection. New York and London are among the definitive centres of the ballet world, Stockholm is not. The relationship between centre and periphery is also especially marked in Garsten's Apple study (which also includes national differences), where the main office in Cupertino, California, occupies a very special position.

In other words, one finds a noticeable interest in comparison in many multi-local studies, where one chooses local units which are comparable (but not necessarily particularly similar). The difference between these studies and what in anthropology are normally called 'comparative studies' is rather that in the latter, there is seldom any emphasis on the units being linked to each other in a more or less coherent structure. On the contrary, sometimes it has been seen as part of the comparative method that the units to be compared should be independent of each other.[9] While in multi-local studies, a central characteristic is thinking in terms of a network.

How does this fit in with my correspondents study? For one thing, many correspondents move between postings, through the network. One year, I spoke with the correspondent of the London newspaper *Daily Telegraph* in Jerusalem. The year after, I met the same newspaper's correspondent in Johannesburg. He was soon to be transferred – and his successor would be his colleague from Jerusalem. Besides, even foreign correspondents have their centre-periphery relations: the editors at home are those who orchestrate the correspondents' reports. Therefore it has been valuable for me also to meet the international editors in the main offices: in Stockholm, Frankfurt, London, New York or Los Angeles.

Something which is also important to point out in the make-up of multi-local projects is that they often include localities that are not easily comparable, that enter into the network in quite different ways. Often, this is due to the mobility of our times. In Wulff's ballet study, one therefore finds four companies, based in four cities. But besides this, companies such as the Opera Ballet in Stockholm travel on tour to Gävle, a Swedish provincial capital, as well as to Japan, making the fieldwork even more multi-local. Galina Lindquist focuses her work on the different types of meeting places where prac-titioners of neo-shamanism get together. In Tommy Dahlén's work, the interculturalists' big international congresses take on central importance. And since we are now said to live in a more or less world-encompassing knowledge society, we should not be surprised that courses and conferences show up as important occasions in one study after the other. Actually, it is often precisely these kinds of temporary meeting places, where participants are only briefly present together, which contribute critically to the formation and enduring cohesion of translocal networks. This is where people who normally live in different places get to know each other, it is through these places that many ideas are spread. The American anthropologist Arjun Appadurai (1996: 192) has coined the term 'translocalities' for places characterised by the fact that people move through them, rather than remaining there for longer periods.[10] Perhaps we should add here that some places are more translocalities for some people – for example, the short-term office personnel in Garsten's Olsten study – than for others. But in translocal research projects, it is often exactly this mobility and flow which is of greatest interest.

TIME IN THE FIELD

The idea of classical fieldwork is strong in the anthropological imagination, and as long as translocal studies stand out as something fairly new, it seems inevitable that they should be compared with it. It can appear that anthropologists worry that this new kind of fieldwork is in some way inferior. Such anxiety is occasionally visible in the studies described here. An important aspect of this anxiety is over how one uses one's time.

In the classical field study, the anthropologist stayed in the same place for at least one year, perhaps longer. There might be several reasons for this. One was that the way of life to be studied was often closely linked to nature. It was therefore often necessary, if one aimed at a comprehensive, 'holistic' picture (as one should), to follow seasonal changes – rainy season and dry season, summer, autumn, winter, spring. In this way, one observed sowing and harvesting, the movements of livestock and all of the calendar's rituals. One should also have time to get a clear picture of everyday repetitive activity. Another reason was that one needed time to build up one's knowledge, to manage the complex interplay between observations and interviews, and to reach such acceptance among the people in the locality that they really would allow the researcher to join in most – preferably all – activities and be confided in concerning sensitive matters. One's observations became more subtle, one's own participation more accomplished (or at least less clumsy), the longer the fieldwork went on.

At one time, let us say the first half of the twentieth century, a further reason to stay for a long period in the single field could have been the nature of travel. If one were to begin one's study by taking the postal ship from Europe to a foreign part of the world, then become acquainted with a colonial establishment and get further prepared, and finally make a plan for setting forth to a village somewhere in a more or less roadless country, one would have invested so much time entering the field one would like to get the most out of it once one was there.

If we are oriented towards doing multi-local fieldwork, how do we stand regarding classical fieldwork standards for handling time? Perhaps one should do the classical kind of fieldwork in each place included in the study? In most cases, however, this is impossible, if only for practical reasons. It would have to be an extremely long project, and, even if the researcher could think of leaving his normal working and living surroundings for such a long time, it might be difficult to convince research funding agencies of the need for such a time-consuming project. More often, it becomes a question of trying to do a multi-local project within a time-frame and a budget that does not differ much from those of other projects, even if we can see that the authors of the various studies discussed have organised their time in slightly different ways.[11]

Now there may be reasons why one should not necessarily see classical fieldwork as a model for activity in each site of a multi-local project. Perhaps one does not have to be present during all seasons because changes in the weather do not greatly affect the ideas, activities and relations one is interested in. It might also be that one does not need to start from scratch in every place, with regard to either knowledge or trustworthiness. Much of what one has learned in one site may be relevant also in the others. Besides, for many of these studies in today's world, one may start with more useful knowledge than, for example, Malinowski had when he went to the Trobriands. This can pertain to some of the commonalities of modern life, and one may also have selected a research topic with which one already has some special connection.

When Henning decided on solar energy's spread as a dissertation theme, she thus already had her background as an environmental activist to fall back on. Huss could certainly move quickly and confidently into his field studies of reggae music, with his background as a record producer, songwriter and *aficionado*. Wulff had had ballet as her main interest during childhood and youth. Besides, she actually had the opportunity to begin her project with a whole season of visiting the Stockholm Opera Ballet, something not so different from the classical model of year-long fieldwork in one place. Garsten was, for her part, at the Apple office in Stockholm for 15 months, as an employee. Of course, no one says that the component studies in multi-local fieldwork need to have precisely the same length, and in several studies it is clear that one of the sites served as the main site – because it was especially important for the problematic involved, or perhaps because it was more easily accessible than the others.

Language can be a particular problem, not least in multi-local projects that are also transnational. Yet this is not necessarily a matter of multiplying the language difficulties of the classical field by the number of sites. In classical fieldwork the anthropologist could arrive with no more than a rudimentary knowledge of the local language – courses, grammar books or dictionaries were perhaps just not available. Then much language learning had to occur during the period in the field itself, perhaps with some help from a local interpreter and assistant, more or less fluent in a European language. In the studies described in this text, the researchers have most often done well with the knowledge of languages they already possessed. Since several of the projects had Swedish ties, Swedish has often been one of the field languages. English has functioned well in several other contexts, French has been employed here and there. Hardtmann studied Hindi as preparation for her project on resistance against the caste system, while Björklund decided not to learn Armenian as in the diaspora one does not find anyone who only speaks Armenian. If he had chosen to do field research in Armenia itself, the need to learn Armenian would have been greater.

And then there is the question of travel. In our times, we can often get around quickly and rather easily. This certainly influences the organisation of multi-local field studies. It might indeed seem like a deviation from the classical fieldwork idea of allowing oneself to be slowly absorbed by local life if one travels in and out, again and again. On the other hand, everyone who has been in the field for a long time knows that travelling away and coming back later can often serve as an intensification of one's relation to the field – it dramatises one's commitment to it. Multi-local fieldwork can involve such returns, but the next trip is often to some other site. And the departure from one site is often a matter of going home, rather than to the next remote field site. To switch between being 'in the field' and 'out of the field' can be practical for many reasons. One might wish to return home in order to be with the family for a while (if it has not come along on fieldwork), or in order to perform other tasks, or in order to think over one's project and its continuation.[12] This may mean that with the multi-local project, even if the total time taken up by fieldwork is about the same as for a project done in a single site, the total time is stretched out over a prolonged period, with numerous breaks. Norman and Henning are among those who emphasise that their field studies alternated with various other types of engagements. Henning insists that this has carried with it a certain advantage – her study achieved a clearer picture of a process, instead of portraying only one slice in time, as is often the case in conventional field studies.

VARIATIONS IN RELATIONSHIPS

To build up acceptance for oneself over time, we stated earlier, has been part of the classical fieldwork model. As a fieldworker, one should participate in just about everything, become a well-known and accepted person – simultaneously 'stranger and friend', as one of Malinowski's first students, Hortense Powdermaker (1966), put it in the title of a volume of field memoirs. And the title shows that this preferably becomes something more than a calculating manipulation of relationships. Anthropologists have often had a very romantic attitude toward their field and the people there. They can find it difficult to describe their informants as informants precisely because they see them rather as friends, and they are often proud and pleased when they can report that they have been adopted by families or kin groups – not only because it indicates that they are skilled field researchers, but because it also has moral meanings. They have surrendered themselves to the field and been accepted on an intimate basis. Developing relationships in the field also helps the researcher on a personal, psychological level – without any close personal ties, being in a remote field milieu can be very lonely.

Can one have such relationships in a multi-local field? According to several of the Stockholm studies under discussion, it is not impossible, but perhaps, as one does not have much time on one's hands, it becomes more difficult. It may be worth pointing out here that this need not be a sign of how successful a study has been – enjoyable as it may be to have close and warm relationships – the question remains as to what the study in itself is about, and what kinds of relationships are actually characteristic of the field.

For one thing, how durable is the field itself? The classical, exotic field site in anthropology had a duration which hardly needed to be problematised. The natives were born, lived their lives and died there – or at least this could be assumed, under normal conditions. The type of relationships which could be built up within the frame of such stability were what the anthropological fieldworker studied and, to a certain extent, had to adapt to, in more or less extensive participant observation. Moreover, as the societies often were not particularly differentiated, so the premise for the fieldworker's search for a picture of 'the whole' was that the same people were engaged in many activities, encompassed by the same multi-stranded social relationships.

In the types of fields we are involved with in contemporary multi-local studies, social reality is often very differently constituted. Garsten's study of contemporary working life shows this most clearly. Quite often, people just come and go, and do not build their relationships on any duration that can be taken for granted. Particularly in the sites we identify as translocalities – for example conferences, courses, festivals – other participants' commitments and personal relationships are perhaps precisely as short-lived as the anthropologist's own. And relationships which stretch over longer periods can still be quite specialised and narrowly defined. Evers Rosander wonders about the lack of intimacy and trust in her contacts with the Mourids on the Canary Islands, and meets a Mourid businesswoman who pointedly tells the anthropologist that she can call when she has become a Muslim. Before this, this trader and her sisters in the movement cannot take time off to spend with this foreign researcher.

Bjørklund seems also to be uneasy about how his diaspora study deviates from the tried and true mark of fieldwork – 'depth and intensity, ethnography's classic virtues, have been left behind ...' – but he also asks a rhetorical question: 'Who can today speak of *any* all-consuming, totalising ways of life?' Here perhaps it is best that we consider his study not as one of all Armenians in the diaspora but specifically as one of its elite, those who are specialists on what is Armenian, and who make special efforts to preserve the culture and extended networks of the diaspora. It may be that something is added to the study by the fact that Björklund could establish a collegial relationship with these specialists as fellow intellectuals. Similarly, for Dahlén's insights into the ideational and practical sides of interculturalism, perhaps his personal relationships to the interculturalists are not of particularly great importance, as long as he is on good speaking terms with them – and the same thing can perhaps be said about my own contacts with foreign correspondents.

Yet some relationships of personal trust can play a special role in multi-local field studies. When one is about to enter a new site, it can be a great help if there is someone there whom one already knows from somewhere else, or at least if, as a fieldworker, one can bring greetings from some credible person somewhere in the wider network. Such 'gatekeepers' between fields show up here and there among the studies. Huss's record producer friend, Ossie Thomas, is found both in London and in Jamaica. In the ballet world, Wulff moves from one company to the next by means of recommendations and through meetings with key persons who move between localities. Dahlén meets other conference participants, who invite him to other institutions of interculturalism. Björklund writes a letter seeking advice from a magazine editor in Watertown, outside Boston, about whom he should meet in Athens. Among foreign correspondents, I notice that it is appreciated, and helps create a sense of mutual understandings, when, even if I do not come with direct greetings, I can mention that I have met colleagues from the same organisation somewhere else in the world, or have even met the editors in the office at home.

On the other hand, the anthropologists themselves can sometimes act as links in the multi-local network. In Stockholm, I can mention to a veteran Swedish correspondent that one of his American contemporaries from Peking in the 1980s, whom I recently met in New York, has got married. Hardtmann finds that she becomes messenger and commentator within the Dalit movement network – not only between continents, but also over shorter distances, such as between Birmingham and Wolverhampton. Wulff may be back in Stockholm, but through telephone, fax and email she is still in contact with the dancers in her four companies, and can also act as intermediary in the informal flow of information between them.

MATERIALS AND OPPORTUNITIES

This leads to one last question. What kind of materials are collected in multi-local field studies, and which situations are part of fieldwork? For example, Wulff might sit at home and talk on the phone with a dancer in Frankfurt. Is this 'participant observation'?

This has been a key term for anthropological fieldwork in the spirit of Malinowski, and has perhaps sometimes been considered a synonym for it. For some people, it may be that participant observation is what defines anthropology. Now and again, it has been pointed out that the degree of participation can certainly vary, and that opportunities for actively joining the locals in some kinds of activities can depend on circumstances over which the anthropologist has no control. Nonetheless, there can be little doubt that opportunities for direct observation have been very highly valued.

In present-day anthropological research this premise may need renewed scrutiny. What observation opportunities do the fields of our time offer, and what other kinds of materials may be of interest?

Clearly, there is much to observe in many of the multi-local fields as well. Wulff had performances and endless rehearsals to follow. Although obviously she could not go along to 'participate' in the performances on stage, she points out that her earlier dance background enabled her to have a special insight into the more practical, bodily and physical aspects of the dance. Lindquist followed neo-shamanism in its rich ritual manifestations, to a great degree also through her own active participation. Huss hung out with reggae people in their complicated passages through the streets of London or Kingston. The conferences and courses which are part of many of the fields also offer many arenas for observation, with more or less participation. Dahlén, who comes to the interculturalists from a neighbouring discipline which is well-known to many of them, became something like their personal expert on anthropology. However, there was some observation which he did not get to do – certain of the interculturalist practitioners would not allow him to come to their lectures and practices, partly because his presence would perhaps interfere with a fragile group dynamic, and partly because their special way of transmitting insight about cultural difference should remain a business secret.

On the other hand there are activities in modern life – and not only within multi-local field studies – which are hardly worth observing. What would be the purpose of sitting, hour after hour, observing someone who sits at his desk in front of a computer screen? Probably it is less rewarding than following Trobriand Islanders to their orchards or the herders around the pastures. This problem shows up, for example, in Garsten's visit to Olsten's regional office in Silicon Valley.

Hugh Gusterson (1997), an American anthropologist who gained attention with his studies of the occupational culture of atomic weapon research, has argued that it is perhaps time to somewhat downplay 'participant observation fetishism' in anthropology, and rather underline contemporary fieldwork's character of 'polymorphous engagements'.[13] Anthropological data collection and data production is somewhat an art of the possible, where one always has to keep an eye out for new opportunities.

In several of the studies here, the observational materials are proportionally more limited than in traditional anthropology, and interview materials more important instead. Björklund points this out about his study of the Armenian diaspora. I myself would not want to miss a chance to be present at an editorial meeting, or to tag along on a reporting mission, but my materials on the work of foreign correspondents consist in large part of long interviews – at home with them, at the office, or at a cafe. In such contexts, it is important (in my study as so often in anthropology) that interviews become conversations, only partially directed, partially developed spontaneously – and seldom a question of going through some questionnaire. Why this concentration on interviews? Perhaps partially for reasons of time – the multi-local fieldworker can be in a bit of a hurry. But it is also because some studies, in knowledge society and in the age of information, to a high degree are about words, words, words; or 'discourses', if you prefer.

This also means that texts and media take up a central space in many contemporary field studies. When I did my fieldwork in Washington a few decades ago, it was still quite unusual for anthropologists to be interested in anything other than the form and content of face-to-face relationships, and I had to ponder over how

I should relate to the black radio stations, and to time spent watching television with my informants. When Garsten set out to study Apple, on the other hand, it was soon apparent that part of the field was made up of AppleLink, the internal electronic network that tied together the company's employees wherever they worked. For Dahlén, the interculturalist's way of employing various forms of communication and media in order to convey cultural difference became an especially strong research interest. And, above all, for many anthropologists fieldwork can now include reading the field's own newspapers and books, using the telephone, keeping an eye on the fax, exchanging email with informants, checking out various web sites and perhaps watching video recordings of events where one could not be present. In a way, this means that the anthropologist never has to be entirely 'out of the field' (we can think about the above citation from Poster here), even if we still perhaps have difficulty imagining a kind of fieldwork without any of the more normal types of face-to-face interaction.[14] In my own project, which is precisely about media people, such materials are naturally quite central. Björklund, for his part, quotes a journal editor who claims that 'wherever one finds two dozen Armenians in the world, they will publish some kind of newspaper'.

If one really feels it is necessary to summarise the pros and cons of fieldwork in the societies of modernity, and specifically in multi-local fields, with the classical anthropological fieldwork in mind, the former does admittedly sometimes offer fewer rewarding opportunities for direct observation of activities and interactions. But, on the other hand, it offers a wealth of types of material which simply did not exist in the Trobriands when Malinowski was there. In its turn, certainly, this may require, and also provide openings for, new skills of composition and synthesis.

Let us also remember that it is media and media materials that so often play an important role when it comes to holding the translocal fields together – they contribute to making them precisely translocal, instead of only multi-local. People can be mobile between localities themselves, and also keep in contact through words·and pictures which move on their own. And the same thing pertains to the work of anthropology.

Translated from the Swedish by Daniel Winfree Papuga.

NOTES

1. I have written more about the project in Hannerz (1998a, 1998b, 1998c).
2. I reported the results of the project in, among other places, my doctoral dissertation (Hannerz, 1969). I also write about the fieldwork in Hannerz (1983: 64ff.).

3. A short explanation of this is found in Hannerz (1973: 24ff.).
4. Such problems are taken up in recent anthropology, for example, by Appadurai (1996: 178ff.), Gupta and Ferguson (1997), and Olwig and Hastrup (1997).
5. More about such migration studies in transnational contexts may be read in, for example, Basch et al. (1994).
6. All of the authors described below have been tied to the Department of Social Anthropology at Stockholm University, even though some of them are now engaged elsewhere. A number of the projects treated here were tied to the umbrella project 'National and transnational cultural processes', which was based at this institution and at the Department of Ethnology at the University of Lund, and was supported by the the the Swedish Council for Research in the Humanities and Social Sciences during the period 1991–96. One of the closing activities of the project was arranged in May 1998, with at workshop on translocal field studies at Villa Brevik, Lidingö, Sweden. Most of the works described below were presented in draft versions there. I wish to take the opportunity to thank the Swedish Council for Research in the Humanities and Social Sciences for its support, Galina Linquist for her work in organising the workshop at Villa Brevik, and Ulf Björklund and Karin Norman for their efforts when it came to taking the first step from workshop to book. A discussion between Galina Lindquist, Tommy Dahlén and myself which was published in *Antropologiska Studier* (Dahlén et al., 1996) also has a place in the preparations for the workshop and book. In addition, an article by Britt-Marie Thurén (1999) has its origin in the workshop.
7. Appadurai (1996) and Hannerz (1996) give examples of such anthropology. Recently, the journals *Public Culture* (started in 1988)and *Identities* (started in 1994) have also paid much attention to this direction. I have treated questions of method within a transnational frame elsewhere (1998d), but these are in large part parallel to what is discussed here.
8. I have written about anthropological uses of the term 'network' in other connections (Hannerz 1980: 163ff., 1992).
9. Comparative studies in anthropology have often not presupposed that the researcher does field studies in all of the places the material is collected from. Instead, many comparisons are built on several researchers' published materials.
10. The French anthropologist Marc Augé (1995) uses a term, 'non-places', which is somewhat looser, but still obviously related to 'translocalities'.
11. It should be pointed out that travel itself does not necessarily make up a particularly large part of multi-local project budgets – anthropologists usually develop a certain competence when it comes to finding cheap tickets.
12. One may wonder whether the need to alternate shorter field visits with periods at home reflects the researchers' different personal practical life situations, and whether it leads to multi-local studies (if they often consist of and easily allow such shifts) attracting other anthropologists than those who enter into long, continuous fieldwork in one place (or whether anthropologists choose different types of fieldwork in different phases of their lives).

13. Gusterson's study of atomic weapon researchers at a laboratory in California is published in Gusterson (1996).
14. Various ways of handling media research, in cultural disciplines but in large part in anthropology, are exemplified in Hannerz (1990) and Marcus (1996), and a survey of the growing anthropology of media is found in Spitulnik (1993). Escobar (1994) gives an early view into the anthropology of cyberspace.

REFERENCES

Appadurai, A. 1996. *Modernity at Large*. Minneapolis: University of Minnesota Press.

Augé, M. 1995. *Non-places*. London: Verso.

Basch, L., N.G. Schiller and C.S. Blanc. 1994. *Nations Unbound*. Langhorne, PA: Gordon & Breach.

Björklund, U. 1981. *North to Another Country*. Stockholm Studies in Social Anthropology, 9. Stockholm: Almqvist & Wiksell International.

Dahlén, T., U. Hannerz and G. Lindquist. 1996. Att definiera ett translokalt fält, *Antropologiska Studier* 54–5: 3–14.

Escobar, A. 1994. Welcome to Cyberia: notes on the anthropology of cyber-culture, *Current Anthropology* 35: 211–23.

Garsten, C. 1994. *Apple World*. Stockholm Studies in Social Anthropology, 33. Stockholm: Almqvist & Wiksell International.

Geertz, C. 1973. *The Interpretation of Cultures*. New York: Basic Books.

Giddens, A. 1990. *The Consequences of Modernity*. Cambridge: Polity Press.

Gupta, A., and J. Ferguson (eds) 1997. *Anthropological Locations*. Berkeley: University of California Press.

Gusterson, H. 1996. *Nuclear Rites*. Berkeley: University of California Press.

—— 1997. Studying up revisited, *Political and Legal Anthropological Review* 20(1): 114–19.

Hannerz, U. 1969. *Soulside*. New York: Columbia University Press.

—— 1973. Lokalsamhället och omvärlden: ett socialantropologiskt perspektiv. In Ulf Hannerz (ed.) *Lokalsamhället och omvärlden*. Stockholm: Rabén & Sjögren.

—— 1980. *Exploring the City*. New York: Columbia University Press.

—— 1983. *Över gränser*. Lund: Liber.

—— 1990. *Medier och kulturer*. Stockholm: Carlssons.

—— 1992. The global ecumene as a network of networks. In A. Kuper (ed.) *Conceptualizing Society*. London: Routledge.

—— 1996. *Transnational Connections*. London: Routledge.

—— 1998a. Other transnationals: perspectives gained from studying sideways, *Paideuma* 44: 109–23.

—— 1998b. Of correspondents and collages, *Anthropological Journal on European Cultures* 7: 91–109.

—— 1998c. Reporting from Jerusalem, *Cultural Anthropology* 13: 548–74.

—— 1998d. Transnational research. In H. Russell Bernard (ed.) *Handbook of Methods in Anthropology*. Walnut Creek, CA: Altamira Press.

—— (ed.) 2001. *Flera fält i ett: Socialantropologer om translokala fältstudier*. Stockholm: Carlssons.

Malinowski, B. 1984/1922. *Argonauts of the Western Pacific*. Prospect Heights, IL: Waveland.

Marcus, G.E. 1986. Contemporary problems of ethnography in the modern world system. In J. Clifford and G.E. Marcus (eds) *Writing Culture*. Berkeley: University of California Press.

—— 1989. Imagining the whole: ethnography's contemporary efforts to situate itself, *Critique of Anthropology* 9(3): 7–30.

—— 1995. Ethnography in/of the world-system: the emergence of multi-sited ethnography, *Annual Review of Anthropology* 24: 95–117.

—— (ed.) 1996. *Connected*. Chicago: University of Chicago Press.

Marcus, G.E. and M.J. Fischer. 1986. *Anthropology as Cultural Critique*. Chicago: University of Chicago Press.

Olwig, K.F. and K. Hastrup (eds) 1997. *Siting Culture*. London: Routledge.

Ortner, S.B. 1997. Fieldwork in the postcommunity, *Anthropology and Humanism* 22(1): 61–80.

Poster, M. 1990. *The Mode of Information*. Cambridge: Polity Press.

Powdermaker, H. 1966. *Stranger and Friend*. New York: Norton.

Spitulnik, D. 1993. Anthropology and mass media, *Annual Review of Anthropology* 22: 293–315.

Thurén, B.-M. 1999. Platsens plats i det antropologiska arbetet, *Kulturella Perspektiv* 8(1): 12–24.

Watson, J.L. (ed.) 1977. *Between Two Cultures*. Oxford: Blackwell.

3 ETHNOGRAPHY AND THE EXTREME INTERNET

Daniel Miller and Don Slater

THE INTERNET AS A GLOBAL PHENOMENON

If one is looking for the best possible image of a global phenomenon, then the internet undoubtedly provides it. But not the internet as either a technology or a practice, but rather the internet as a discourse. Recall the scene circa 1999, the globe, that is all that part of the population that was concerned with this phenomenon speaks with one voice, no exceptions, no dissent, one voice, one certainty, one clear vision of the future. From Alaska to Australia you are being told that if you want even to be part of that future, to actually be present in it at all, then boy you had better be on the internet. If your business wasn't largely online within a couple of years, you might as well pack up your bags and give up. Who is saying these things? Just about every intelligent well educated person there is, anyone who ever got the top marks in their university degree, the high-flying management consultants from McKinsey and Andersen, the finest economists determining the pattern of investments and government policies, the hardest-nosed capitalists and their vanguard, the venture capitalists and, behind them all the rest of us, academics, journalists and the person with the loudest mouth at the dinner party. The future is the internet. It was impossible to think otherwise. Fortunately we don't need to rely on a collective memory, nor give references. The point is that you can take any major influential writing at that time, from the *Harvard Business Review* to the *McKinsey Quarterly* and look now (with considerable embarrassment) at what was being written at that time, you will have to look pretty hard to find dissent.

We should know – in 1999 we were busy trying to write about the future, to fill in all the details from the rather vaguely sketched image of how things would be. We had spotted our niche. In all this certainty about what the internet was going to be, there had been remarkably little attempt to find out in any detail what it had already become. There were no scholarly monographs describing how people actually used the internet. Soon of course there would be hundreds, but we were going to be the first. With the sensibility of anthropology we were also going to strike a kind of ethical blow on behalf of the diverse populations of the world. The first proper description of the future was not going to come from Paris, London or New York. We were asserting a global right to have a stake based on the demonstrable prescience of those dismissed as peripheral. We had a kind of vicarious pride in the idea that the first description fleshed out in the detail of actual humanity in all its complex struggle to appropriate and forge a new technology, a picture one could see the faces in, would come from Trinidad.

Fortunately our primary concern was not the extreme internet, this fabulous global certainty. By deciding to conduct our work ethnographically and with respect to what was specific and local about the internet we were ideally placed, with a stake firmly embedded in one fixed point, to resist the flood. In this chapter we will consider the highly localised aspects of the internet but, at the same time, as with any ethnography, this was a study of discourse as well as practice and we were in an excellent position to observe the extreme internet. Even in Trinidad the biggest claims to perspicacity, the people who really were certain about the future and the centrality of the internet to it, were the top-notch management consultants. There were plenty of firms such as KPMG that were busy taking time out from the US or Europe to send missionaries to places like Trinidad and tell them how to become part of the future. As part of our ethnography we tried to sit in and listen to some of these workshops, missionary activity of one kind or another is quite central to contemporary Trinidad, and we needed to observe it directly.

At such seminars we heard the local captains of industry being informed that it was commerce that should and indeed was taking the lead. It was venture capitalists who were marshalling the billions of dollars being poured into the internet forge, the crucible from where the future would take shape. It was businesses that were to set up the mature internet, integrating all their office work, their accounts, their supplies, and of course their sales, since who would sell anything if it wasn't available online? A new language about back-office integration and B to B (business to business) connectivity was emerging. We could also see how this impacted upon the local discourse of being global. Trinidadians were no more resistant to this discourse than were the British or the Americans. They too believed that if Trinidad was to be part of the future then this would be the quickest route. Indeed the hope was that they could use their skills to leapfrog their way into becoming an off-shore centre for high value-added work such as web-site construction and finally take what they saw as their rightful place as a metropolitan centre within the global world. Pouring scorn on nearby Barbados for its commitment to low-level data-entry work (see Freeman, 2000) Trinidad was going to use its educational capital to come in at the high value-added side of activities such as web-site construction. As we put it in local terms in 1999 the internet was 'hot' in Trinidad (Miller and Slater, 2000: 32–5).

In the midst of this, we were busy trying to gain a sense of the present, that is the everyday practice of internet use to set against this discourse. We knew that Trinidadians were indeed using the internet. At that time we reckoned as high a proportion of people were finding some kind of access in Trinidad as in the UK, which, given the income differentials, was nothing less than astonishing. We could also see, however, that they had managed to find a hundred ways of getting things free for everyone where they were paying for anything. We knew that the software was being copied, that web sites were being cannibalised from others, and that the main usage was communication and relationships and not purchase. We do not want to claim that we achieved some marvellous prescience that flew in the face of this global certainty. All we did was to acknowledge our own findings. Looking back on our publication of this material the statement that the internet was at least as much evidence for the growth in decommoditisation as commoditisation (Miller and Slater, 2000: 169–71) now looks pretty impressive in the degree of scepticism this demonstrated as against the prevalent discourse. But it could hardly be said to have exposed the sheer tide of what is now called 'irrational exuberance' and was rather cautious as against what finally transpired. It was difficult to reach conclusions on the implications of this evidence for decommodification in the face of the insistence by the global discourse that the pundits couldn't be that wrong – sooner or later they would work out the right business model, the way to get people to pay upfront, that they would crack it and, even if things were rather overhyped, this was the big one.

What is remarkable from the point of view of 2002 is the sheer velocity of change. Actually the dotcom crash now seems like ancient history. We are now collectively surveying the wreckage, with the help of well-written surveys such as Cassidy's book *Dot.Con* (2002). We now read about the financial aspects of the internet largely in the light of the South Sea bubble and what seems like mindless speculations in the eighteenth and nineteenth centuries. But even with Dutch tulips and never actually built railway speculation as precedents, we have to acknowledge that the internet bubble was far more extreme. There never has been such a vast misuse of capital as in the last few years; so many people so ungainfuly employed and then unemployed. There are lessons to be learned, but they may not be about the nature of the internet *per se*. Rather, with hindsight we can see how the entire world economy was in hock to what, in effect, was an abstraction that claimed to be founded upon the internet as practice but was re-cast in terms of financial leverage. The missionaries who came to Trinidad were strongly connected to the world of venture capitalism and the stock market, which creates wealth by multiplying the potential of a given asset. What developed was a kind of outbidding around the possibilities of speculation, such that an abstract concept of the internet became more important than its practice. This is an example of what can be termed 'virtualism' (Miller, 1998) where this refers not to a property of the internet but a property of modern finance. Once huge sums are invested around the confidence about what the internet is going to become, the missionaries' role is to try and make sure the practice starts looking a bit more like the abstract model of what it is supposed to be. As the theory of virtualism argues, this is actually quite central to the role of economics and finance more generally. This so-called irrational exuberance (Shiller, 2001) is not best understood as some aberration around the internet but a description of ordinary contemporary capitalism.

What would be quite wrong is for us as academics to pretend that we were ahead of the game. There is certainly no evidence for this in the record of academic writings about the internet. The best-known and praised academic work was all about this new 'network society' (Castells, 1996, 1997, 1998). Our book was published in 2000, and it is only now, in 2002, that one is waiting for the first book to offer a fully sceptical take on the internet: Woolgar's edited collection *Virtual Society* (2002). This is a book that includes papers such as 'They came, they surfed, they went back to the beach'. But academics, even the best of them, were no more prescient than anyone else at the time we started our work. Indeed, we were wrong about the academics too. When we conducted our study we were convinced that our monograph was surely going to be the first of a flood. Everyone could see that what was needed was detailed accounts of what people in one place were actually doing with the internet. That is what gave us the impetus to get the thing out while it could still be part of the action. Our book duly came out in the summer of 2000. And the flood that we were so certain was about to be unleashed? Well actually three years down the line we are still waiting to see monograph number two!

So, at first glance, the phenomenon of the internet provides a wonderful glimpse of globalisation. It shows that more or less the whole planet, without exception and irrespective of place or perspective can actually unite in almost total self-delusion. That the brightest brains and most informed journalists could tell the mere population that anyone who didn't understand that the internet was the future was a moron. It's almost impossible without squirming with collective embarrassment to recall that certainty and lack of dissent. Do we learn from these mistakes? Try going to a seminar on mobile phones in 2003. You will here the same buzz, the same excitement. Tales about all the things we are about to start doing with mobile phones, all of us. The way we are all now linked up, how older forms of communities are now really buzzing down the lines. Perhaps most extraordinary is the G3 phenomenon which arose when the major telecom companies vastly overbid to secure control over third generation mobile phone contracts in major states, only to find themselves today some of the biggest losers in corporate history. All this happened within a year or two of the internet crash. Does this suggest that those who had most to learn, and were once bitten, were now twice shy? Hardly. But there is nothing insignificant about self-delusion, and the capacity of the world to engage in it is extraordinarily instructive. This is not an argument against globalisation, quite the contrary; it is just a sobering representation of what globalisation at its height actually looks like. On the whole, childish, excitable and pretty stupid.

None of this is to suggest that the internet is unimportant or has not made a major impact, or isn't going to be part of the future. It only looks paltry when placed against the vast claims that were made and the fact that humanity actually did put its money where its mouth was, almost rocking the global economy as a result, with the subsequent collapse of high-technology shares. If the original claims had only been modest we might be sitting here marvelling at all the important things the various technologies that make up the internet have become. At least now the dust has settled we can hopefully gain a better sense of landscape, the actual hills and troughs. The internet that we spent most of our time studying in Trinidad was extraordinarily impressive in terms of the impact it had made in a remarkably short time on people's lives. This is what our book was largely about, and, on reflection, we feel we were right to have been impressed and we see a similar impact on a wide range of countries that is badly in need of similar investigation and acknowledgement.

Underneath the extreme internet, there is a much more sober and equally important case to be made for the internet itself as a localised global phenomenon in terms of its infrastructure and its technical ability to link up places in the world. That is to say, its importance is not so much as technology itself – one could already contact most parts of the world by telephone – but rather it was that this radically changed the price structure of communication. So that while one had previously to think very hard about making contact between

Argentina and Australia and keep the communication to high-value minimalised forms, an Australian who wanted to contact an Argentiniean online could be as relaxed and thoughtless about it as they liked since the cost was identical to contacting their neighbours online. The point of our book is that this shift within the ease of global connectivity had quite clear local consequences. Indeed, if anything, the effect was as much in the self-conception of a place as local as it was to the sense of the world as global, since people could become more aware of their relative position vis-à-vis the rest of the world. It is to the study of this impact on localisation that we now turn, by way of contrast to the above. The way the internet pushed further the tendencies to localisation and to the definition of one's identity in relation to the particularity of place, since this is far less intuitively obvious or indeed reported. Indeed, we are just as clear about the need to conduct new research on the impact of the mobile phone, we are applying for the grants to do so. The global may look like the science fiction it is, but the local still needs studying.

THE INTERNET AS A LOCAL PHENOMENON

This section, which summarises a larger presentation of the evidence in chapter 4 of our book (Miller and Slater, 2000; see also www.ethnonet.gold.ac.uk) examines the internet as a means by which Trinidadians refined their sense of themselves as Trinidadian. We argue that there were two main manifestations of this tendency the first we call being Trini and the second we call representing Trinidad.

Being Trini

Participants routinely went to great lengths to make the internet a Trini place, a place where they could be Trini and perform Trininess. Indeed, in the case of diasporic Trinidadians, this was often put forward as the major reason for being on the Internet in the first place: to make contact with Trinis, talk about Trini things and also do Trini things like lime, banter, talk music, food, drink and sex. For example Trinidad-Online.org provides a range of Trinidad-related facilities: bookshop, music store, penpal and personals service, postcard centre, web-based email facility, a chat room hosted on Yahoo with accompanying photographic archive and membership list, it is also part of the Trinidad-Online webring, it has an email list (Trinbago-Now) as well as a hard-copy magazine called *Kalypso*.

Its chat room 'de Rumshop Lime' represented a rival to the largest dedicated Trinidadian ICQ list – 'de Trini Lime' ICQ or 'I Seek You' is a way of knowing which of your friends – that is people on your list – happen to be online at the time you choose to go online. Today it has largely been replaced by MSN. Here Trinis (and a few non-Trinis with some connection or affection for the place) place their nicknames and a few details as a basis for contacting Trinis online, either individually or via a collective chat room. The controller (a Trini based at MIT) proudly proclaimed them to have come from 40 different countries. Our analysis of this information showed that there were more, though not a whole lot more, men, and participation leaned towards the young. It was dominated by home-based Trinis with the rest roughly equally split between the USA and Canada.

The names of these chatrooms – de Rumshop Lime, de Trini Lime – evokes a core concept within Trinidadian cultural life. The 'lime' especially evokes the street corner where males traditionally exchanged innuendo and banter with passing females and aimed to hear about whatever was happening The rumshop is a local, down-market drinking place, in the old days dominated by dominoes and rum, today often filled with ear-splitting music and Carib beer. Limers hope to fill their time with skilled banter, drifting onwards to other places (a street corner, a club, someone's house, another island, ideally perhaps dancing and sex). The term 'lime' is regarded as quin-tessentially Trini – both peculiar to the place and definitive of its people – and was regularly cited as the Trini pleasure they most wanted to recover on or through the Internet. In fact, 'liming' was the word generally used to describe all chatting online and other non-serious uses of the internet, as it would describe any similar hanging out. The internet comes to be seen as simply extended liming into just another space. Indeed Trini youth, could pursue their lime from school to home to street to ICQ (either at home or in a cybercafe, which was also a place to lime face to face), that is, they would chat, then meet at a local mall, then return home and chat some more.

The term 'lime' highlights the free-flowing sociability of chat sites. An observer could look inside to find no-one there; all of a sudden someone else has spotted them and joined, a crowd would gather, people would drop in and out, regular characters were described and discussed. Characters were important: individual eccentricity plays out the stock Trini types found in literature such as Naipaul's *Miguel Street* and in Carnival characters. So here LouistheLover performed the most outrageous version of the red-hot, flirtatious predatory Trini male (and was constantly, affectionately, described as a real Trini 'type'), but every chat room had its equivalent BigSexy or xxx who was essential in keeping things going in what was seen as a specifically Trini way. There was endless talk of how hard one had partied last night, or wanted to party but couldn't because of work or being stuck in Toronto, or even how late de Rumshop Lime had gone on the night before. Indeed, given that so many people were liming from North America, with its very different lifestyle and time structure, they might lime online at some personal cost. The endless banter and what is called 'ole talk', has clear local rules, for example although the banter can be – indeed should be – filthier and more outrageous with every additional remark, there is a complete ban on swear words or indeed any explicit sexual reference: the skill and pleasure is entirely in the use of the most extensive and creative forms of innuendo. There is also the basic shared nationalism which means they can together praise but perhaps more often disparage Trinidadians (politicians, institutions, web sites, etc.) with the underlying affinity to Trinidad that would make the same negative comment by an outsider seem highly offensive.

This was made explicit in the response to someone who made the grave mistake of putting the local soca music in the same sentence as rap. One of the angry responses was:

Our music is suggestive but we have what rap and other modern music [don't] have ... respect for the listeners and class. Think of that the next time you listen to Biggy, little Kim and the majority of the artists today before you compare our slightness with their blatant porn.

People show an astonishing facility for switching between 'proper English' and patois, I gave a paper on this material in Bristol and a Bajan – that is, Barbadian – told me afterwards he had had to relearn his local patois in order to go online. Much of the content of the discussion concerns the defining features of being Trinidadian, as seen in the self-description of the participants. A home-based Trini says: 'I live for West Indies Cricket, love to listen to David Rudder, love all things Trini, liming, drinking, feting, and did I mention liming, drinking, and feting? And let's not forget the Trini woman, dbest in the world!' While another, living abroad, says 'All alyuh boy up here studyin' in dis cold ass country. Ah real missin' de limin on de block, eatin' doubles dong by UWI wit ah beastly cold in meh head, alyuh drop meh ah line nah and make meh feel like ah home again.'

For the Trinis in the UK this opportunity to lime online came with a sense of relief, since they felt the banter, insult and flirting, which is seen as intrinsic to their being Trini would most likely be misunderstood or misconstrued (e.g. as sexist and racist) if it took place within any other context than one framed specifically as Trinidadian. So that, as with the traditional 'lime', there is a sense that people can relax, or be themselves while engaged in this activity, free from the stress of having to watch themselves their behaviour and conversation. This, then, is what we mean by 'being

Trini', with the internet as a critical place for its performance by Trinidadians irrespective of where they happen to live.

For Diaspora Trinidadians who do not enjoy chat and ICQ, an almost ubiquitous feature of online use is access to the internet versions of the two daily papers. There were also more seasonal uses, such as extensive interest in the Carnival sites, from which people might choose a costume if they are intending to return for Carnival. Several UK Trinis had at least tried to look at the live webcam that was set up over the Savannah, which is the high point of the carnival parade; indeed, one enterprising Trinidadian, who had gone back to play mas that year, subsequently went through the archive online and found and downloaded the section where he and his wife were filmed crossing the Savannah stage! Overall, UK-based Trinis reckoned that around 50 per cent of their surfing was directed to Trinidad-related sites. Finally, one should note that this was not used to form any actual UK Trini sociality. It was not a catalyst for developing an offline community here in the UK. It did not matter whether the online chat was coming from Canada, Trinidad or here, it allowed them to retain a strong sense of the specificity of Trinidadian culture and practice within any particular location.

Representing Trinidad

There is also a hyper-awareness that one is also constantly 'representing Trinidad'. This might be peculiar to Trinidad – an island culture, culturally and economically ambitious but on the periphery of North America and so on – but then that would be precisely our point: that we cannot exclude spatial and even national identities from Internet studies, either on the basis of theoretical assumptions about disembedding or on the basis of extrapolations from exclusively US and European experiences of the internet. It would be hard to imagine a mid-western American student including in their web-site links to the local chamber of commerce or to government information sources, as Trini students would normally do, informing people about the country, putting its music or sports on the global map.

Although Trinidadians are used to metropolitan peoples, random ICQ exposes them to the wider ignorance of the larger world, as in these quotations.

What I usually find with new people, they don't know about Trinidad. Their reaction is where is that, or what is that? It is some thing to them not some where. I think especially with what happened last night. The Miss Universe Pageant [which was held in Trinidad while we were conducting fieldwork] it has opened up a lot. I think from now I should be getting a different response from people when I say Trinidad. 'Was that where the Miss Universe was held, we thought the culture was nice and everything'. I think that is the exposure we have got from last night.

Some of them have the idea that Trinidadians live up trees and swing from branches. I am big 'real world' fan from MTV and tell them we have real world. Our schools are different, we wear uniforms. I don't show them specific web sites or anything, I just tell them about it. They think the Caribbean is natural rain forest like the Amazon.

Thus, at the same time the internet opens the gates to a potential cosmopolitanism it also exposes a global parochialism and makes people feel insecure in their own nationality as constituting a recognised place in the world at large. This is not quite the same as what has recently been called glocalisation, which focuses on the reception of global goods in a local context. What we have been describing is a projection of nationally conceived projects and identities into a newly available global context. Moreover, Trininess in particular is an identity which, in crucial respects, has been conceived of as naturally global and cosmopolitan long before the internet appeared. Trinis see the trait of cosmopolitan confidence as itself highly Trinidadian. In other words, unlike many others, Trinidadian nationalism has for a long time been extremely cosmopolitan, which we suspect is one of the reasons they take so readily to the internet. The point is that if Trinidadians see themselves as more cosmopolitan than other nationals, then it follows that it is precisely evidence of their openness to global forms for which they take pride in national terms. So a good Trinidadian is not someone who just loves soca music, but who loves soca music as the best of global music of which they are particularly aware. Obviously this bears no relation to a simplistic literature that assumes nationalism must be parochial or opposed to cosmopolitanism.

One of the most striking examples of representing Trinidad comes in the post-teenage personal web sites. The assumption is often that to understand the individual the viewer must first understand what it means to be Trinidadian. At its simplest this means the home page is replete with various core symbols of that country, such as its flag, crest, a map and some basic statistics, while links lead to photographs and further information about Trinidad. This may even include the playing of the national anthem on the home page, or opening onto a Trinidadian beach with the sound of waves crashing on the shore. Core symbols include those evocative of Carnival, calypso and soca music, Carib beer or key Trinidadian personalities. One page opens with:

Whoa! That was a big wave! Glad you surfed on in here ... never mind the dents you put in the coral reef! Hi I'm Sharon, and I am thrilled to welcome you to my little piece of Paradise! I live on a tiny island (not much more than a blob covered with grass and trees, surrounded by water) called Trinidad, which is in the Caribbean.

What is striking is how many of these sites are actually run by Trinidadians currently at colleges in the US. Yet unless one is looking hard, the surfer would assume they have landed on Trinidad and not at a US college such as Cal-Tech.

In some cases, the process goes much further than this simple presentation of the nation-state. Specifically Trinidadian idioms can be employed for the process by which the stranger is drawn into acquaintance with the world of Trinis. For example, in Weslynne's Big Lime, she shows how the process of surfing can be translated into local terms. The surfer joins her on a lime, or is teased for being *macotious*, that is nosy about her private affairs, or is accused of being too *fass*, which implies that one is getting to know her more quickly than is considered civil in offline relationships. In a way, this draws attention to the very lack of control the web-site constructor has over those who visit, and some ambivalence about the often very personal information that is included.

The sites that have been described so far are still recognisably personal web sites. There is, however, another genre of sites that take the dominant trend much further. These are individuals who have taken upon themselves the role of producing national homepages and have completely subsumed their own presence within the larger concern to present the nation. In the most extreme cases, the site will have a name such as the Unofficial Trinidad Home Pages, and the only sign of the individual concerned is at the base of the home page where it states who the site is maintained by. Some sites have a more individual style in the way this is done. For example, a site called 'A Workbook on Trinidad and Tobago' presents itself in the form of a traditional Carnival figure. It introduces itself in the following style: 'For I am Chanticleer, cock-of-the-rock, master of this barnyard: your Tourguide. I am the herald of the new and the old. My diversity, magnificent in the rising sun as I announce the new day, gives rise to the multitude of opportunities the day offers.' That is, typical Carnival figure banter. Then there is 'Click on the "Welcome" balloons for an enjoyable Virtual Tour of Trinidad & Tobago. To see and hear how we celebrate Christmas, go to "Visit our Christmas Page" where there are recipes for preparing foods and drinks enjoyed in Trinidad & Tobago during the Christmas season.' Other sites include small dictionaries of favourite Creole terms or instructions on how to compute the local currency. Overall, they either try to include hundreds of links to other Trinidadian sites to become virtual portals, or loads of photos and descriptions as virtual guidebooks.

Surprisingly few of these sites are used for any sort of commercial purposes. In Miller and Slater (2000) we go into the nuances of how Trinidadians' culture is represented, for example the differences between Carnival, soca music and steelband. These show considerable continuity with previous media. Carnival is directed most to the outsider, with the hope of selling costumes to tourists and others; steelband is focused most on the insider, which includes foreigners but usually those who have an intense interest in steelband, play it and study it, so the sites are more like encyclopaedia articles, with vast amounts of data, directed at the cognoscenti and education. Such distinctions are critical in opposing any glib assumption that the internet would make culture either more inauthentic and alienated, or indeed profound and inalienable. We find both trends here, the point being that web sites, email and chat extend and transform much longer trajectories and are firmly embedded in their offline equivalents. But they are all variants upon this overall theme of representing Trinidad.

ETHNOGRAPHY AS THE MEDIATION OF THE LOCAL AND THE GLOBAL

In the previous two sections we have considered in turn the extreme examples of the most global and the most local aspects of the internet. In this third section we want to consider the challenges this poses to the practice and theory of anthropology itself, and in particular, the way it impacts upon ethnography as methodology. One of the most influential arguments in recent years in terms of anthropological methodology came from Marcus (1995), with the promulgation of the ideal of multi-sited ethnography. I have absolutely no desire to detract from these ideas. Many of our PhD students are conducting commodity chain analysis, which requires just such a following of the object to see how it connects up people. But in this respect our book on the internet comes over as somewhat anachronistic, since it is entirely geared to an old-fashioned notion of place. Indeed, it might be regarded as anthropologically quite conservative since it constantly generalises around the concept of the Trinidadian as was evident in the previous section, and yet we were clearly aware of the discourse of the internet as a global form as indicated by our first section. Were we somehow being perverse in our refusal to take this new opportunity for global research and subject to it something closer to the traditional – what some might see as rather outmoded – forms of ethnographic enquiry? Certainly most of the other works that have been published on the methodological implications of the internet see this as an evident route to quite novel forms of research, largely conducted by following connections online and almost irrespective of more traditional conceptualisations of place (e.g. Hine, 2000).

There is an issue raised by the difference between what Marcus argued for, at least as it seems to evidently apply to the study of the internet (see also Marcus, 1996), and what we actually did. It is an issues about the nature of ethnographic inquiry itself, and therefore the role of anthropological work in mediating local and global articulation. Where is one going – literally – in internet research? Is sitting in one place and surfing to sites constructed on the other side of the planet a form of single-sited research or a form of multi-sited research? Is this more local (you remain in your house) or more global (you connect with all other places) than interacting with, for example, all the members of a village?

This in turn brings out one of the key problems that students have encountered when contemplating research influenced by Marcus's ideal of the multi-sited. If I work in several places over the time period when previously I would have been in only one place, is my fieldwork necessarily more superficial and lacking in the richness of context that traditional ethnography claimed? This issue of context has in turn become critical to the self-reflection by anthropologists about the nature of their research. In recent years, writers such as Latour (1996, 1999: 104, 110) and Strathern (1999, 2002) have questioned the separation of inquiry into objects or subjects on the one hand and their contexts on the other, as though these were separate entities which the ethnographer as analyst somehow puts back together. Behind their critique of simple concepts of context, Latour and Strathern clearly see that an effect of this separation is a reification of something called 'society' which is taken to be the context for whatever is being studied. They oppose the idea that, for example, one could have a study of art works where society is specified as context, or a study of class relations where the political economy is defined as the context. They imply that ethnography should form part of a struggle to dissolve any such dualism and recognise that the relationship of phenomena and their contexts be seen as reciprocal; that is, in any given study, what from one perspective is the object of study A and its context B, could from another perspective have been object of study B and its context A. One can study cars in their social context but one can equally study the kind of society that develops within a cultural milieu in which cars have a prominent role (Miller, 2001).

In terms of the internet, this general point may be grounded by focusing upon the specific question of the relationship between the study of this phenomenon as essentially an online investigation or an offline investigation. This is because the most immediate response to such a distinction between online and offline is to think of the actual investigation of the internet as constituted by the online part of the research with the offline component relegated to that context which is required to account for it. It should be clear that the ethnographic commitment to 'putting things in context' has to avoid the danger of reifying the object (in this case the internet) as much as the danger of producing an analytically reified context (e.g. society). To go beyond this immediate dualism and follow the strictures of Latour and Stathern seems to imply a recognition that the internet as an ethnographic phenomenon might comprise different social relations, rather than regarding it as a single 'object' with inherent properties that might, at most, be variously expressed in different contexts.

The place where the extreme internet as discourse tended to reify the very distinction that we are trying here to set ourselves against, came with the development of the concept of the virtual. The concept of the virtual privileged the experience of online to such a degree that it came to be regarded as an other-worldly sphere which thereby separated itself from offline life. Indeed, it went much further than relegating offline worlds to mere context, it implied that one could consider the internet as, in effect, decontextualised altogether, a self-sufficient world grown out of but largely autonomous from that inhabited by offline peoples. Of course, the virtual can be studied as a discourse that effects internet use. There may well be people who are treating these media *as if* they were virtual and doing all in their power to separate their online relationships from offline ones. That is an important topic which is coming to the fore in the study of areas such as MUD and MOO, the Multi-User Dimensions whose theoretical implications were pointed out by Turkle (1995). But there is a huge difference between starting an online ethnography from the *presumption* that the internet inherently comprises 'virtual' relationships and can therefore be studied as a self-contained setting (ignoring offline 'contexts'), as opposed to finding – in the midst of an ethnography – that some people use it to create their sense of the virtual. The idea that we can critique the assumptions behind the concept of the virtual while accepting that there may be a 'native' experience of or construction of the virtual replays many familiar anthropological debates.

We are looking, then, for something more subtle than simply a distinction between online and offline experience, or a study that simply treats the latter as the context of the former. It follows that we cannot come to what might seem to be the most obvious conclusion from our work, which is to favour research that includes an offline component as ensuring that we do not retreat to this presumption of the virtual. That this is too simplistic a conclusion is evident if we bring into the frame of consideration not just our

Trinidad work but also the previous studies conducted by Slater on other examples of internet use. The reason for this is that Slater's studies (1998, 2000) which looked at the exchange of sexually explicit materials ('sex pics') on Internet Relay Chat (IRC) was conducted entirely online. It exemplifies this multi-sited/single-sited distinction since he was working as much with housewives based in the USA as with people in the UK, even though the work took place entirely from his home in London. But what gave that work its ethnographic sensibility was not the question of place but the question of the relationship between online and offline activity.

Slater worked entirely online but had to pay constant attention to the references online participants made to their offline activities and, above all, to how participants themselves constructed highly diverse, complex and fluid distinctions between their online and offline lives. For example, to understand what some US housewives were doing when they spent hours engaged in this trade in sex-pics depends upon understanding their offline relationships, often with their partner. This in turn explains one of the most surprising results, which was that, rather than being a vanguard of libertarianism, many of those involved have tight, sometimes quite conservative views on the morality of the activity they are engaged in. For example, they may become quite upset at those who cheat on the ratios of exchange that have been agreed (Slater, 2000), or who trade pictures that are considered beyond the pale of their conventions as to proper or morally justified sex pics. In short, this is not a study in which there is simply a phenomenon – the online exchange of sex pics, to which offline is the context that explains it. Rather, there is a recognition of the complex and nuanced relationship between online and offline worlds which produces the normative structures of both of these worlds.

The point is that such work, while insisting upon the importance of offline activity and notwithstanding that the research was conducted entirely online, does not treat offline worlds merely as the context for understanding online worlds. Each feeds upon and helps constitute the experience of the other in reciprocal rather than hierarchical fashion. Furthermore, such a study refuses to separate off the internet as technology from the process of exchange. Most early studies of the internet saw certain properties as intrinsic to this new media. Indeed, it was precisely areas such as sex-pic exchange with an apparent premium on fantasy and anonymity, as well as a new libertarian and performative relation to personal identity that was proclaimed as evidence of this technical foundation to the new world of virtuality. Slater's research certainly provides plenty of evidence for where and when the virtual develops as a feature of internet use. But at the same time it shows that this is not some intrinsic property of the technology. This critique of virtuality was to become central to the subsequent work on Trinidad (Miller and Slater, 2000: chapter 1).

So, in making our commitment to carry out an ethnography in Trinidad, we started with a joint commitment to working both online and offline, but not on the basis of a simplistic or dogmatic claim that no research conducted entirely online could ever count as a proper ethnography. Rather, it was with a mind to the deeper implications of relating online and offline worlds, without seeing either as the context for the other. It would not be a study of technology in a social context, but a study in the formation of normative and transient cultural forms that dissolved simple dualisms of subject and object. The ideal was that the Trinidadian internet could be understood as the product of Trinidad itself, just as the contemporary culture of Trinidad is becoming a product of, amongst other things, its relationship with the internet.

In the light of this discussion, we can now return to the relationship between the first two sections of this chapter. As already noted, our book looks unusual in its willingness to countenance descriptions of place that are generally seen as suspect within contemporary anthropology. In particular, we provide a defence of our use of the term 'Trinidad' and indeed 'Trinidadian'. We agree that the use of the general term 'Trinidad' could only be warranted where it was a product of the ethnographic encounter. We were well aware of yet another critique of traditional anthropological forms of inquiry that follow from a single-sited stance. Current anthropological theory and fashion has been increasingly sceptical about the use of such a term as 'Trinidadian' on the grounds that it ignores the diversity of peoples and that it reproduces nationalistic discourse. But we would no more assume that it was now an 'improper' thing to use a term such as 'Trinidadian' where it appears warranted than we would assume that we could/should use the term where it clearly obfuscated those differences and the diversity that were salient to our inquiry. Indeed, a central conclusion of our research was discussed in the second section of this chapter, which is that, far from dissipating a sense of national identity through exposure to a global media, the internet has become a primary means for refining a specifically national genre of being.

As one might expect, the terms 'local' and 'global' are in many respects mutually dependent. It was the experience of going online and meeting people from Latvia who had never heard of Trinidad that fostered the sheer nationalism within the Trinidadian response. That is to say, they became more self-conscious of their locality, and the need to strongly identify it, identify with it and then place it as a presence online, because of the extreme nature of the global encounter they were now subject to. We may be distressed by such nationalism, but we see our task as understanding it, not pretending that it doesn't exist. For us, the point of critiques of national labels, or indeed of the word 'culture' itself, is to force ethnographers to discriminate in their use of such terms and apply them only where they are clearly salient, not to determine a priori what we want or 'need' to encounter in the field. So a quite unexpected conclusion from this examination of ethnographic work on the internet would be to defend the use of such localised terminology where appropriate.

An almost symmetrical point could be made with reference to the use of the term 'global'. In many respects, by undertaking a localised ethnographic study, we might be seen as acting in opposition to the increasing use of the term 'global' or the presupposition of phenomena such as the internet as global. But, just as our defence of local terms such as 'Trinidadian' is based on the ethnographic discrimination between appropriate and inappropriate uses of this term, so also with the term 'global'. Where it refers to the ethnography of practice it appears an unwarranted presupposition that can be discarded in the light of ethnographic research, but as discourse, for example as a symbol of modernity of quite extraordinary potency around 1999, then if the term 'global' is ever merited, this was the phenomenon that best merited the term.

So internet research may help clarify the appropriate use of both local and global terminology. We would also hope that these discussions of the internet are particularly interesting in the way that they throw open the discussion that had already developed about the role of the anthropologist in mediating between local and global connections. In the previous sections, this was manifested most clearly as a difference between the study of discourse, the subject of our first section, and the study of practice, the subject of our second. But we do not want to reify this dualism any more than the others we have described, since in both cases there is a constant interaction between the two. In particular, the study of the local nature of practice turns out to be in many respects a response to discourse, the concept of the global and the way the sense of oneself as local takes on a particular discursive presence in relationship to that. Similarly, to call the global element a discourse should not hide the materiality of investments and failures that also exist as unemployment and poverty as much as excess and wealth. It is, after all, a fairly pointless task to try and specify whether the identification of being Trinidadian is a matter of practice or discourse.

So, instead of re-casting local/global mediation as that between practice and discourse, we have preferred – in this third section – to consider what we take to be more subtle arguments that have arisen through the critique of the concept of context, which, we have argued, in turn puts a more interesting gloss on the argument between an ideal of single-sited and multi-sited ethnography. As such, this study clearly falls within the contemporary response to a more flexible set of encounters which problematised the more traditional concept of the fieldsite (e.g. Gupta and Ferguson, 1997; Marcus, 1995) in general, and with respect to the internet in particular (e.g. Hakken, 1999: 58–60). In many respects, what our studies have retained is a commitment to a much older ideal of holism, a structural sense of the relationship between as many different aspects of people's behaviour and the forces that impact upon them as possible. Such a holistic commitment seems the best prospect for avoiding the hierarchisation implied by the concept of context. This holistic commitment recognises that offline can inform on online as much as online on offline, and that an enrichment of understanding can come equally from following relationships by studying them in many different places as from the traditional single-sited ethnographic aim of deepening of the number of relationships that bear on the site. As such, what internet research suggests is that we should not pit online against offline research, or single-sited as against multi-sited and, in particular, not pit the internet as a research object against society seen as its context. Rather, we treat the phenomenon as material culture, something that constructs both its social and material effects.

Finally, by examining the extremes of local and global that the internet constructed we are also able to consider again the role of the anthropologist as a mediator, as someone who could almost be defined in terms of their role as the representative of the local to the global. At this level there is a striking parallel between the internet and anthropology itself. Anthropology has constantly tried to force the global to acknowledge cultural and regional diversity and specificity, and thereby attempted to define it and identify with it. There are obvious parallels with the way Trinidadians were found to be doing much the same thing in their reconfiguring of local identity in the second section of this chapter. But anthropology also has an ambition towards generalisation about the nature of humanity and the using of local studies within comparative studies in order to make higher levels of generalisations that bring us quickly to the level of the global as in itself an academic ambition. Indeed, anthropology is constantly poised within the contradictions that have been the subject of this chapter, and their defence has tended to be that it is much safer to engage in such generalisations when one is grounded in the ethnographic encounter with the specific. The main argument of this chapter has been that the study of the internet helps to highlight such contradictions and reveal how they bear on such specific questions as the nature of the methodology we use to try and safely navigate towards an ideal which could be said to be the pursuit of generality in the absence of virtuality, both in the sense of Miller (1998) and of Miller and Slater (2000).

REFERENCES

Cassidy, J. 2002. *Dot.Con: The Greatest Story Ever Sold*. New York: Harper-Collins.

Castells, M. 1996. *The Rise of the Network Society*. Oxford: Blackwell.

—— 1997. *The Power of Identity*. Oxford: Blackwell.

—— 1998. *End of Millennium*. Oxford: Blackwell.

Freeman, C. 2000. *High Tech and High Heels in the Global Economy*. Durham, NC: Duke University Press.

Gupta, A. and J. Ferguson. 1997. Discipline and practice: the 'field' as site, method and location in anthropology. In A. Gupta and J. Ferguson (eds) *Anthropological Locations*. Berkeley: University of California Press.

Hakken, D. 1999. *Cyborgs@cyberspace? An Ethnographer Looks to the Future*. London: Routledge.

Hine, C. 2000. *Virtual Ethnography*. London: Sage.

Latour, B. 1996. *Aramis, or the Love of Technology*. Cambridge, MA: Harvard University Press.

—— 1999. *Pandora's Hope*. Cambridge, MA: Harvard University Press.

Marcus, G. 1995. Ethnography in/of the world system: the emergence of multi-sited ethnography, *Annual Review of Anthropology* 24: 95–117.

—— (ed.) 1996. *Connected*. Chicago: University of Chicago Press.

—— 1998. *Ethnography Through Thick and Thin*. Princeton, NJ: Princeton University Press.

Miller, D. 1998. A theory of virtualism. In J. Carrier and D. Miller (eds) *Virtualism: A New Political Economy*. Oxford: Berg.

—— (ed.) 2001. *Car Cultures*. Oxford: Berg.

Miller, D. and D. Slater. 2000. *The Internet: An Ethnographic Approach*. Oxford: Berg.

Shiller, R. 2001. *Irrational Exuberance*. Princeton, NJ: Princeton University Press.

Slater, D. 1998. Trading sexpics on IRC: embodiment and authenticity on the Internet, *Body & Society* 4: 91–117.

—— 2000. Consumption without scarcity: exchange and normativity in an Internet setting. In P. Jackson, M. Lowe, D. Miller and F. Mort (eds) *Commercial Cultures*, pp. 123–42. Oxford: Berg.

Strathern, M. 1999. *Property, Substance and Effect: Anthropological Essays on Persons and Things*. London: Athlone Press.

—— 2002. Abstraction and decontextualization: an anthropological comment. In S. Woolgar (ed.) *Virtual Society: Technology, Cyberbole, Reality*, pp. 302–13. Oxford: Oxford University Press.

Turkle, S. 1995. *Life on the Screen: Identity in the Age of the Internet*. New York: Simon & Schuster.

Woolgar, S. (ed.) 2002. *Virtual Society: Technology, Cyberbole, Reality*. Oxford: Oxford University Press.

4 GLOBAL PLACES AND PLACE-IDENTITIES – LESSONS FROM CARIBBEAN RESEARCH[1]

Karen Fog Olwig

A cartoon published in the weekly magazine *The New Yorker* in 2001 showed two middle-aged men chatting in a local bar. One of them, obviously on his way home from work, is bald and is wearing a suit, white shirt and tie, and is holding a drink. The other has longer hair, is wearing a T-shirt and drinking beer, and seems to be rather out of touch with the pulsating life in the wider world. The beer drinker says, 'Look, I've got nothing against globalization, just as long as it's not in my backyard' (Mankoff, 2001). The cartoon is amusing not least because it plays on the NIMBY (Not In My Back Yard) cliché: 'I have nothing against XX (refugees, immigrants, foreigners, blacks, children, dogs) as long as they are not in my back yard.' 'Back yard', in this context, refers not only to the area behind the house, but also to the area that is one's particular domain, that is, where one has control or where one feels at home. The cartoon therefore presents a person who imagines his little back yard to be a place of liberty, where he can be himself, undisturbed by the wider world under rapid transformation by global forces that he has no control over and with which he therefore wants nothing to do.

We know that it is impossible to make such a neat distinction between the local – home, where one is one's own boss – and the global, changing world where external forces rule. We are all deeply implicated in globalisation, and there are many effects of globalisation in our own back yards and homes. The effects are there in the form of garden furniture made of tropical hardwoods, clothes made with cheap labour in the far East, fresh fruit and vegetables flown in from industrial producers under southern skies, satellite or cable TV that gives access to a string of international TV stations all over the world, internet, email, and so on. Globalisation becomes even more apparent when one leaves the private sphere for the public sphere, where one encounters population groups from various parts of the world, such as migrants and tourists, transnational corporations that produce for the international market or international chains of shops and restaurants that appear to offer the same consumer goods no matter where they are in the world.

At the same time as globalisation seems to level out regional differences to the extent that it can sometimes be difficult to distinguish one place from another, place is being celebrated as an increasingly important source of identification. This notion of places is based on the view that there are, in fact, different places that have their own distinct and meaningful characteristics. Such places are not only people's private homes and back yards, but also public areas ranging from neighbourhoods to villages, regions and nations.

Anthropologists have noted the apparent paradox that the more global our lives seem to be, the more we insist on the existence of demonstrably different places where we are socially and culturally anchored. A number of anthropologists have pointed out that the focus on place and its great social and cultural significance is not contrary to globalisation, but is actually one of globalisation's features. One can therefore argue that it is not *despite of*, but rather *because* we live in a world that has become so closely interwoven, that place has become so significant.

SPECIFIC GLOBAL PLACES

Akhil Gupta and James Ferguson (1992, 1997) have argued that the world has long been characterised by global connections marked by complex constellations of power and hierarchical relations which crystallise in close ties between central and peripheral areas. From this point of view, local places do not exist as autonomous economic, social, cultural or political units. Place is created when local communities appear within the broader world system and constitute themselves in particular areas. Gupta and Ferguson thus understand place as a cultural construction, created in the light of global consciousness of the meaning of local experience. For Gupta and Ferguson it is therefore important that anthropologists study how people create a place for themselves based on its particularity, separateness and special identity within a world that is, in many ways, a connected space.

Arjun Appadurai, like Gupta and Ferguson, also starts from the position that places must be defined, bounded and given meaning in relation to broader structures. Appadurai (1996) identifies two different kinds of places. One concerns what he calls 'neighbour-hoods' and he refers to 'actually existing social forms in which locality, as a dimension or value, is variably realized', though not necessarily in local communities. The other kind of place he terms a 'locality' and he describes this as 'primarily relational and contextual' and of emotional, symbolic value (1996: 178–9). 'Localities' may not necessarily lead to the formation of actual social forms tied to particular physical sites, but may take a more imagined form. Thus, diasporic people celebrate a distant homeland as their place of identification, but their attachment to this locality may not necessarily result in the development of an actual, situated social form. From a modern, global point of view, place is therefore not only a geographically delimited space where people live their lives and to which they therefore attribute particular meanings. It has also become an anchoring point where modern mobile people can find a source of identification across appreciable distances in a changeable world.

In earlier research on the former Danish and British Caribbean, I carried out an historical-ethnographic study of how places may be created within a broader global space of social, economic, political and cultural influences. This research detailed how Afro-Caribbean communities of social relations and cultural values, connected with particular places, emerged among the African slaves and their descendants, as they began to engage in family-based subsistence activities, often in marginal areas of the plantations (Olwig, 1985, 1999). These areas, where the slaves essentially fed themselves and brought up their families in their free time, were an integral part of the European colonial society, but as local manifestations of Afro-Caribbean culture, which in many parts of the Caribbean eventually led to the establishment of free villages, they were also defined in opposition to European culture and the interests of European colonial powers (see Mintz, 1974; Mintz and Price, 1992/1976). This dual nature of the places is perhaps most apparent in the institution of family land that emerged in many of these villages.

Family land refers to property, originally acquired from the white plantation owners by the African-Caribbean population, which has been passed on to the descendants of the original owner and which is held in common by the family. The land is often of a modest extent, and it is therefore often used only for residential purposes. Since a large kin group often shares the land, however, most relatives will never be able to settle on it. Ten children, who inherit between them a family plot of 2 acres, could hardly eke out a living as small-holders on this small piece of land. The ten children might acquire small house plots for themselves, but there would not be enough land for their children, in turn, to have house plots of their own. Many Caribbean people who grow up on family land therefore leave it and migrate to economic centres, often in the West, where they can obtain waged employment. But the very same Caribbean places of family land that the migrants must leave behind in order to make a living can acquire important symbolic value as cultural and social points of identification for the migrants. For the migrants, the family land symbolises stability, continuity and rootedness in the Caribbean, because it is a concrete manifestation of their Caribbean origins where they, and their descendants, maintain a right to return as members of the family that owns the land, whenever they wish to do so. Since few actually move back to the Caribbean, it may be possible for a large group of family members to maintain the idea that a tiny plot of family land offers a safe home in the Caribbean for all of them (see Besson, 1987). Indeed, family land only makes sense as a cultural site that most people leave behind and cherish *in absentia*. While descendants born and reared abroad in principle maintain the right to return to the family land, their use right in practice depends on their having cultivated their ties to the land, for example by helping the family pay taxes on the land. Many do not do this, and the family land therefore, in effect, ceases to be a concrete place to which they can return. The descendants of the Caribbean migrants relocate in their place of birth, and the family of origin – if they still know about it – becomes a genealogically as well as geographically distant place.

Those who are born in the Caribbean, on the other hand, usually maintain a close relationship to the family that they have left behind in their place of origin, and today, with improved and less expensive modes of transportation, they often return periodically for visits. In recent decades an increasing number of migrants, wishing to retire to their place of origin, have begun to build their own house in the place of origin. They may do this on the inherited family land, if it is large enough. In many cases this will not be possible, and they will therefore build their house on land that they purchase with money earned abroad. Since the migrants continue to live and work abroad, these houses stand empty most of the time. While the collectively owned family land symbolised a family's rootedness in a particular village, often concretised in the visible graves of the family members who had lived and died on the land, the individually owned houses are concrete evidence of the owners' absence from their place of belonging. Furthermore, the houses that migrants build to demonstrate their continued ties to the Caribbean, and thereby their Caribbean identity, are often built of concrete blocks in a Western style and equipped with an electric stove, a refrigerator, freezer, washing machine, TV and video, even though the local infrastructure often is far from sufficient to support the use of so many modern Western consumer goods. One could say, therefore, that these migrants turn the *New Yorker* caption on its head, and say, 'I have nothing against globalisation as long it *is* in my backyard.' In other words, they can accept globalisation as long as they can domesticate it in their own home.

In this example, home, as a local place of belonging becomes a global place in so far as it closely reflects the global world that migrants and their families attempt to domesticate. One could posit, somewhat provocatively, that the difference between the American in the *New Yorker* cartoon, who lives in his own house in his own country, and the West Indian migrant who builds a Western house in his or her Caribbean homeland, is that while the American believes that his home in the American suburbs can be kept outside the realm of globalisation, the West Indian migrant considers the house in the Caribbean homeland to be that particular domain of the global arena, which has been brought under control and mastered. One might add that this domestication of the global carries a rather high price, in that migrants often spend most of their lives in the service of globalisation, working as cheap labour for the same organisations that profit from producing the very goods that the migrants are so keen to domesticate.

GENERALISED GLOBAL PLACES

So far I have discussed places that are global in the sense that they are constructed within a larger global space of which they are a part, whether this space is defined primarily in relation to the capitalist world economy (Gupta and Ferguson), to global modernity (Appadurai) or to a historically colonial, present-day Third World region such as the Caribbean (Olwig). These global places have emerged as people give special meaning and purpose to specific sites – villages, family land, houses – thus transforming them into places of their own. The significance of such specific places may therefore not necessarily be recognised, or understood, by others. This can be a problem for migrants who have moved to the Western world, where they may encounter notions of place that may be quite different from their own. As migrants they will, by definition, come from an elsewhere that will be defined in relation to notions of place of origin that are predominant in the receiving society. Furthermore, migrants and their descendants may continue to be socially categorised according to this place of origin, whether or not they themselves identify with this place. Migrants, and their descendants, in other words, will be perceived, and sometimes treated, in relation to a global place of belonging that conforms to dominant 'structures of common difference, which celebrate particular kinds of diversity while submerging, deflating or suppressing others' (Wilk, 1995: 118). Such global places, I shall argue, are, to a great extent, defined in accordance with the global order of nation-states and the concept of territorially defined cultures that is closely related to this order.

A large body of research has described the nation-state's origins and development under specific historical conditions. It goes without saying, therefore, that the nation-state is a historical-cultural construction and not a natural phenomenon. Even so, it is often assumed to be a universally natural and obvious framework of human life. The nation-state is, no doubt, extremely important, because the world has become divided into a large number of political and administrative systems, believed to correspond to autonomous nation-states that both coexist independently of each other and unite in an international community of nation-states such as the UN. A nation-state provides an important framework of life for the native population, because it defines, to a very great extent, the political and social rights and economic opportunities that individuals may enjoy. A nation-state, however, is not merely a politico-legal structure that makes it possible to divide global space into smaller administrable units. As Anderson has pointed out (Anderson, 1991/1983), a nation-state is also conceptualised as continuing a community of people believed to share a unique culture and history that forms an important basis of identification for those who live within its boundaries. While such national ideologies may have formed an important basis for the historical development of nation-states in some parts of the world, such as Europe and North America, they may not necessarily have been so prominent in many areas of the developing world, where nation-states have been established recently in the wake of decolonisation. This means that places of belonging tied to nation-states of origin may not necessarily be of particular relevance to migrants from the developing world. The case of Nevis may illustrate some of the problems that emerge when one conceptualises migrants in relation to a nation-state.[2]

The little Caribbean island of Nevis was colonised by the British in 1628 and was a part of the British West Indies until it became an independent state in union with the neighboring island of St Kitts. Independence implied not only the establishment of a political and administrative system but also the creation of a nationally bounded social, cultural and historical entity. It was not difficult to make a national flag, a national anthem and a national coat of arms; the flag and song were chosen through a local competition and the coat of arms was designed by a British firm specialising in such matters. It was much more difficult to create a St Kitts–Nevis history which brought together the people of two islands, because the history of the two islands had been quite different in important ways. Both islands have a past of sugar plantations owned by European planters and cultivated by slave labour forcibly imported from Africa. When the independent nation-state of St Kitts–Nevis came into being in 1983, St Kitts was still noted for its large-scale sugar production and it had a large population of landless plantation workers who were unionised. On Nevis, however, large-scale sugar cultivation had disappeared early in the twentieth century, and the island had a long history of farming and fishing by people living on their own land. Despite major social and economic changes on the two islands in recent decades, the two island societies were very different, and it was difficult for the local population to accept the idea that a nation-state of St Kitts–Nevis could be a natural entity. Furthermore, throughout the nineteenth century, both islands had developed a marked tradition for migration to areas with better economic and social opportunities, and the population therefore did not think of St Kitts–Nevis as a meaningful framework of life. The local population, in other words, nourished no particular feeling of belonging to the independent national union of St Kitts–Nevis. The union was strange, not only because the two islands were in fact quite different and therefore difficult to conceptualise as one country, but also because it did not seem realistic to the population to think of St Kitts–Nevis as an autonomous economic, political, social or cultural entity that might constitute a natural framework of life. Most continued to see migration as the way forward, and for them the most significant aspect of the establishment of St Kitts–Nevis as an independent nation-state was the potential for an increased immigration quota to the USA in relation to the quota allowed when the islands were under British rule. The new independent union therefore was seen to offer greater freedom of movement on the global scale where people from St Kitts and Nevis had long been active, whether as students at British universities, nurses in Canadian hospitals, cab drivers in New York City, or hotel receptionists in St Thomas. St Kitts–Nevis was meaningful as a nation-state for people to leave, but not as a place where people could live their lives, nor as a place with significant symbolic value with which they could identify. The population traditionally lived beyond the limits of the two islands that became the nation-state, and their local identity seems not to have referred to the nation-state that was a new and peculiar union.

One could choose to portray the nation-state of St Kitts–Nevis as no more than a marriage of convenience given that it is made up of two small islands that were brought together for no better reason than that they happened to be close to each other and were governed by the same colonial power. In fact, their greatest similarity was probably the fact that they were both marked by an unusually high degree of emigration. As an example of the arbitrary construction of nation-states during the decolonisation of the developing world, however, St Kitts–Nevis is not at all unusual. In the Caribbean context, St Kitts–Nevis can be understood as a fairly unremarkable example of the construction of place which gives the two islands a place in the global order of nation-states, but which does not necessarily correspond to the field of relations or the place-identities that the local population has built up during a long colonial history of connections with the rest of the world. Still, as an established nation-state, St Kitts–Nevis is a reality that the population must live with, not only as a political-administrative institution, but also as an entity with a particular cultural meaning, at least globally. It is precisely in this global space outside St Kitts–Nevis, navigated by so many of its people, that the implications of the global definition of place become apparent.

One might question quite fundamentally what migration actually means. People move through space all the time. At what point does one decide whether or not to call this movement migration? In the dictionary, to migrate is defined as 'to move from one country, place, or locality to another' (*Merriam-Webster*, 1996). This begs the question of when one can say that a person has left one place, or locality, for another, and when they simply move around within the same place. What factors have to be present before movement is called migration? Historically, migration has been identified with movements from the countryside to the towns in Europe, from tribal place of birth to mining districts in Africa, from poor, racist southern states to northern industrial regions less marked by racial discrimination in the USA, and of course from various countries, particularly in Europe, to the New World in North America. In the last half of the twentieth century, however, migration research has focused mainly on international migration. The connection between migration and international population movements has been consolidated by the introduction, in the course of the twentieth century, of immigration regulations by nation-states that attempt to control the ever more comprehensive and widespread population movements. In the nineteenth century there was little control of the international migration from Europe to North America. At the beginning of the twentieth century, however, restrictions were put in place in North America to stem the flow of mass immigration which had by then begun to incorporate people from countries outside Europe as well. Despite these restrictions, and the instituting of intensive patrolling of political borders, mass immigration to North America has continued, much of it illegally. Various European countries have also put restrictions in place since they, too, have become important migration destinations. At the same time as the regulation of population movements over political borders has been tightened, which has led to the redefinition of migration as unusual and requiring special permission, increasing attention has been paid to the cultural aspects of migration. Migration poses not only judicial and administrative problems but is also about cultural ties. Migrants are perceived as people who leave the nation-state where they belong not only legally and administratively, but also culturally. Nation-states, in other words, have become global places that define where one is in one's element, and where one can be perceived as foreign.

While migration in and of itself is loosely defined as movement from 'one country, place, or locality to another', it has effectively become limited to refer only to international movements from one country, or nation-state, to another. This has had two important consequences for the perception of migrants in destination countries. First, migrants are often perceived as people who come from a qualitatively different place, and who are therefore radically different culturally. That is, the identities that migrants share with the local population, for example as a cook, schoolchild, neighbour, etc., are underplayed in relation to their cultural identity, rooted in another nation-state, which marks them as different. This means, second, that migrants are perceived as being outside their place of origin, where their roots are and where they really belong. This intense focus on the meaning of migrants' place of origin, defined by the nation-state where they or their ancestors were born and grew up, is reflected in some of the recent theories on transnational and diasporic relations.

In traditional migration research, not least in the USA which may well be the country in the world that has received the most immigrants, interest has focused on the processes whereby migrants have been 'integrated' into the society of a new nation-state. This integration has been conceptualised in terms of three phases (see, for example, Waters, 1999: 192–6):

1. The immigrant arrives and settles in an immigrant ghetto, often with people who came from the same place.
2. Their children become integrated in the new society and move out of the ghetto.
3. Their grandchildren, who are now completely integrated, become interested in their roots and ethnic identity.

Being interested in one's ethnic background therefore is a way to be an American like most other Americans who also have their roots in another place. The exception is obviously the 'Indian' population, that did not come from another place within historical memory, and therefore paradoxically are not regarded as ordinary hyphenated Americans, but as 'native', and therefore unusual Americans. Black

Americans are also a special case. They are there because of their ancestors' forced migration to North America several centuries ago, and they often find it exceedingly difficult to ascertain a particular place of origin that can be located on a map. Even though they may be able to establish some connection to Africa, it is extremely difficult to interpret this tie in relation to contemporary African conditions. While Native Americans and African-Americans cannot become ordinary Americans, because they cannot document having left another place, Anglo-Americans who have well-documented English backgrounds going back many generations, and whose place of origin is a kind of motherland for the USA, are almost Super-American. They become the embodiment of Americans.

Since the 1980s, the three-generation integration model has been criticised by researchers who argue that it is too simple and inappropriate in a modern world characterised by global fields of movement, networks, communication, and so on. It no longer makes sense to talk of migration as a one-way journey from one place to another, since migrants often retain intimate contact with their place of origin through frequent visits, communication with families and friends in the place of origin by telephone and email, and the watching of TV programmes from their homeland transmitted via cable or satellite. Migrants therefore often continue to regard their place of origin as an important social, cultural, economic and political place of belonging. Since this place of origin has been defined, in the migration research, as a different nation-state, the migrants' identification with a place of origin has come to be seen as identification with another nation-state. This has therefore led researchers to raise the question, what kind of Americans will these migrants be, and will they become American at all? Two concepts have been particularly important in this debate: transnationalism and diaspora.

TRANSNATIONAL AND DIASPORIC PLACES

In 1987, the American anthropologist Constance Sutton launched the concept of transnational sociocultural systems in her introduction to the book *Caribbean Life in New York City: Sociocultural Dimensions* (Sutton, 1987). She argues here that contemporary Caribbean migrants in New York, unlike earlier European immigrants, experience a 'continuous and intense bi-directional flow of peoples, ideas, practices, and ideologies between the Caribbean region and New York City' (1987: 20). According to Sutton, the existence of a transnational sociocultural system means that Caribbean migrants do not experience the same incorporation into

American society as the earlier European migrants. Although the earlier European migrants cultivated their European roots and ethnicities, they did so in the private sphere within the destination country. Caribbean migrants, however, cultivate their particular culture and identity in the public sphere where they develop transnational sociocultural systems linked with the Caribbean. These systems are been made possible by improved international communication, but they have become so prominent because they have become an integral part of ethnic politics in the destination country, the USA (Sutton, 1987: 20). Migrants, in other words, are not only attracted to their country of origin because of their personal connections with it. They are pushed back to the country they have left by the receiving society because they are categorised and perceived in this country in terms of their origins in another nation-state. This affiliation with another nation-state is expected to give them a particular cultural orientation that marks them as different, and in a receiving country like the United States, that recognises dual citizenship, it also allows them to be active in the political life of two different nation-states. The immigrants, in other words, are perceived to be transnational.[3]

A great number of works examining various aspects of transnational social relations and cultural values were published during the 1990s in the USA (for an overview of the literature, see Kearney, 1995; Mahler, 1998; Marcus, 1995; Schiller et al., 1992; Vertovec, 1999). These studies have emphasised the close connections between transnational sociocultural systems and ethnic politics, and have shed light on the relationship between migrants' identities and their social and cultural ties to the two nation-states with which they are connected. In their theoretical article on transnational sociocultural systems, Nina Glick Schiller, Linda Basch and Cristina Szanton-Blanc write that such systems both nourish and are nourished by ethnic politics in the destination country. These authors perceive transnational identity as a form of resistance by migrants who face incorporation into an often racist and repressive destination country (Basch et al., 1994; Schiller et al., 1992). Similarly, Michael Kearney sees transnationalism as an alternative to the hegemony of the nation-state and emphasises that transnational identities escape the either/or categorisation that is otherwise implicit in national identities (Kearney, 1995: 528, 558). These anthropologists also agree that transnationalism carries elements of resistance: migrants do not wish to become integrated into the destination country because of their marginal social, economic and cultural condition there, but prefer to remain a part of the country of origin.

In a critical discussion of studies of transnationalism, Sarah Mahler (1998) has noted that the concept of transnationalism is so broadly defined that it is difficult to decide exactly what it means. She points out that Schiller et al. define it, for example, as those processes by which immigrants form social fields that link their place of origin with their destination. This implies the development of many kinds of relations – familial, economic, social, organisational, religious and political – which transcend boundaries. The definition is so broad, however, that it tells us little about the content, intensity or significance of transnational links, says Mahler (1998: 74). Mahler concludes, therefore, that it is necessary to undertake much more specific, as well as broader, comparative studies of transnational social fields in order to investigate themes such as:

1. the various ways in which individuals, groups and institutions construct and maintain relations across borders – what does transnationalism mean at the level of concrete relations? (1998: 81)
2. the meaning of gender, class, age/generation, mobility and regionalism in transnational social fields – how is a transnational field differentiated, and are there forms of belonging that eclipse the meaning of the transnational, for example, gender, age, social background, regional origin, experiences from other places?
3. the interests aroused by transnationalism – there is a tendency to add a rather romantic gloss which emphasises grassroots, anti-hegemonic systems, but is this the whole story?
4. the relation between transnationalism and identity – this has been an important theme in a number of studies, but sociocultural systems that cross nation-state borders, and identities connected to two different nation-states are not necessarily compatible.

These last two points, the interest in migrants' continued identification with their place of origin and the interpretation of identification with a place of origin as resistance to integration in the society of the receiving nation-state, have been discussed in terms of the concept of diaspora, which has become increasingly important within migration research in recent years. Thus the strong focus on the importance of the native country to migrants has meant that the concepts of transnationalism and diaspora are being merged so that it has become commonplace to describe migrants as belonging to diasporas from their native country. In a review of theories of transnationalism, Steven Vertovec, for example, writes that 'Social formations spanning borders' have become known as 'ethnic diasporas' (1999: 449) and suggests that the theoretical debate has been primarily concerned with 'diasporic awareness' among people with 'two or more identifications' (1999: 450).

The conceptualisation of transnational sociocultural systems as 'ethnic diasporas' has been severely criticised by scholars who have worked with the notion of diaspora. The editor of the American journal *Diaspora*, Khachig Tölöyan, has, for example, expressed surprise and concern over the broad understanding of the notion of 'diaspora' that has been apparent in the manuscripts he has received for publication in the journal since it was founded under his editorship in 1992 (Tölöyan, 1996). According to Tölöyan, who himself belongs to the Armenian diaspora, the concept of diaspora no longer refers specifically to what he calls 'exile nationalism'. By this he means the sense of belonging to a homeland that some exiled groups, such as Jews or Armenians, retain many generations after leaving their nation of origin, and which forms the basis of their continued existence as a people despite being scattered in many countries. The concept of exile now also refers to what Tölöyan calls 'diasporic transnationalism' and defines as migrants' transnational connections to a country of origin (Tölöyan, 2001: 1). Most authors, according to Tölöyan, use the term 'diaspora' in this latter meaning of the word, and he finds this use of the concept deeply problematic because 'Diasporic identity has become an occasion for the celebration of multiplicity and mobility – and a figure of our discontent with our being in a world apparently still dominated by nation-states' (1996: 28).

When Tölölyan writes 'our', it is clear that he is not referring to people in general, but to intellectual elite of migration researchers who themselves have an experience of migration and are concerned with the forms of identification that this generates. He therefore raises the question, do migrants in general, or the destination country's population more broadly, also celebrate 'mobility' and 'multiplicity'? Or is it primarily a small group of intellectuals and politically active migrants who see mobility and cultural complexity as a form of resistance to the continued hegemony of the nation-state? This leads to further questions concerning whether it is justifiable to characterise people's ties to places of origin as transnational. Are migrants, for example, maintaining contact with friends and family left behind in a place of origin or are they creating transnational connections that allow them to take advantage of their position as legal citizens and members of national communities in two different nation-states? In the remainder of this chapter I shall explore these questions by the way of a study of three family networks of Caribbean background that I studied during the 1990s.[4]

GLOBAL PLACES IN FAMILY NETWORKS

The families consist of the descendants of three couples that had their home on the islands of Jamaica, Dominica and Nevis respectively. The aim of the research was to learn about the sorts of lives that family members had had in different parts of the world, and they ways in which they chose to interpret and represent these lives in the life histories they told to me. I interviewed approximately 150 people from four generations of relatives living in the Caribbean, Great Britain, Canada and the USA. In other words, these were people who have been deeply affected by what we refer to as migration, and who therefore might be expected to have developed transnational sociocultural systems and corresponding transnational identities linked to the two nation-states. How do these family members depict their lives, the places they are connected to and the social fields of relations and cultural values they are part of? They do this in many different ways, which is to be expected given their very different social, cultural, economic, political and geographic conditions. However, there are some consistent themes that are relevant in this context.

Family Networks

All the persons interviewed knew about their family's background in the Caribbean and all were pleased to talk about the various relatives they knew around the world. It was clear that they knew many of these relatives well through visits, telephone calls, letters and now emails, and that they had a close relationships with at least some of them. Many of the family members were quite dispersed; thus I found descendants of the Dominican couple in places as far-flung as Bridgetown (in the Caribbean nation-state of Barbados), Toronto (in the Canadian province of Ontario), Charlotte (in the American state of North Carolina) and Ipswich (in the East Anglia region of England) as well as in Dominica. There was even a relative somewhere in India who I never reached but who had close contact with his family via email. In all family networks most relatives had visited the place where the family home was located and had enjoyed their visits there. By far the majority of their links with the Caribbean, and the various places where the family members lived, were private. Even though family members' networks of relations criss-crossed up to several nation-state borders, and therefore were transnational from a formal political point of it, it seems rather misleading to denote these private family relations as 'transnational'.

Personal Identities

While the oldest generation in the family, who actually emigrated, held on to their identity defined by their original place of origin, many of the second and third generations in the family networks attached little importance to belonging in the Caribbean as such. In fact there were some who rather played down their Caribbean background, not because it held no significance for them, but because so much public attention was paid to their being Caribbean that they felt trapped by the categorisation. This became particularly apparent when I interviewed young family members who were born and brought up in societies with active multicultural policies, such as has been the case in Canada during the past decades. A question about identity directed to a woman of 19 who was born and brought up in Canada led to the following response: 'Do I have to identify myself in any particular way? I say I am a person.' She was clearly tired of being categorised as 'ethnic'. Other young people were less negative about the categorisation they were subjected to, but they found it difficult to understand why it was important to have an ethnic identity. One said:

'Close friends have asked whether I am Black. Like if I am from Africa or something. I don't know what to say. I say that I am West Indian. [...]'
[What does West Indian mean?]
'Being Black. I know I am Black. I am not sure what I am. People say they are Polish, so I say I am West Indian, just to say something. It means little.'

My research shows, therefore, that many people, even if their family can be traced to another place, do not necessarily identify with that place. Or if they do, that identification is linked to personal relations that they do not necessarily translate into ethnic categories.

Places of Belonging

The Caribbean identification points that the family members had developed were strongly influenced by the stories that family members related about the place the family came from and the ties that the family had to these places. There were individual variations within the families, but it was quite clear that particular histories were created within the three different networks about the families' places of origin that created common points of identification for the relatives of significance to the way they related to one another. The Smith family emphasised that they were descended from small-holders in a village in Nevis and that, since the 1950s, the children and grandchildren had sought waged employment abroad in order to support the remaining family in Nevis through remittances of money, clothes and food. Members of the family therefore identified strongly with their childhood homes and the village. The Gaston family described their origins in a teacher's family in a village in Dominica. They were not particularly well off, but were able to keep their children in school and strongly encouraged education and their Catholic religion. The children were sent to secondary school in Dominica's capital Roseau and since the 1950s most of them have left on for higher education at universities of repute in the Caribbean, USA and Britain. Some of them returned to Dominica and obtained prominent positions in the independent nation-state that emerged in the late 1970s. The family therefore identified with the nation-state Dominica, rather than with the house they grew up in. Indeed, this house was sold some years ago since none of the family had any remaining connections with it. Individual family members' identification with the nation-state of Dominica, however, was strongly mediated by the particular family ties that they had developed. The Muir family's history revolved around their origins in a little harbour town in Jamaica. The family belonged to the middle class of the British colonial system, and was part of the respectable middle classes. The children began emigrating in the 1940s in order to obtain a higher education. Family hopes that one of the sons would become a medical doctor were not fulfilled, but some of the family members received an undergraduate education and most settled abroad in their own homes. None of them returned to Jamaica apart from one who earned enough in the USA to purchase a small hotel in Jamaica. While nobody lives in the small harbour town in Jamaica, which has undergone a period of decline since the collapse of the sugar industry early in the century, the childhood home is still owned by the family and family members visit it regularly. The older generation, who grew up in the family home, identify principally with colonial Jamaica where they were part of the colonial middle classes and it is difficult for them to place themselves in the modern, racially aware nation-state which, at least officially, favours its Black, African, non-colonial identity. The three families have thus developed quite different forms of identification in the Caribbean that are difficult to reduce to categories such as Caribbean or to their belonging to different nation-states of origin.

One of the reasons my research uncovered little trace of transnational or diasporic identities or practices is that my field was located within the private domain of family relations. Much of the recent migration research on transnational and diasporic relations has focused on cultural identities asserted in the public domain. There have been few studies of the forms of cultural identity that are articulated in the private sphere of the home, where ethnic politics is less influential. Research on migration has therefore overemphasised migrants' preoccupation with the potential transnational identity they can derive from the nation-states they once came from, or with homelands as a focus for an exiled group within a diaspora. It might well be argued that transnational and diasporic relations are

under-represented in my research. This may well be the case, but it
is thought-provoking, at the very least, that when people are offered
the opportunity to talk about themselves and their lives, ethnic
identities, transnational belonging and diasporic homelands do not
appear to play a significant part in their lives. This does not imply
that these people have been deterritorialised, or that they have no
place-identity. The life histories reflect a number of place-identities
linked both to the areas where people live and to the geographical
locations where they can trace their family backgrounds. These geographical locations have, broadly speaking, become meaningful as
places of origin through the social and cultural values given to them
within family networks, but their significance in the lives of the
various family members around the world varies enormously. In
other words, it is important that people's place-identities are studied
in all their complexity and not only in relation to those global
categories of proper places of belonging.

CONCLUSION

In this chapter I have discussed the notion of global place as (1) a
specific cultural site that attains particular meaning and purpose in
relation to the global space that provides a contrastive context for
the formation of place, and (2) as a generalised, dominant model for
place and place-identity that is closely related to the globalisation of
the order of nation-states. On the basis of research on global places
among Caribbean people or people of Caribbean origin living in
different areas of the world, I have shown that specific and
generalised meanings of global place may vary significantly. In a
Caribbean context, global places attain their value because they
provide a cultural site of identification within the global space of
social and economic relations where people of Caribbean origin
carve out a living for themselves. These global places are therefore
not expected to be self-contained entities where people may live
their lives in their own backyards undisturbed by the ravaging global
forces that surround them. The places are rather anchoring points
that enable people to both explore opportunities in the wider world
and to maintain a sense of rootedness on firm ground – until they
decide to let go of these places and root somewhere else.

The generalised global places that people of Caribbean origin
encounter in the Western world are conceptualised in terms of
autonomous, territorialised sociocultural communities that are
expected to provide a framework of life for the local population.
Within this thinking, people cannot be affiliated with two places at
one time, and migrants will be expected to undergo a long and

difficult processes of integration into a new place of residence – a process that may be completed by future generations. If migrants continue to maintain close bonds with their place of origin, this process of integration is seen to be hampered, so that migrants may never become fully part of their adopted place of residence, but develop transnational or diasporic sources of identification. This perception of migrants, however, is based on a sense of place as an exclusive national entity that bears little relation to the sense of place as a safe vantage point for inclusive and exploratory excursions to different parts of the world held by many people of Caribbean origin. Furthermore, it does little justice to the multi-faceted relations to place that people develop both in the course of their everyday lives and in the context of the extensive networks of personal interrelations that they may develop with family, friends and acquaintances living in different parts of the world.

There is every reason to examine the role of place as source of belonging and identification in the increasingly globalised world. We are just beginning to understand the nature of global places and the complex ways in which they may be culturally constructed in different social, economic and political contexts.

Translated from the Danish by Simone Abram and the author.

NOTES

1. An earlier Danish version of this article was published in *Norsk Antropologisk Tidsskrift* 12(4), 2001.
2. The following analysis is based on Olwig (1993a, 1993b).
3. In a discussion of the concept 'transnational', Ulf Hannerz (1996: 6) has emphasised that it can be useful since it has raised awareness that nation-state actors cannot be active in relations between nation-states. It has, thus, been an important alternative to the concept 'international', which points to nation-states as the most important actors in relations between nation-state units.
4. This research is published in Olwig (2001, 2002a, 2002b, 2002c).

REFERENCES

Anderson, B. 1991/1983. *Imagined Communities: Reflections on the Origin and Spread of Nationalism*, revised edn. London: Verso.

Appadurai, A. 1996. *Modernity at Large: Cultural Dimensions of Globalization*. Minneapolis: University of Minnesota Press.

Basch, L., N.G. Schiller and C.S. Blanc. 1994. *Nations Unbound: Transnational Projects, Postcolonial Predicaments and Deterritorialized Nation-states*. Langhorne, TA: Gordon & Breach.

Besson, J. 1987. A paradox in Caribbean attitudes to land. In J. Besson and J. Momsen (eds) *Land and Development in the Caribbean*, pp. 13–45. London: Macmillan.

Gupta, A. and J. Ferguson 1992. Beyond 'culture': space, identity, and the politics of difference, *Cultural Anthropology* 7: 6–23.

—— 1997. Discipline and practice: 'the field' as site, method, and location in anthropology. In A. Gupta and J. Ferguson (eds) *Anthropological Locations: Boundaries and Grounds of a Field Science*, pp. 1–46. Berkeley, Los Angeles and London: University of California Press.

Hannerz, U. 1996. *Transnational Connections*. London: Routledge.

Kearney, M. 1995. The local and the global: the anthropology of globalization and transnationalism, *Annual Review of Anthropology* 24: 547–65.

Mahler, S. 1998. Theoretical and empirical contributions: toward a research agenda for transnationalism. In M.P. Smith and L.E. Guarnizo (eds) *Transnationalism from Below*, pp. 64–100. New Brunswick, NJ: Transaction Publishers.

Mankoff, R. 2001. Cartoon, *The New Yorker*, 8 June.

Marcus, G. 1995. Ethnography in/of the world system: the emergence of multi-sited ethnography, *Annual Review of Anthropology* 24: 95–117.

Merriam-Webster's Collegiate Dictionary 1996. 10th edn. Springfield, MA: Merriam-Webster.

Mintz, S.W. 1974. *Caribbean Transformations*. Chicago: Aldine Publishing Company.

Mintz, S.W. and R. Price 1992/1976. *The Birth of African-American Culture*. Boston, MA: Beacon Press.

Olwig, K.F. 1985. *Cultural Adaptation and Resistance on St. John: Three Centuries of Afro-Caribbean Life*. Gainesville: University of Florida Press.

—— 1993a. *Global Culture, Island Identity: Continuity and Change in the Afro-Caribbean Community of Nevis*. Studies in Anthropology and History. Reading: Harwood Academic Publishers.

—— 1993b. Defining the national in the transnational: cultural identity in the Afro-Caribbean diaspora, *Ethnos* 58(3–4): 361–76.

—— 1999. Caribbean place identity: from family land to region and beyond, *Identities* 5(4): 435–68.

—— 2001. New York as a locality in a global family network. In N. Foner (ed.) *Islands in the City: West Indian Migration to New York*. Berkeley: University of California Press.

—— 2002a. A respectable livelihood: mobility and identity in a Caribbean family. In N.N. Sørensen and K.F. Olwig (eds) *Mobile Livelihoods: Life and Work in a Globalized World*, pp. 85–105. London: Routledge.

—— 2002b. The ethnographic field revisited: towards a study of common and not so common fields of belonging. In V. Amit (ed.) *Community Revisited: A Review of the Relationship Between Community, Place and Culture*, pp. 124–45. London: Routledge.

—— 2002c. A wedding in the family: home making in a global family kin network. *Global Networks* 2(3): 205–18.

Schiller, N.G., L. Basch and C.S. Blanc (eds) 1992. *Toward a Transnational Perspective on Migration*. New York: The New York Academy of Sciences.

Sutton, C.R. 1987. The Caribbeanization of New York City and the emergence of a transnational socio-cultural system. In C.R. Sutton and E. Chaney (eds)

Caribbean Life in New York City: Sociocultural Dimensions, pp. 15–30. New York: Center for Migration Studies.

Tölölyan, K. 1996. Rethinking diaspora(s): stateless power in the transnational moment, *Diaspora* 5(1): 3–36.

——— 2001. Elites and institutions in the Armenian transnation, paper presented at Conference on Transnational Migration: Comparative Perspectives, Princeton University, 30 June–1 July.

Vertovec, S. 1999. Conceiving and researching transnationalism, *Ethnic and Racial Studies* 22(2): 447–62.

Waters, M.C. 1999. *Black Identities: West Indian Immigrant Dreams and American Realities*. New York: Russell Sage Foundation.

Wilk, R. 1995. Learning to be local in Belize: global systems of common difference. In D. Miller (ed.) *Worlds Apart: Modernity through the Prism of the Local*, pp. 110–33. London: Routledge.

5 INTO OUR TIME:
THE ANTHROPOLOGY OF POLITICAL LIFE IN THE ERA OF GLOBALISATION[1]

Christian Krohn-Hansen

Let us suppose that there is some value in trying to shape an anthropology of the present ... (Sidney Mintz, *Sweetness and Power*)

How can anthropologists usefully examine and write about the contemporary world? How should we study political life in the era of globalisation? The purpose of this chapter is to sketch a set of answers to these questions. Given the questions' high level of abstraction and enormous scope, anybody would be foolish to imagine that he or she could offer more than partial solutions.

A reinvigorated anthropology about the world at present must recognise how indispensable it is to explode a deep-rooted theory about the world. Too much anthropology still contributes to the maintenance of the old (historical, political, economic and cultural) distinction between the West and the rest. Yet from the beginning, the distinction between Western and non-Western societies was blurred. On sheer empirical grounds, the differences between the West and the rest are now more blurred than ever before (Cooper and Stoler, 1997; Trouillot, 1991). This is an old piece of news. Most, if not all, anthropologists accept this. Yet as Akhil Gupta and James Ferguson have argued, much anthropological activity continues none the less in practice, to too large an extent, to portray the world, not in terms of a historical, global web of interconnections, but, instead, as if it were made up of discrete, originally separate place-based societies. Gupta and Ferguson write:

On the one hand, anthropology appears determined to give up its old ideas of territorially fixed communities and stable, localized cultures, and to apprehend an interconnected world.... At the same time, though ... anthropology has come to lean more heavily than ever on a methodological commitment to spend long periods in one localized setting. What are we to do with a discipline that loudly rejects received ideas of 'the local,' even while ever more firmly insisting on a method that takes it for granted? (Gupta and Ferguson, 1997: 4)

A very large part of mainstream twentieth-century anthropology was virtually ahistorical. It was little interested in tracing and analysing the implications of historical global connections – global history (Thomas, 1996). Had it taken a much deeper interest in centuries of global history, it would have been compelled to think and study the world, less as discrete, territorially rooted societies, and more in terms of an interconnected universe.

A strengthened anthropology about the present must acknowledge the need to work better on the past. This may seem as a paradox. I firmly believe that we have to make an anthropology about the world today, not about yesterday's societies. But this requires that we study global history far more seriously than mainstream anthropology in the twentieth century did. As Sidney Mintz has argued, much anthropological work, by some strange sleight of hand, whisked out of view 'any signs of the present and how it came to be'. It seemed to want to 'maintain the illusion of ... "the uncontaminated McCoy"' (Mintz, 1985: xxvii). Too much anthropology in the twentieth century played down or even ignored the historical construction of the West in all its guises. It thus played down or ignored the historical processes that shaped the world we all live in, the world today, an interconnected world. The insistence on a continued need to get rid of the ingrained distinction between the West and the rest is, to a large extent, an outcome of my own background. It is a product of something like an anthropological *credo*. I have worked anthropologically in the Hispanic Caribbean. From its inception, the anthropology of the Caribbean challenged the anthropological hegemony. It defined its object of study, life in the Caribbean, as an integral part of its own history, its own world.

Were we to push things to extremes, we could perhaps summarise much anthropology in the twentieth century as having been permeated by a wish: 'Stop the world! I want to get off.'[2] This resembles a wish to suppress or get out of time. Anthropologists ignored, neglected and froze time (Cohn, 1987: 19–20, 42–9; Hastrup, 1992: 4; Thomas, 1996: 120). So did nationalists. Both anthropologists and nationalists in the nineteenth and the twentieth centuries created and depicted social entities outside concrete time. Both categories of actors produced and naturalised orders of spatially segregated communities and localised cultures. This chapter stresses the existence of a historical link – the link between the twentieth-century construction of anthropology and the making of nationalisms. Twentieth-century anthropology was far more saturated by the nation-building project than has usually been acknowledged.

I have claimed that we must reject a part of the anthropological heritage. Yet this is not the whole story. Many writers on contemporary globalisation tend to treat long-maintained academic ideas as if they formed part of a sort of *ancien régime*. I shall adopt an altogether different position. I shall argue that we still need many insights developed by the classic anthropology of the twentieth century. We need many of the central ideas of mainstream twentieth-century symbolic anthropology.[3] Anthropologists should use these ideas in order to analyse contemporary social life as it unfolds in a transnational world. The two parts of the argument are equally important. Researchers should use some of mainstream twentieth-century symbolic anthropology's well-tried comparative insights if they wish to understand the world at present. But it would be indefensible to lean on that tradition uncritically. Most of the conventional symbolic anthropology showed almost no will to analyse historical global flows, the forces of globalisation.

Below I hope to substantiate these very general claims. I shall limit myself to political analysis.

Let us start with a group of questions: What is political analysis? How can we usefully conceptualise the object of study for inquiries into contemporary political life? The answers to these questions depend much upon how one chooses to reply to a third question: How should we understand the modern state?

Philip Abrams long ago claimed that we should understand the modern state as a historically constructed and contested 'exercise in legitimation, in moral regulation' (Abrams, 1988: 77). I share his views. Abrams acknowledges the extreme importance of the state as a reification. At the same time, he suggests that the whole analytical involvement with the problem of the state may be in an important sense a fantasy. He makes two decisive moves. First, he criticises work based on an intellectual separation of 'the state' and 'society'. He claims that by positing a mystifying separation of the political and the social, analysts have objectified and personified the state. Analysts, politicians and citizens have given the state a misplaced concreteness. Second, Abrams proposes we focus not so much on the state but on power, daily life and the construction of meanings (1988: 58, 77, 81–82).[4] In a fresh essay on the anthropology of the state, Michel-Rolph Trouillot claims, and I agree, that the presence of the modern state is far from as empirically obvious as often thought. He argues that the state 'has no institutional or geographical fixity' on either theoretical or historical grounds, and that 'state effects never obtain solely through national institutions or in governmental sites' (Trouillot, 2001: 126).[5]

As I see it, the typical notions of what constitutes the political, or politics, have become narrow, sterile and misleading. Political life, not least as it unfolds in the heart of Europe and the United States, has been understood far too much based on a hegemonic separation of the political and the cultural, of the building of the state and the construction of meanings. Rational-choice theory has exerted a much greater influence on the usual ways in which we perceive politics than has symbolic anthropology. I believe that is unsatisfactory.

In the next two sections, I shall insist that we use a part of anthropology's classic heritage in order to make sense of politics. Each section reflects on how an anthropologist has chosen to analyse – in my view, in thought-provoking ways – political life in the world at present. My first example tells a story from Eastern Europe after 1989. It focuses on what may be described as the reconstruction of collectivities and subjectivities in a transformed political and social landscape. In the second case, I look at what can be called the contemporary debate concerning European integration and the 'problem' of Third World immigration. This example focuses on the construction of race in a transformed Western European landscape. Both examples speak of borders, territories, collectivities, individuals, movement, and the forces of globalisation. Since both examples are drawn from Europe, I can be said to be Eurocentric. I would argue that the European bias is both a potential strength and a limitation. Europe has been *the* site for academic reflection on the nature of politics. I have chosen to try to make my case on a part of ethnocentric, Western political theory's home ground. The limitation is obvious. Social and political processes in today's United States, for example, are different from those in Europe. And so are the social and political processes on the rest of the American continent, in Africa and in Asia. Yet the aim is not to do justice to the variety of political forms today. The intention is to argue in favour of a general position; it is to claim that we should employ insights derived from classic symbolic anthropology in order to analyse some of the most hotly debated political issues of our times.

IDEAS ABOUT DESCENT AND LAND

Key authors on today's globalisation tie what they regard as a shift from earlier to contemporary forms of global connections to the year 1989 – to the fall of the Berlin Wall and the collapse of Communist Party rule in Eastern Europe, and soon thereafter in the Soviet Union. One example is Zygmunt Bauman in his book *Globalization* (1998). Another example is Ulrick Beck. Beck opens his recent study *What is Globalization?* in the following way:

With the peaceful fall of the Berlin Wall and the collapse of the Soviet empire, many thought that the end of politics was nigh.... [B]ut the current scareword 'globalization' ... points not to an end of politics but to its escape from the categories of the national state, and even from the schema defining what is 'political' and 'non-political' action. (2000: 1)

These writers tell us that after 1989, the analysis of political life is in deeper trouble than it used to be. In Beck's view, we lack a satisfactory language, a language which can be used to describe and explain what goes on. The categories we relied on are no longer valid in the wake of the collapse of the Communist regimes.

Katherine Verdery's recent book *The Political Lives of Dead Bodies* (1999) offers an ethnography and an analysis of some of the massive changes in Eastern European and post-Soviet society and culture. I believe it is useful to read her text in the light of the ideas of authors such as Beck and Bauman. She provides us with a different perspective on contemporary forms of globalisation. Not only does she give us rich insights into everyday and political processes in the former Eastern Bloc. Her book also argues that we need a part of anthropology's classic heritage – anthropological thinking about the significance of ideas about descent and place, kinship and land – in order to be able to make sense of politics in the global era. Unlike Beck, she conveys the message that important features of political life after the fall of the Berlin Wall can fruitfully be examined by means of old categories – those developed and used by an anthropology which sought to analyse, not forms of globalisation, but myths of authority and practices in small-scale societies. I am not saying, and I stress this, that there is nothing new under the sun or that we should not search for better ways of analysing. Rather I am saying that contemporary forms of globalisation manifest historical continuities, or at least transformations of earlier forms, and that we should try to meditate on the implications of this. I wish now to briefly sketch aspects of Verdery's analysis, and then attempt to reflect further on its general ideas – what I believe it says about political analysis in the era of globalisation.

Since 1989, scores of dead bodies across the former East Bloc have been exhumed and brought to rest in new grave sites. Verdery's book, subtitled 'Reburial and Postsocialist Change', investigates why certain corpses have taken on political life in the years following the collapse of the Communist Party rule. It examines what their roles are in revising individuals' and collectivities' histories. Bones of ancestors and heroes may be key vehicles of validation in power struggles, struggles which simultaneously concern identities and lands. Being 'objective' artefacts, bones root, incorporate and authorise territorialised identity claims. Bones *are* the past, the ancestors. By controlling them one can exercise a certain control of the past and the future.

The making of nationalisms, our world's 'profane religions', entails construction and reconstruction of ideas about roots. The ideas anchor the sacred national community with its fixed territory in burial places, the ancestors of the collectivity. Many nationalisms are closely linked to particular grave sites (Mosse, 1979, 1990). In each country of the former Eastern Bloc, the bodies of leaders, heroes, artists and other luminaries, as well as more humble folk, have been taken from their graves – and in many cases repatriated – to be reinterred in new locations. In her book, Verdery indicates the sheer magnitude of the phenomenon by summoning up a veritable parade of corpses on the move from the entire region.

The conspicuous materiality of human remains makes them means of *localising* particular ideas about social relations and particular ideas about rights. Bones of ancestors can easily be transported, displayed and placed. But a dead body is meaningful not in itself but through cultural idioms. The political significance of bones has primarily to do with their symbolic properties. As symbols, dead bodies have the capacity to evoke a variety of understandings. Their notorious ambiguity renders them effective in politics; they can help create and maintain ideas about unity. Corpses have two important additional advantages as symbols. They evoke ideas about kinship and about correct burial. Notions of descent are powerful organisers of cognition and emotion in all societies. Ideas about national collectivities harness descent idioms. In so doing they capitalise on the power of imageries of kinship. Representations of proper burial tie notions of kinship to understandings of order in the universe – ideas about the cosmos and about what it means to be human.

The socialism of the former Eastern Bloc did not suppress ethnic and national identifications. Rather it reinforced them (Smith, 1990; Tishkov, 1994; Verdery, 1996). In the post-socialist period, mobilisation based on ethnic and national identifications has played a key part in the transformation of politics and everyday life. The Yugoslav and Soviet federations were dissolved, and new nation-states were created. Political and social life in this region at the end of the twentieth century demonstrates that modern political collectivities produce 'roots'. The striking traffic in bones in the postsocialist landscape shows us that bearers of national ideologies anchor the collectivity in particular places, in grave sites. The tombs, and the dead bodies in them, represent not only specific ideas about history – about the collectivity's past and present. They also articulate ideas about geography. Since 1989, the former Eastern Bloc has been in a situation where political geography and relations of property – or

state borders and rights to economic resources – have been re-
negotiated in spectacular and violent ways. The intensified flow of
remains of ancestors formed part of, expressed, dramatised and
helped ritualise the massive changes. The processes that caused the
collapse of Communist Party rule generated new needs. In the
former Eastern Bloc, many felt a need to revise ideas about the relationship between a particular territory and a particular category of
people. Leaders and masses exhumed, moved and reburied ancestors.

Are these processes a part of contemporary globalisation? The
answer is 'yes'. The changes in Eastern European politics and society
had an important economic dimension (Boswell and Peters, 1990;
Burawoy, 1985; Humphrey, 1995; Kornai, 1992). Verdery has herself
analysed in detail the spectacular economic changes that have taken
place in the region (Verdery, 1996: 19–38, 133–228; 1991). For the
last three decades or so, we have been living through an important
shift in the world economy. Among its elements is a change in the
operation of capitalism. Some have called it a change to 'flexible
specialization' (Harvey, 1990). It has produced significant changes
in the global economic landscape. One testimony to that was the
1989 collapse of Communist Party rule in Eastern Europe, and soon
thereafter in the Soviet Union. In the 1980s, the Soviet system
became more fully connected with international capital flows; as a
result, both the socialist political economies and their place in global
capitalism changed (Verdery, 1996: 20–37). Dead-body politics in
the former Eastern Bloc since 1989 has been an integral part of, not
outside of, global flows of ideas, capital and commodities.

A number of the bodies reinterred in new locations in the former
Eastern Bloc have been repatriated. They have been brought back
from their place of exile – in Italy, Spain, the United States and other
countries. Some 'corpses on the move' in the postsocialist world
were *in themselves* striking signs of transnational flows – global
connections.

The point is that we should not see the reburials of ancestors –
and the ethnic, national and other struggles of which they are a part
– as a return to sorts of 'premodern, irrational forms'. Nor should we
see these phenomena as a sort of revival or return to primordial
loyalties. The reburials are forms of a complex, dynamic modernity.
The reburials are a part of the construction of contemporary forms
of globalisation. Jean and John Comaroff have argued in a similar
way about contemporary globalisation and forms of ritual, witchcraft
and sorcery in parts of Africa (1994). And Paul Stoller has done the
same in his fascinating analysis of ritual and political life in
independent Niger (Stoller, 1995).

Verdery's focus is anchored in classic – one could say old-
fashioned – anthropology, but she uses it to attempt to understand

the present. Anthropology's close yet shifting relationship to the study of kinship has existed ever since the mid-to-late nineteenth century, when Morgan and his interlocutors invented the study of kinship. Morgan saw so-called primitive societies as based on 'blood' and kinship, and our own ('advanced') society as based on 'soil' and the state. Later work showed that his neat dichotomy was spurious – that his two types of societies, one based on kinship and the other on territory, presented a false dichotomy. We can see this, for example, from two classic ethnographies – Firth's (1936) study of Tikopia and Bloch's (1971, 1982) work on the Merina. In both cases descent merges with locality; in both cases kinship merges with land, territory. Traditional Tikopians lived on the borders of their tombs and took their identity from what was essentially a necropolis. In Bloch's view, tombs, ancestral land, ancestors, unity and blessings were to the Merina so many aspects of the same thing: the good. The Tikopians and the Merina experienced their collectivity as a kinship society. Their tombs secured and represented the tie to the past – or a community which contained the living and the ancestors. The dead bodies objectified and symbolised a particular past and oriented the future. The agents' identities were territorialised. The Tikopians and the Merina saw themselves as rooted, not only in their dead, but also in a particular place – the ancestral soil or 'the homeland'. The grave site sealed rights – claims on political and economic resources. The control of the ancestors provided leadership and decision-making among the living descendants with a blessed, sacred authority.

Dead bodies and burial places may be of great significance also today. In the national order of things, agents formulate and reformulate specific notions of roots (*in* ancestors and homelands). On the threshold of the twenty-first century, we should recognise (1) the lasting, perhaps even expanding, power of the nation form across the globe,[6] and (2) that we ought to understand national ideologies and nations as a sort of (patrilineal) ancestor cult. National mythologies are replete with kinship metaphors. Many national ideologies represent the nation as a descent group, a group which commemorates its (usually male) founders and culture-makers as the origin and ancestors of the community. As authors such as Benedict Anderson, Carol Delaney, Bruce Kapferer, David Schneider and Brackette Williams have forcefully brought out, we should seek to understand the nation form as if it formed an example of kinship and religion (Anderson, 1991/1983; Delaney, 1995; Kapferer, 1988; Schneider, 1977; Williams, 1995). We should attempt to understand nations as examples of cosmologies. Bearers of national world-views anchor the collectivity in ancestors. The graves, and the human remains in them, seal a naturalised and fetishised connection between the nation's two 'natures', the nation's place and the nation's people, the territory and its population. Modern collective identities are territorialised. The Tikopians and the Merina saw themselves as anchored in the land of their ancestors. Nationalists understand themselves as rooted in a particular soil, the national territory; localisations of ancestors' bodies authorise such understandings.[7]

Massive transnationalism does not eliminate the need to study how agents construct histories about roots and how in this way, they shape political practices and processes. Ethnographies of international labour migrants and of political refugees demonstrate this (Appadurai, 1996: 158–199; Fuglerud, 1999; Malkki, 1992; Olwig, 1993: 137–208, 1997). Most researchers today attempt to deconstruct and deterritorialise histories, cultures and identities (by undermining the belief in their natural link to specific ancestors and homelands). But this does not prevent millions of people who have left, or been expelled from their homeland naturalising, essentialising and reterritorialising their histories, cultures and identities. Notions of kinship and soil are important; they give form to belonging in a world of flows. Territorialised descent operates as a key idiom of our times.

CLASSIFICATION SYSTEMS

An important overlap exists between my first and second example. 'Kinship' can and should be understood as a classification system and as a set of ideas about origins and shared substance. The same can be said about 'race'; race too is a classification system and a discourse on origins and shared substance. Both classification in terms of kinship and classification in terms of race articulate ideas about the flow of substance and the distribution of rights (Williams, 1995). My second example is one anthropologist's analysis of a change in the semiotics of race in the middle of contemporary Western Europe. I wish to use this analysis in the same way I used that from Eastern Europe. That means I shall not dwell on the study of the making of race in itself. Instead I intend to underscore something more general – that we need classic anthropology's strong interest in the construction of categories and systems of classification if we wish to understand some of the most fundamental power struggles of our times, the battles which define forms of citizenship (Holston and Appadurai, 1999).

Anthropology should use its strength – comparative insights into how the naturalisation of hierarchy and power differentials operate in the construction of classification systems – in order to examine how citizenship and civic rights are organised and negotiated.

Analysts of civic rights often distinguish between the formal and substantive aspects of citizenship. The formal refers to membership in a political community – in modern history, pre-eminently the nation-state. The substantive concerns the array of civil, political, socio-economic and cultural rights people possess and exercise. Ethnographies of the construction and operation of classification can shed light on both these aspects.

Most capital investments today take place in limited parts of the world. People from the Third World and Eastern Europe travel to these areas – in particular to these areas' cities – in order to attempt to sell their labour-power at a better price than it obtains in their home country. As new residents – people from the Caribbean, Latin America, the Middle East, Asia and Africa – occupy cities of North America and Western Europe, clear-cut tensions and conflicts arise in the receiver countries. One sign of that is the alarming spread of new ideologies of exclusion – new essentialist discourses – which basically support the slogan 'Foreigners Out!'

The spread of hostility in Europe against immigrants from the Third World has generated much soul-searching over the resurgence of the old beast of racism in a new guise. A thought-provoking contribution to this debate has been offered by Verena Stolcke. In an essay, 'Talking culture: new boundaries, new rhetorics of exclusion in Europe' (1995), Stolcke claims that an ideological shift has taken place in parts of Western Europe. She argues that it is misleading to understand the contemporary anti-immigrant discourse of the Western European right as a new form of racism or a racism in disguise. Instead she emphasises that what she describes as 'cultural fundamentalism' should be understood as a phenomenon in itself, as a new construction of exclusion suited to a climate marked by both growing globalisation and increasing stigmatisation of racism. Yet let me be crystal clear. Stolcke's intent is not to belittle intolerance. Far from it. She writes:

> Not for a moment do I want to trivialize the socio-political import of this novel exaltation of cultural difference, but to combat the beast we need to know what sort it is. To this end we need to do more than uncover the strategic motives for the right's disavowal of racism and analyze the conceptual structure of this political discourse. (Stolcke, 1995: 4)

Stolcke draws on one of mainstream twentieth-century symbolic anthropology's strengths. She shows how the naturalisation of asymmetries and power differentials operates in the construction of specific forms of social classification. In so doing, she sheds light on key practices and processes that shape political life in the heart of today's Europe.

Stolcke claims that the political right in Europe in the 1980s developed a rhetoric of exclusion in which Third World immigrants were construed as posing a threat to the national unity of the 'host' countries because they were culturally different. Rather than asserting a hierarchy of human races, this discourse postulates a propensity in human nature to reject strangers. In Stolcke's words:

> From what were once assertions of the differing endowment of human races there has risen since the seventies a rhetoric of inclusion and exclusion that emphasizes the distinctiveness of cultural identity, traditions, and heritage among groups and assumes the closure of culture by territory. (Stolcke, 1995: 2)

Stolcke writes as if her analysis applies only to the political right. This is to be too modest – or, if one wishes, it gives too much comfort. Cultural fundamentalism is a very flexible concept. It is used *both* by the right *and* by the left. It has a broad social basis. It is used not only to legitimate xenophobic cultural fundamentalism, but also an often equally fundamentalist multiculturalism. Since the 1980s, a whole spectrum of political positions have spoken in its common language (Strathern, 1995: 16; Turner, 1995: 17).

Stolcke compares straight or old-fashioned racism to cultural fundamentalism. She regards them as two different conceptual structures, two different symbolic logics. '"Equality" and "difference" tend to be arrayed against each other in political discourse in both cases, but the "difference" which is involved and the meaning with which it is endowed differ' (Stolcke, 1995: 5). Racism is a system of asymmetric classification. Cultural fundamentalism, by contrast, postulates a set of symmetric counterconcepts, that of the foreigner, the stranger as opposed to the national, the citizen. Racism operates with a particularistic criterion of classification – 'race'. Notions of 'races' challenge the claim to equal humanness by dividing humankind into inherently distinct groups organised hierarchically, one group advancing a claim to exclusive superiority. Cultural fundamentalism works in a different way. It assumes that all humans by their nature are bearers of culture. 'But humanity is composed of a multiplicity of distinct cultures which are incommensurable, the relations between their respective members being inherently conflictive because *it is in human nature to be xenophobic*' (Stolcke, 1995: 7, italics added). Cultural fundamentalism naturalises people's propensity to reject strangers. In turn, it uses this natural trait, this 'human universal', to account for the inevitability of cultural fundamentalism.

The difference between the two discourses can also be sketched in another way. The racist denies mutual recognition between himself or herself and the 'other'. Mutual recognition is impossible precisely because the 'racial' defect is not shared by the 'self'. The cultural fundamentalist is different. He or she constructs a cultural 'other', the Third World immigrant as stranger, and as such a potential 'enemy', out of a trait which is shared by the 'self'. The two are equal; they belong to the same humanity; as humans they are both bearers of culture. Instead of conceptualising different cultures as a hierarchy, cultural fundamentalism segregates them spatially, each culture – or nation – in its place. It anchors cultures in territories; it provides them with roots.

Both racism and cultural fundamentalism are part and parcel of modernity – the forces of globalisation. The two ideologies share an important trait: both make it possible to legitimate and naturalise asymmetries and enormous power differentials between agents in a world system shaped by European imperialism and global capitalism. We should see racism and cultural fundamentalism as modes of thinking that both reflect, in different ways, attempts to symbolically resolve a historically constituted contradiction – the contradiction in the modern liberal democratic state project between universalistic values and the need to both explain conspicuous social inequality and limit the nation-state to its territorial boundaries.

Stolcke examines political discourses and processes in today's France and Britain by means of a set of conventional ideas – ideas which state that a good way to examine the exercise of power in a given social setting is to analyse how its justification operates in the production of classification systems. Anthropologists developed these ideas almost exclusively through studies of so-called small-scale societies. Yet Stolcke's analysis speaks for itself (and so do a number of other works which employ similar ethnographic strategies in their attempts to understand political life in a world of global flows [Domínguez, 1986; Handelman, 1998; Malkki, 1995]). Her work reveals powerful ideology in today's Western Europe. In so doing it shows a set of key factors that affect both how the 'problem' of Third World immigration is dealt with by authorities and ordinary citizens, and how the new residents themselves – the immigrants – act in order to achieve civil, political, socio-economic and cultural rights.

In her book *Purity and Exile*, Liisa Malkki has said that ethnographers of contemporary forms of power should attempt to politicise the anthropological study of classification (1995: 6). I agree. We need some of anthropology's old comparative insights if we wish to understand politics in the global era. Some analytical tools used earlier can still do a good job. But if we want to fully politicise the anthropological study of meanings, we have also to historicise it. It is not enough to put to use ideas employed by most symbolic anthropologists in the twentieth century in order to examine contemporary politics. We must also examine meanings as parts of a global history. It is to the need for history – global history – that I now turn.

BETWEEN GLOBAL HISTORY AND SYMBOLIC ANTHROPOLOGY

I have argued in favour of a position which can be described as conservative. I have claimed that we need an analysis of modern forms of power which uses concepts derived from a mainstream twentieth-century symbolic anthropology. I wish now to qualify this position. Mainstream symbolic anthropology ignored the forces of globalisation. If it is right to say that we should use ideas drawn from symbolic anthropology in order to exercise a necessary critique of a certain reductionist homogenising globalisation theory, it is also correct to maintain that we must criticise symbolic anthropologists for having neglected, and silenced, global history. Global flows did not form part of a hegemonic symbolic anthropology's object of study.

Between, say, the end of the First World War and the early 1940s, an expanding modern anthropology turned the social and cultural forms of Melanesia and the Antilles respectively – two different clusters of islands, two different regions – into its objects of study. This happened in a very different way in the two cases. The peoples of Melanesia and those of the Caribbean were studied by anthropologists differently. They were incorporated into anthropological knowledge in strikingly different ways. These regions were historically and sociologically extremely different. What I am interested in, however, is not so much these empirical differences. Instead I wish to underscore what was a radical difference in anthropological perspective. From the beginning Western metropolitan anthropologists who worked in these two regions conceptualised the relationship between globalisation and what they examined, their object of study, in a different way. They not only studied two different regions, they constructed the world differently. As Gupta and Ferguson have written, with the Malinowskian revolution in fieldwork, anthropological naturalism came to be asserted in a strong form.

> Through an active forgetting of conquest and colonialism, fieldworkers increasingly claimed not simply to *reconstruct* the natural state of the primitive, but to *observe* it directly. Thus did social anthropology become defined as 'the study of small-scale society – ahistorical, *ethno*-graphic, and comparative'. (Gupta and Ferguson, 1997: 7)

Malinowski conceptualised Melanesia in the early twentieth century as outside his own society. He understood Melanesia as outside global history; the Melanesian political, social and cultural forms he studied were, in Thomas's words, 'out of time' (Thomas,

1996). Herskovits, by contrast, examined the Caribbean in the first decades of the twentieth century as an integral part of his own world. He understood the political, social and symbolic forms of the Antilles as shaped by centuries of global flows – a global history. Caribbeanists defined their object of study as a component of the historical construction of global networks.

In an essay from 1995, Fernando Coronil has discussed the relationship between Malinowski and Fernando Ortiz, the Cuban ethnographer and historian who wrote the classic *Cuban Counterpoint: Tobacco and Sugar*. *Cuban Counterpoint* was published for the first time in 1940 with a preface by Malinowski (Ortiz, 1995/1940). Coronil shows the profound difference in interests between these two writers (Coronil, 1995). Ortiz's 'field' was not a bounded localised community, but, instead, a multistranded transatlantic traffic that shaped a Cuban experience. *Cuban Counterpoint* examines commodities, relations and meanings on Cuba as the outcome of a history of transculturation processes in a global system. The book shows us the Cuban social reality as a part of a global history – the history of Western imperialism and world-embracing capitalism. Yet, in his preface to the book, Malinowski completely silenced this essential dimension of Ortiz's work. Instead he packaged and marketed Ortiz as a 'good functionalist' with only a small dash of added history.

Far too much symbolic anthropology in the twentieth century did as Malinowski did; far too much anthropology remained silent on concrete history and global connections – on how its objects of study, socially embedded meanings, were integrated into (perhaps even part and parcel of) processes of globalisation. In the course of the last couple of decades, this has changed. Yet the Malinowskian tradition is still powerful. Much anthropological work on meanings is still carried out with too little awareness of the world as an interconnected system (Gupta and Ferguson, 1997: 4, 35–40; Thomas, 1996: 102–27; Thomas and Humphrey, 1996: 1–12). I have drawn on analyses by Verdery and Stolcke. Both have devoted a tremendous attention in their work to global processes – global history (Stolcke, 1974; 1988; Verdery, 1983, 1996). Yet both have also shown that we need anthropology's classic insights, insights derived from ethnographies of so-called small-scale societies.

Anthropologists need perspectives on the global. But do we need 'history'? Do students of politics have to historicise? Why should we shape an anthropology of globalisation that is historical? Why do we have to work, not only on global flows, not only on global connections, but on global history?

To historicise is essential. If we don't historicise, we weaken the power of our analyses; we deprive them of a critical political function.

Let us for a moment return to Verdery and Stolcke. Both these writers claim that crucial power continues to be based on territory – that modern political processes are based on the land. This can be formulated more strongly. In his latest book, Keith Hart writes acridly:

> Western states are no more liberal than the Soviet Union was Marxist. At least the old regime of agrarian civilization called itself what it was.... Ours is a corrupt *ancien régime* that must soon find a new democratic revolution.... The form of social organization underpinning this universal crisis for humanity in the twentieth century has been state capitalism, the attempt to manage markets and money through nation-states.... The institutions of agrarian civilization, developed over five millennia ... are our institutions today: territorial states, landed property, warfare, embattled cities, money and markets in their traditional form, world religion, racism and the family. (2000: 66–7)

Authority, decision-making and identities continue to be tied to the land. Ours is an agrarian universe, a world society divided into national fragments – patrilineal ancestor cults. As Bruno Latour has put it, we have never been modern.

Verdery shows that bearers of national ideologies root the collectivity in grave sites, ancestors. Stolcke argues that cultural fundamentalism operates as a key idiom for construction of inclusion and exclusion in parts of contemporary Europe. As a cognitive and emotional system cultural fundamentalism segregates cultures/nations spatially, each culture/nation on its land. Both authors claim that modern political processes are marked by attempts to relate the nation to nature, to bind up the two parts of the nation, that of the people and the land. The construction of the relationship between the people and the place is based on uses of root metaphors – imageries of ancestries, trees and sedentarism (Malkki, 1992).

What does this have to do with a need for history? Anthropologists and those who construct states and nations have a common intellectual history. They share many influences. Anthropologists, too, used to relate society to nature, and bind up the two bodies of the society, that of the people and of the place. Ethnography, as well, segregated societies spatially, each society on its territory. Anthropology, too, was oriented towards the land; in the words of Gupta and Ferguson (1997: 8), it was, and continues to be, permeated and shepherded by 'agrarian metaphors'.

Given this, we should attempt to anchor anthropological work better in time. We should examine concrete historical processes that produce particular social forms. The processes which generate a 'natural' tie between a place and a people, a territory and a community, are historical; they are rooted in time. We ought to use history as a tool. We should use it in order to deconstruct the reified, the fetishised – such as the naturalness of a relationship between a particular collectivity and a particular place. Instead of studying contemporary myths of authority by means of ethnographic snapshots, or as if they were out of time, we should seek to anchor and inscribe them in history, in the historical possibility for change. We should use examinations of concrete processes over time in order to show that what has come to be viewed as natural, and explains a given social order, is part of a large-scale history – a history that embraces (but is not reducible to) boundary-crossing flows and globalisation. This is not the place to begin to outline a view of historicity. Nor is it the place to answer in detail the question 'What sort of history should anthropologists do?'[8] Suffice it to say that history is never just about the past, and not only a tool. History, as Trouillot has argued, is material, tool and context of anthropological discourse (1995). It is material, because not only researchers but all social actors – individuals and collectivities – produce memories and histories. Yet all narratives about the past are historical. They are anchored in time; they have to be viewed historically. History is also a context – a setting for anthropology. As I have already emphasised, anthropological narratives about the world are outcomes of particular historical processes. The point that I wanted to emphasise above, however, is simply that anthropologists must use history as an implement. They must understand social and political life historically. This should have implications for the data collection. The anthropologist ought to work, not only in the field, but also on the historical sources. The anthropologist needs to work in archives and libraries. He or she needs to study the past as it exists in documents, objects, buildings and landscapes.

It's not that this hasn't been said before. Evans-Pritchard, for example, said it more than 50 years ago; he claimed that anthropology had to become history or nothing (Evans-Pritchard, 1962/1950: 21–5, 1962/1961: 64). Dependency researchers, world-systems theorists and neo-Marxists, as well, argued that it was indispensable to historicise. The point is that it still needs to be said. If we wish to understand today's political processes, we have to historicise them.

CONCLUSION

It is essential not to become a prey to one of the expanding, powerful ideologies of our times, an a-historical 'globalitarism', a discourse on the ongoing rapid emergence of a new world with few or no boundaries. Much of what goes on politically today manifests far from wholly new phenomena. Things change, to be sure; they always did. But we still need comparative insights drawn from the core of mainstream twentieth-century symbolic anthropology; we need its ideas about descent and place, and about classification systems. Politics is of a deeply symbolic nature. Contemporary political entities are shaped by, and shape, practices which entail that agents classify and order the world, express ideas about purity and hybridity, and attempt to sanctify conceptions of descent, notions of roots. Contemporary political life unfolds by means of its own myths of authority.

Globalisation has been understood as the end to almost anything. It is definitely not the end to difference and distance – to conflict, intolerance and exclusion. In our world of global flows, the human interest in genealogies is enormous. The interest in blood is tremendous. The same can be said about place. The interest in place and soil in our world of departure and movement continues to be huge. I have drawn a tragic picture; I am a European anthropologist and I do not see why that means I have to be an ostrich. Globalisation entails change. But difference and distance continue to be experienced through imageries of kinship and land.

NOTES

1. The first draft of this chapter was presented to the seminar 'Globalisation studies: epistemological and methodological considerations from anthropology' held in Oslo, 7–8 June 2001. I am grateful to the participants of this seminar for their comments and support. Special thanks are also given to Thomas Hylland Eriksen, Keith Hart, Erik Henningsen, Signe Howell, Marianne Lien, Sarah Lund and Marit Melhuus who have taken the time to read drafts and discuss the topic with me.
2. I owe this to Keith Hart, who in a conversation proposed this summary of twentieth-century anthropology.
3. Anthropologists often associate 'symbolic anthropology' with a late twentieth-century American school led by Clifford Geertz and perhaps Marshall Sahlins. I do not intend to be as specific as that. In this chapter, I am not interested in the issue of how to separate symbolic from cultural or even social anthropology. As will become apparent, by 'mainstream twentieth-century symbolic anthropology' I mean a strong intellectual tradition; I mean an anthropology considerably devoted to studies of ideas about kinship and locality, classification systems and meanings.
4. Abrams was influenced by Radcliffe-Brown. Radcliffe-Brown invited anthropologists to forget the state. To him the state did not form an object of study. As he wrote, the modern state, in the sense of an entity over and above the human individuals who make up a society', is a fiction of the philosophers. What does exist is ... a collection of individual human beings connected by a complex system of relations' (Radcliffe-Brown, 1987/1940: xxiii). The history of anthropology shows that most of the discipline's practitioners complied with Radcliffe-Brown's wishes. Few anthropologists, even few self-professed political anthropologists, studied

the modern state, yet this is changing (see, for example, Blom Hansen and Stepputat 2001; Coronil 1997; Joseph and Nugent 1994; Nagengast 1994; Nugent 1997; Trouillot 2001).

5. In the same essay, Trouillot outlines an ethnographic strategy for studies of states. He invites us to examine the many sites in which state processes and practices are recognisable, as he writes, through their *effects*. He suggests we focus on the production of four different effects: an isolation effect, that is, the making of atomised individual subjects moulded for governance; an identification effect, that is, a re-incorporation of the atomised individuals into collectivities, a legibility effect, that is, the construction of a language for governance and of tools that classify and regulate collectivities, and a spatialisation effect, that is, the production of boundaries (Trouillot, 2001: 126). As I read him, however, much of what these effects cover can also be investigated under other headings. To me it seems that the production of these effects has very much to do with the production of collective and individual identities, with the making of classification systems, and with the construction of territorialised boundaries. Twentieth-century symbolic anthropology worked on these themes.

6. As David Harvey, for example, has written:

The transition from Fordism to flexible accumulation, such as it has been, ought to imply a transition in our mental maps, political attitudes, and political institutions. But political thinking does not necessarily undergo such easy transformations.... The serious diminution of the power of individual nation-states over fiscal and monetary policies, for example, has not been matched by any parallel shift towards an internationalization of politics. Indeed there are abundant signs that localism and nationalism have become stronger precisely because of the quest for the security that place always offers in the midst of all the shifting that flexible accumulation implies. The resurgence of geopolitics and of faith in charismatic politics ... fits only too well with a world that is increasingly nourished intellectually and politically by a vast flux of ephemeral images. (1990: 305–6)

7. Elsewhere I have attempted to analyse in detail the relationship between dead-body politics and the construction of a hegemonic, territorialised racial-national identity in a part of the Hispanic Caribbean, the Dominican Republic; the same work also analyses a correlate: legitimation of discrimination and violence on the national territory against 'second-rate citizens' (black Dominicans) and 'immigrants' (Haitians), those held to lack the necessary roots (Krohn-Hansen, 2001).

8. See, for example, Cohn (1987: 1–77); Comaroff and Comaroff (1992: 3–48); Price (1983); Thomas (1996: 117–22); Trouillot (1995: 1–30).

REFERENCES

Abrams, P. 1988. Notes on the difficulty of studying the state, *Journal of Historical Sociology* 1(1): 58–89.

Anderson, B. 1991/1983. *Imagined Communities*, revised edn. London: Verso.

Appadurai, A. 1996. *Modernity at Large: Cultural Dimensions of Globalization*. Minneapolis: University of Minnesota Press.

Bauman, Z. 1998. *Globalization: The Human Consequences.* New York: Columbia University Press.

Beck, U. 2000. *What is Globalization?* Cambridge: Polity Press.

Bloch, M. 1971. *Placing the Dead: Tombs, Ancestral Villages and Kinship Organisation among the Merina of Madagascar.* London: Seminar Press.

—— 1982. Death, women, and power. In M. Bloch and J. Parry (eds) *Death and the Regeneration of Life.* Cambridge: Cambridge University Press.

Blom Hansen, T. and F. Stepputat. 2001. *States of Imagination.* Durham, NC and London: Duke University Press.

Boswell, T. and R. Peters. 1990. State socialism and the industrial divide in the world economy, *Critical Sociology* 17: 3–34.

Burawoy, M. 1985. *The Politics of Production.* London: Verso.

Cohn, B.S. 1987. *An Anthropologist among the Historians and Other Essays.* Delhi: Oxford University Press.

Comaroff, J. and J. Comaroff. 1992. *Ethnography and the Historical Imagination.* Boulder, CO: Westview Press.

—— (eds) 1994. *Modernity and its Malcontents. Ritual and Power in Postcolonial Africa.* Chicago: University of Chicago Press.

Cooper, F. and A.L. Stoler. (eds) 1997. *Tensions of Empire.* Berkeley: University of California Press.

Coronil, F. 1995. 'Transculturation and the politics of theory: countering the center, Cuban counterpoint', introduction to Fernando Ortiz's *Cuban Counterpoint. Tobacco and Sugar,* pp. ix–lvi. Durham and London: Duke University Press.

—— 1997. *The Magical State: Nature, Money, and Modernity in Venezuela.* Chicago and London: University of Chicago Press.

Delaney, C. 1995. Father state, motherland, and the birth of modern Turkey. In S. Yanagisako and C. Delaney (eds) *Naturalizing Power: Essays in Feminist Cultural Analysis.* New York and London: Routledge.

Domínguez, V. 1986. *White by Definition: Social Classification in Creole Louisiana.* New Brunswick, NJ: Rutgers University Press.

Evans-Pritchard, E.E. 1962/1950. Social anthropology: past and present (The MarettLecture, 1950). In E.E. Evans-Pritchard, *Essays in Social Anthropology.* London: Faber & Faber.

——1962/1961. Anthropology and history. In E.E. Evans-Pritchard, *Essays in Social Anthropology.* London: Faber & Faber.

Firth, R. 1936. *We the Tikopia.* London: George Allen & Unwin.

Fuglerud, Ø. 1999. *Life on the Outside: The Tamil Diaspora and Long-distance Nationalism.* London: Pluto Press.

Gupta, A. and J. Ferguson. 1997. Discipline and practice: 'the field' as site, method, and location in anthropology. In A. Gupta and J. Ferguson (eds) *Anthropological Locations.* Berkeley, Los Angeles and London: University of California Press.

Handelman, D. 1998. *Models and Mirrors: Towards an Anthropology of Public Events.* New York and Oxford: Berghahn Books.

Hart, K. 2000. *The Memory Bank: Money in an Unequal World.* London: Profile Books.

Harvey, D. 1990. *The Condition of Postmodernity.* Oxford: Blackwell.

Hastrup, K. (ed.) 1992. *Other Histories.* London and New York: Routledge.

Holston, J. and A. Appadurai. (eds) 1999. *Cities and Citizenship.* Durham, NC and London: Duke University Press.

Humphrey, C. 1995. Creating a culture of disillusionment: consumption in Moscow, a chronicle of changing times, in D. Miller (ed.) *Worlds Apart: Modernity Through the Prism of the Local.* London and New York: Routledge.

Joseph, G.M. and D. Nugent (eds) 1994. *Everyday Forms of State Formation. Revolution and the Negotiation of Rule in Modern Mexico.* Durham, NC: Duke University Press.

Kapferer, B. 1988. *Legends of People, Myths of States: Violence, Intolerance, and Political Culture in Sri Lanka and Australia.* Washington, DC: Smithsonian Institution.

Kornai, J. 1992. *The Socialist System: The Political Economy of Communism.* Princeton, NJ: Princeton University Press.

Krohn-Hansen, C. 2001. A tomb for Columbus in Santo Domingo: political cosmology, population and racial frontiers, *Social Anthropology* 9(2): 165–92.

Malkki, L. 1992. National geographic: the rooting of peoples and the territorialization of national identity among scholars and refugees, *Cultural Anthropology* 7 (1): 24–44.

—— 1995. *Purity and Exile: Violence, Memory, and National Cosmology among Hutu Refugees in Tanzania.* Chicago: University of Chicago Press.

Mintz, S.W. 1985. *Sweetness and Power: The Place of Sugar in Modern History.* Harmondsworth: Penguin.

Mosse, G. 1979. National cemeteries and national revival: the cult of the fallen soldiers in Germany, *Journal of Contemporary History* 14: 1–20.

—— 1990. *Fallen Soldiers: Reshaping the Memory of the World Wars.* Oxford: Oxford University Press.

Nagengast, C. 1994. Violence, terror, and the crisis of the state, *Annual Review of Anthropology* 23: 109–36.

Nugent, D. 1997. *Modernity at the Edge of Empire: State, Individual, and Nation in the Northern Peruvian Andes, 1885–1935.* Stanford, CA: Stanford University Press.

Olwig, K.F. 1993. *Global Culture, Island Identity. Continuity and Change in the Afro-Caribbean Community of Nevis.* Reading: Harwood Academic Publishers.

—— 1997. Cultural sites: sustaining a home in a deterritorialized world. In K.F. Olwig and K. Hastrup (eds) *Siting Culture: The Shifting Anthropological Object.* London and New York: Routledge.

Ortiz, F. 1995/1940. *Cuban Counterpoint: Tobacco and Sugar,* Introduction by Bronislaw Malinowski, with a new Introduction by Fernando Coronil. Durham, NC and London: Duke University Press.

Price, R. 1983. *First-time: The Historical Vision of an Afro-American People.* Baltimore, MD and London: Johns Hopkins University Press.

Radcliffe-Brown, A. 1987/1940. Preface. In M. Fortes and E.E. Evans-Pritchard (eds) *African Political Systems.* London and New York: Kegan Paul International/International African Institute.

Schneider, D. 1977. Kinship, nationality and religion: toward a definition of kinship. In J. Dolgin, D. Kremnitzer and D. Schneider (eds) *Symbolic Anthropology.* New York: Columbia University Press.

Smith, G. (ed.) 1990. *The Nationalities Question in the Soviet Union.* London: Longman.

Stolcke, V. [Martínez-Alier]. 1974. *Marriage, Class, and Colour in Nineteenth-century Cuba: A Study of Racial Attitudes and Sexual Values in a Slave Society.* Cambridge: Cambridge University Press.

—— 1988. *Planters, Workers, and Wives: Class Conflict and Gender Relations on São Paulo Plantations, 1850–1980.* Oxford: St Antony's/Macmillan.

—— 1995. Talking culture: new boundaries, new rhetorics of exclusion in Europe, *Current Anthropology* 36(1): 1–24.

Stoller, P. 1995. *Embodying Colonial Memories: Spirit Possession, Power and the Hauka in West Africa.* London: Routledge.

Strathern, M. 1995. Comment on V. Stolcke's 'Talking culture', *Current Anthropology* 36(1): 16.

Thomas, N. 1996. *Out of Time: History and Evolution in Anthropological Discourse,* 2nd edn. Ann Arbor: University of Michigan Press.

Thomas, N. and C. Humphrey (eds) 1996. *Shamanism, History, and the State.* Ann Arbor: University of Michigan Press.

Tishkov, V.A. 1994. Inventions and manifestations of ethno-nationalism in Soviet academic and public discourse. In R. Borofsky (ed.) *Assessing Cultural Anthropology.* New York: McGraw-Hill.

Trouillot, M.-R. 1991. Anthropology and the savage slot: the poetics and politics of otherness. In R. Fox (ed.) *Recapturing Anthropology: Working in the Present.* Santa Fe, TX: School of American Research Press.

—— 1995. *Silencing the Past: Power and the Production of History.* Boston, MA: Beacon Press.

—— 2001. The anthropology of the state in the age of globalization, *Current Anthropology* 42(1): 125–38.

Turner, T. 1995. Comment on V. Stolcke's 'Talking culture', *Current Anthropology* 36(1): 16–18.

Verdery, K. 1983. *Transylvanian Villagers: Three Centuries of Political, Economic, and Ethnic Change.* Berkeley and Los Angeles: University of California Press.

—— 1991. Theorizing socialism: a prologue to the transition, *American Ethnologist* 18(3): 419–39.

—— 1996. *What was Socialism, and What Comes Next?* Princeton, NJ: Princeton University Press.

—— 1999. *The Political Lives of Dead Bodies: Reburial and Postsocialist Change.* New York: Columbia University Press.

Williams, B.F. 1995. Classification systems revisited: kinship, caste, race, and nationality as the flow of blood and the spread of rights. In S. Yanagisako and C. Delaney (eds) *Naturalizing Power: Essays in Feminist Cultural Analysis.* New York and London: Routledge.

6 SHIFTING BOUNDARIES OF A COASTAL COMMUNITY: TRACING CHANGES ON THE MARGIN

Marianne E. Lien

Anthropology, known by disciplinary neighbours for dealing with practically every aspect of human society, has been remarkably slow in coming to terms with global forms of connectedness. This is in spite of a recent theoretical turn in the discipline away from the idea of what Gupta and Ferguson (1999) call the paradigm of 'peoples and cultures', and in spite of analyses that convincingly demonstrate the salience of transnational connections historically and today (e.g. Mintz, 1985). The implications of such insights for anthropological research practice, however, remain unclear. Anthropologists' unease in relation to global connectivities clearly may be understood as a result of the way anthropology has traditionally delineated its object of study in time (synchronic studies, ethnographic present) and in space (a community, a culture): a discipline which builds its epistemology on immersing oneself in a single place (over a period of a year or more) is hardly well-suited for dealing with global connectivities and transnational flow. This methodological disadvantage becomes no less problematic when the most privileged places or regions within our discipline are those that have traditionally been made to appear stable, homogeneous and thus 'unaffected' by the heterogeneity that is brought about as things, ideas and people move.

Michel-Rolph Trouillot (1992) has addressed similar issues in his writings on the Caribbean. According to Trouillot, *historicity* and *heterogeneity* are both crucial dimensions for an understanding of the Caribbean region, but at the same time, they are the very features that have made the encounters between Caribbean studies and anthropology uneasy. The unease that he describes in the encounter between anthropology and the Caribbean appears to have much in common with the unease of the encounters between anthropology and the topic of globalisation.

As has been pointed out by several scholars recently, an understanding of globalisation requires a reassessment of the value of the anthropological method. We need to rethink the role of fieldwork in defining our discipline, the kinds of places we choose, and also the basic idea in anthropology that one single place must be chosen. Alternative approaches to constructing the field have been suggested, offering various strategies for combining the advantages of intimate knowledge and face-to-face social interaction with enhanced attention to global connectivities (see for instance Gupta and Ferguson, 1997, 1999; Hannerz, 1996; Hastrup and Olwig, 1997; Kearney, 1995). Among the more controversial proposals is George Marcus's concept of *multi-sited ethnographies*. According to Marcus, this approach 'moves out from the single sites and local situations of conventional ethnographic research designs to examine the circulation of cultural meanings, objects, and identities in diffuse time-space' (1998: 79).[1] Launching the concept of multi-sited ethnographies, Marcus moves beyond the strategies applied in anthropological studies of history and material culture that literally 'follow the thing' (Appadurai, 1986; Mintz, 1985). While these approaches, according to Marcus, represent the 'obvious cases' of multi-sited ethnographies,[2] the more radical approach that he advocates are the 'cases where there is very little actual contact or exchange between two sites but where the functioning of one of the sites depends on a very specific imagining of what is going on elsewhere' (1999: 7). Central to Marcus's argument is the notion of actual 'empirical changes in the world', expressed as 'transformed locations of cultural production' and the need to construct multi-sited ethnographies to deal with such changes. In other words, empirical changes are to be discovered by looking more closely at discontinuties in space, that is, by juxtaposing different 'places' (or field-sites) with little actual contact.

In this chapter, I shall explore a methodological strategy that literally inverts the approach advocated by Marcus, but nevertheless remains close to the overall aim of situating the ethnographer in a position of an enhanced awareness of connections between a chosen locality and the rest of the world: rather than arguing for multi-sitedness, I shall suggest an approach to the field based on *multi-temporality*. Instead of juxtaposing field-sites that differ in *space*, I juxtapose the configurations of a single field-site as it differs over *time*.

The idea of 'going back to the field' is by no means a novel idea.[3] I will argue, however, that it is particularly well-suited to deal with epistemological and methodological challenges that anthropology currently faces. What I suggest is, in a sense, an old solution to a novel range of problems. These problems relate to the challenges of grasping what I will refer to as the transformative potential of transnational flow.

THE TRANSFORMATIVE POTENTIAL OF TRANSNATIONAL FLOW

In literature on globalisation, an important distinction is made between globalisation as process and globalisation as experience. Ulrich Beck, for instance, distinguishes the term *globalising processes*, which denotes those mechanisms that enable or facilitate the movements that we refer to transnational flows, from the term *globality*, which he refers to as the reflexive awareness that we are 'living in a world society' in the sense that the 'notion of closed spaces has become illusory' (Beck, 2000: 10). In accordance with this distinction, one of the challenges in anthropololgy is to trace, in ethnographic terms, the relationship between the former and the latter.

This relationship is never simple and one-to-one. People have consumed substances brought to them from across long distances for centuries while retaining their focus on local concerns, and without much awareness of living in a 'world society' (consumption of sugar is a case in point). Similarly, the production of goods for export does not necessarily involve the internalisation of a 'global gaze', although it might.[4] The transnational flow of objects, in other words, does not necessarily imply a change of perspective or practice by people situated locally at either end of the objects 'route', or even at their passage points.

This point is particularly relevant in relation to localities that have historically been constituted by connectivities to places far away, such as the Caribbean, and, I would add, some localities along the north Norwegian coastline. In such empirical contexts, a strict dichotomy of the local and the global as two separate domains appears to be not a very fruitful conceptual model. Nevertheless, the question of how these connectivities constitute localities is still a relevant question to ask.

Studies of globalisation often tend to draw attention to the obvious. Phenomena like the expansion of McDonald's in post-communist countries, or the consumption of Coca-Cola in Papua New Guinea succeed remarkably in drawing the attention not only of the general public, but also of anthropologists, and are often referred to as 'icons' of processes of globalisation. In this chapter, I will argue that the transformative potential of globalising processes is much too important to be collapsed into such easily observable, or even spectacular pehnomena. More precisely, I suggest that we conceive of transnational flows as a vast array of movements, including some that are noisy and loud, and others that are quiet, subtle, not measurable and hardly noticeable, let alone a topic of local discourse. I contend that we, as anthropologists, are particularly responsible for catching such quiet movements, and for grasping the almost not-noticeable changes that may happen as people are busy drawing attention to something else. This is partly because we share a disciplinary training that makes us particularly well equipped to notice such subtleties, but also because the cultural significance of such quiet movements may, in some instances, be much more important than 'another McDonald's', even if it is not as readily apparent.

When I use the term *significance* in this context, I seek to draw the attention to the complex coexistence of continuities *and* discontinuities that accompany transnational flows. In their book *Global Transformations*, David Held et al. (1999) operationalise the concept of globalisation by pointing to four dimensions of global relations: extensity, intensity, velocity and impact.[5] By the term *significance* I seek to capture something similar to what Held refers to as *impact*, but with an important modification: while impact may be operationalised as change, an event may be interpreted as significant even if it does not immediately bring about observable change. By making this distinction, I seek to draw the attention to the *transformative potential* of globalising processes, while also recognising that this potential may not necessarily be realised. In other words, if globalising processes are culturally significant beyond their aggregate effects as facilitators of transnational flow, it is because these movements represent a potential discontinuity in the lives of people involved, even if this discontinuity is not yet immediately observable as change.

How then do we as anthropologists, approach these complexities? How do we position ourselves in order to discover the transformative potential of transnational flow? How do we grasp those moments of signficance when change becomes a possibility? If global connectivities may be traced by a multi-sited approach, their transformative power cannot. An anthropological understanding of globalising processes ought to be able to catch those moments, or meeting points (in time and space) when a transformative potential is present, even if this potential impact is not actually released. I suggest that one way of achieving this aim is by approaching those moments when a transformative potential emerges with a keen awareness of what boundaries are at stake – physical, social or conceptual. We need to ask: in what arenas do boundaries emerge or disappear, and what measures are being taken in order to make them stable? Furthermore, how are the movements and distributions of people and functions separated or confined to certain places, by whom and to achieve what ends? In particular, we need to address which larger contexts, networks or units are aligned, or made relevant, by the emergence or the disappearance of local boundaries.

Dealing with these issues requires a contextual sensitivity which, I will argue, is strongly enhanced by a multi-temporal approach.

In this chapter, I will present three cases which are selected in order to highlight such moments – or meeting points – when the transformative potential of globalising processes is significant . The cases that I present are recent events that took place in Båtsfjord, a coastal community in northern Norway, where I did extensive fieldwork in 1985, made several visits during the years that followed, and conducted short intensive fieldwork again in 2000. In other words, my focus on shifting boundaries is based on multi-temporal approach, and reflects, as well as advocates, the analytical possibilities inherent in long-term engagement in a single locality.

A 'MARGINAL' LOCALITY

Båtsfjord (literally 'Boats'-fjord') is a settlement of approximately 2,500 inhabitants[6] situated on the Varanger peninsula of the Northern Norwegian coastline in the county of Finnmark. Finnmark borders Russia and Finland, and is Norway's most northern and eastern county. Unlike most communities in Norway, Båtsfjord[7] has practically no arable land. Consequently there are no farms, and the hereditary land-ownership is of minor importance. The viability of the community is due entirely to its favourable harbour and a vital fish-processing industry. The growth of Båtsfjord roughly coincides with the expansion of motorised fishing vessels and the introduction of freezing technology. Although Båtsfjord did exist as a small settlement even before the Second World War, its main expansion took place during the 1960s and 1970s. During this period, households dependent on fishing left exposed settlements along the rugged coastline, in order to take part in the rapid industrial expansion of communities like Båtsfjord. Since the 1970s, many fishing communities in the region have experienced economic decline and a net loss of inhabitants. In Båtsfjord, however, several successful fish-processing plants have contributed to what is at times a vibrant economy, ensuring employment and economic strength in the community.

Most descriptions that take Norway or the Nordic countries as their basic unit of analysis render Båtsfjord as a marginal location. Practically any standard map with a Euro-centred or nation-centred perspective will necessarily place the Varanger coastline on the very periphery of Norway, or of Europe. The significance of the coastline is thus reduced to a marker of the border of civilisation in the north-east, while the vast geographic distance between this coastline and almost any European centre is visually exposed. In this way, a hegemonic image of marginality is reproduced.[8]

An alternative presentation of this area is a map in which the national boundaries in the inland are erased and replaced by a large transnational area called Sàpmi, indicating the contested nature of national hegemony in the region, and the presence of the indigenous Saami population, who constitute a majority in parts of the inland area, but a minority on the coast. However, this map is also slightly misleading from the perspective of Båtsfjord, in the sense that it would not account for the multi-ethnic character of the region. Although dominated by a Norwegian-speaking population today, Finnmark has been heterogeneous for centuries, consisting of at least three ethnic groups, distinguished by different languages, the Saami,[9] the Norwegian and the Finnish migrant population ('*Kvæn*'). A notion of ethnic hybridity dominates local discourse on the coast, emphasising precisely 'being a mixture' as the characterising trait (Megard, 1999).

The political effort to strengthen economic and cultural exchange across the Barents Region has led to the production of an alternative map that challenges the Euro-centred dichotomy of centre and periphery. I came across this map during the summer of 2000, in the offices of the Barents Region 'secretariat' in Kirkenes, Finnmark, and later came across a similar version on the web pages of the Norwegian Ministry of Foreign Affairs.[10] On this map, the Varanger peninsula is centrally situated as a 'natural' point of connection between northern Sweden, northern Finland, Finland, north-east Russia, the Finnmark inland area and the Barents Sea. The map thus indicates how geographical surroundings allow transnational flows across land and across the ocean, and is part of a political effort at revitalising transnational exchange and multilateral cooperation in the Barents Region in the 1990s. During the 1980s, when Norway bordered what was then the Soviet Union, the term 'Barents Region' was rarely used. In the early 1990s, however, following the emergence of a post-communist Russia, and the gradual opening of the Norwegian-Russian border for traffic in tourism and trade, the idea of the Barents as a transnational region became a political aim, with strong proponents in the Norwegian Ministry of Foreign Affairs. The 'Barents Cooperation', a foreign policy initiative, was formed in 1993, with an overarching aim of ensuring political stability in the region. The notion of the Barents Region involves a recognition of historical ties across national boundaries prior to 1917, and the strengthening of such ties, now achieved by funding and support for cultural and commercial exchange. Although the map of the Barents Region is offically recognised in the Ministry of Foreign Affairs it appears to be not very widely circulated and remains itself a marginal construction of space, even in the north. To summarise, the geographic marginality of Båtsfjord is constructed and naturalised through three competing cartographic rhetorics: the Euro-centred that highlights nation-states and the ethnicity-based (Sàpmi) that highlights homogeneous ethnic unity, while the map of the Barents Region challenges this image of marginality through implicit references to regional migration and trade.[11]

In his book *Places on the Margin*, Rob Shields demonstrates how geographic marginality has a social component. Rather than simply reflecting a neutral topography, marginality is the result of 'a complex process of social activity and cultural work' through which places are ordered according to a stratified hierarchy of high and low, or centre and periphery (1991: 4). Janet Nadel-Klein (1995) develops a similar argument when she claims that anthropology has contributed to the construction of marginal localities of what she refers to as the 'Atlantic Fringe of Europe', through community studies that emphasise the rural–urban contrast. Such studies, she argues, exemplify how:

dichotomizing categories such as rural/urban, simple/complex, traditional/modern and even periphery/core contribute to an essentialized, occidentalized, vision of Western society as having 'margins' that harbour pre-modern ways of life. (Nadel-Klein, 1995: 124–5)

This rural–urban contrast is not a simple complementary opposition, but a 'duality that is inherently hierarchical', and is based upon differences in class and power. According to Nadel-Klein, such dualities are crucial elements in the cultural construction of what we call 'the West', an imagined territory, governed by urban, bourgeois, cosmopolitan values. Such essentialising processes, however, depend upon images of the other. These may be found both outside, as Said (1978) has argued (orientalism), or within, through images of insular, pre-modern local communities that represent the internal Other. Nadel-Klein writes:

orientalist and occidentalist images interact dialectically to produce a particular construction of the West that situates both rural/local and non-Western communities as crucial opposites to what it defines as modern, industrially technological and middle-class. (1995: 112)

Within the Nordic context, examples of such hierarchical dualities are easily found, such as for instance between the densely populated, partly urban inland of the south, and the sparsely populated coastal communities of the north. The self-evidence of such dualisms is fully illustrated in the famous short story by the Danish author Karen Blixen called 'Babette's Feast',[12] first published in 1958 (Blixen, 1977). The story is situated in the explicitly remote coastal community of Berlevåg, which in fact happens to be Båtsfjord's

neighbouring community, located a few kilometres west of Båtsfjord
on the Varanger peninsula. In this story, Berlevåg is cast as a
backward, insulated and strongly pietist parish with very little
knowledge of the joys of modern life in general, and of high cuisine
in particular. This world of ignorance is transcended, however, when
the French woman Babette arrives and gradually reveals, through
her presentation of an extraordinary gourmet dinner, her profound
genius as a former chef at the Parisian Café Anglais. Through this
meal, the achievements of European civilisation are brought to its
periphery through elements like vintage wine and turtle soup.

The relevance of this story for the present argument is the way in
which Berlevåg serves as an icon of marginality for the European
urban audience. The author's choice of Berlevåg should come as no
surprise. Considering the hegemonic spatial image of Europe,
Berlevåg is as remote as you can get, and therefore a perfect location
for the story Blixen had in mind. However, this very choice also
confirms the *social* marginality of the north Norwegian coast within
the European or Nordic literary discourse. If Karen Blixen and her
cosmopolitan readership had been slightly more informed about this
region, they would have known that the description of Berlevåg as
a very religious pietist parish is strongly misleading. On the contrary,
Berlevåg and its neighbouring settlements on the Varanger coast are
traditionally far more secular, with few traces of the self-imposed
restrictions that Blixen suggests. Furthermore, the alleged isolation
of Berlevåg hardly takes into account the traffic brought by fishing
vessels that made Berlevåg one among many passage points for a
transnational system of connections that dates back to the Middle
Ages. Karen Blixen's use of Berlevåg thus exemplifies the way geographically marginal locations in the north have served as internal
'Others' in narratives about modern, cosmopolitan Europe. This
function overrides any consideration of factual correctness to the
extent that marginal locations are rendered not only marginal, but
also subject to the creative imagination of the urban cosmopolite.[13]
In order to serve as a suitable location, whether in northern Norway
or in coastal Denmark, any emergent cosmopolitanism on the
margins must therefore systematically be denied. For, as Nadel-Klein
writes 'the fully Western person is a cosmopolitan person' who
thinks, lives and acts independently of local customs and kinship,
free from the parochial constraints of any particular community.
Consequently, the 'Other' within must do just the opposite.

TRANSNATIONAL CONNECTIONS

Unlike better-known localities on the north Norwegian coast
(notably Lofoten and the North Cape), Båtsfjord has very few

tourists. Nevertheless, it is a very dynamic place, attracting both visitors and migrants from near and far. During the last couple of decades, Båtsfjord has witnessed various shifts in flows of people. The most significant is perhaps the successive replacement of Finnish by Tamils in the late 1980s, and the subsequent relacement of Tamils by Russians in the 1990s as the most important group of immigrants. These represent the most recent waves of immigration, and contribute significantly in making up Båtsfjord's rather hetero-geneous population. This is reflected, for instance, in the two local elementary schools where basic language training in native languages other than Norwegian ('*morsmålsundervisning*') is offered to as much as 15 per cent of 290 pupils, and includes Finnish, Tamil, Russian, Somali, Polish and Thai.[14]

Furthermore, a vital fishing industry dependent on export involves transnational relations on a massive scale. Seasonal production of capelin roe during the 1980s and 1990s has brought Japanese wholesalers to the community, where they have stayed for weeks to inspect production. Managers and marketing professionals from the local fishing industries also travel frequently to visit foreign customers or to present their products at international food exhibitions in, for example, Paris, Cologne and Brussels. In addition, young trainees are sent abroad to learn more about potential markets. Since the early 1990s, Russian trawlers have arrived with fish caught within the Russian fishing zone (so-called '*russefisk*'), contributing significantly to keeping industrial production going during years of reduced quotas, and creating a steady presence of Russian crews on the docks and in public spaces.[15] Finally, Båtsfjord has a higher percentage of people moving in and out of the community than most places in Norway.[16]

Other flows are related to consumption and the media. In a sense, Båtsfjord has experienced roughly the same type of diffusion of consumer goods and media entertainment that we may find in most parts of Western Europe during the last decades, and whose trajec-tories could be mapped and interpreted as it is appropriated in different places. Rather than representing discontinuities, these flows serve to reaffirm, for a large part, the Euro-centred and nation-state-oriented 'natural order of things' in the sense that they present images that reify a hierarchic duality between the north and south of Norway, or between an urban, cosmopolitan way of life and 'Otherness' on its alleged margins. To summarise, Båtsfjord is a place where flows of people and goods are not a novel phenomenon, in fact it has been based upon such flows ever since its establishment as a major fishing port. In spite of this, in relation to Norway, the Nordic countries and Europe, it represents, in many ways, a locality 'on the margin'.

With this in mind, we may return to the issue of globalising processes. Clearly, the flow of goods and of people does not constitute a discontinuity in – or by – itself. How then, do globalising processes become significant in a locality like Båtsfjord? Is it possible to identify moments or arenas in which a transformative potential is present? And if so, what kinds of discontinuities emerge?

Boundaries do not disappear as a result of globalising processes, but they may be altered and, as new boundaries emerge, others may silently disappear. I suggest that it is precisely through localised analyses of shifting boundaries that the transformative potential of globalising processes may be traced and understood. The following section highlights three cases concerning different empirical contexts in which the transformative potential of globalising procesess may be analysed. I shall draw attention to the issue of boundaries, the shifting understandings of what belongs together and what needs to be kept apart, and their relationship to globalising processes. All cases concern the investment of physical spaces with certain meanings and functions, and their social implications. I suggest that these cases are significant, as they bring us closer to those moments or meeting points when the transformative potential of globalising processes is present and might 'make a difference'.

CASE 1   THE AIRPORT

In September 1999, a new airport was established in Båtsfjord. It represented a great improvement in terms of safety, as it has a longer runway than the previous airport. The new airport building is made of wood; it is spacious with a high ceiling, but otherwise it looks like any other modern small-town airport in northern Europe. The waiting lounge is separated from the adjacent ticket office by a solid wall made of wood and glass. Through the glass, the travellers can watch the staff and vice versa. On this wall is a ticket counter, and a circular frame built into the glass wall that allows travellers to speak to staff. Left of the ticket counter, there is a door that allows staff to pass into the waiting lounge.

In March 2000, six months after the airport had been opened, a handwritten poster was still temporarily taped to the glass door, with the message: '*Adgang forbudt, kun for ansatte*' ('No entrance – staff only'). One of my friends told me that the sign had been put up just after the airport opened because local travellers kept walking in and out to have coffee and chat with the staff. I immediately recalled the old airport building, which was about the size of a small living room, and in which the one person on duty would be doing his paperwork at a desk practically in the middle of the room, surrounded by friends and neighbours chatting and sharing coffee, until the Twin Otter plane was ready for departure, and the pilot would turn up at the door, saying something like: 'OK, we're ready, come on, follow me....'

If Båtsfjord is analysed as a small, peripheral society striving to become modern, the new airport represents a huge achievement. It does not bring any more flights or international connections, but it allows each flight to be undertaken within the format of international standards regarding safety and bureaucratic procedures. In a sense, since September 1999, Båtsfjord has become comparable to other airports of similar size all over the world. Local solutions to the challenge of public transportation have given way to a standardised format.[17] However, such enlistment is only achieved to the extent that local travellers are willing and able to participate, that is, to separate their roles as customers or travellers from their roles as neighbours, kin or friends, and to let the former role replace the latter as soon as they enter the airport waiting lounge. As the temporary poster indicates, the architectural structure of the waiting lounge is not (yet) sufficient to discipline all local travellers to participate in achieving this.

CASE 2 'FISKEBRUK'

'*Fiskebruk*' is the name of the premises where fish is brought ashore and transformed to frozen products for domestic sale and export. In the year 2000, there were five such premises in Båtsfjord. A *fiskebruk* is always located right at the dock. Outside and on the docks, there will be vessels and trawlers, containers of fish and huge entrances to the building that allow smaller trucks to bring the fish inside. On the other side of the building, facing the street, there are one or more entrance doors for staff, but these tend to be small and usually with no signs attached.

During the last 10–20 years, most *fiskebruk* in the region have gradually been transformed from a public space to a private, commercial space reserved for staff only. Traditionally in this region, the *fiskebruk* was a place to meet, and a place for both young and old to work a few hours ('*egne lina*'), to buy some fish, get fish for free or simply to hang around.[18] Since the 1970s, these multiple and locally defined functions of such places have gradually given way to the more exclusive and overarching goals of providing products that fulfil quality standards of international trade regulations. This implies that *in principle* no one can enter the premises (neither inside nor outside) except staff currently on duty. The argument for this regulation is related to hygiene and food safety. An effect of this is that *in principle* fish is no longer sold from the *fiskebruk*. In practice, this principle is frequently violated. Local managers do feel a responsibility for providing fish to the local population, and as there is no formalised sale of fresh fish in Båtsfjord, many feel obliged to find ways of stretching or even breaking the rules in order to meet these needs.

The question of how to supply fresh fish to the local inhabitants has been an issue of some debate for many years, and, in spite of the gradual construction of more and more efficient boundaries – socially and physically – between local consumers and fish, the issue still remains unsettled. One effect of this is that an unspoken but significant distinction between locals and newcomers from outside the region is erased. In the 1980s, fish was readily available for most local people, but acquisition required a certain social network and subtle, implicit knowledge about a wide range of practical details such as where to enter the *fiskebruk*, who to talk to, how to wrap the fish and so on. These requirements served in practice to exclude many newcomers from actually taking part in consumption of local fresh catch[19] (Lien, 1989). As a result, a newcomer's ability (or lack of ability) to acquire fish served as one among several markers of social integration in the community, and thus in practice signified the distinction between the (working class) 'us' and the (middle class) 'others', while at the same time subverting that very hierarchical order. Today, with the local adaptation to national and international trade regulations that legally restrict such informal exchange, this signifier is no longer as meaningful.[20] As a result, a significant mediator of distinction between 'us' and 'others' has partly disappeared.

Having a new airport and complying with international trade regulations at local fish-processing plants does not make Båtsfjord any less marginal, socially or geographically. However, to apply the terminology of Edwin Ardener, it might make it *less remote*. According to Ardener, the term 'remoteness' cannot simply be reduced to a notion of centre and periphery.[21] One of the dimensions that characterises remote areas relates to change and invention, and the way the remains of failed innovations scatter the landscape as a result. This could be an apt description of parts of the coastal landscape of Båtsfjord. Another issue emphasised by Ardener is what he refers to as 'event-richness'. He writes:

In the large stable systems of dominant central areas ... there are equally large regularities ... in which only in periodic 'prophetic situations' do major singularities occur. They are event poor. Event richness is like a small-scale, ... continuously generated set of singularities which are not just the artefact of observer bias ... – but due to some materiality I define to be the enhanced defining power of individuals. (Ardener, 1987: 222)

The cases above indicate that a maintenance of a self-generated set of social definitions in Båtsfjord is threatened. Although Båtsfjord remains 'remote' according to most (but not all) of Ardener's qualifying criteria, we may nevertheless interpret each case of compliance with universal regulations of traffic and trade as a step towards a less overt 'self-definition', towards more regularity and thus a gradual movement towards making Båtsfjord slightly less 'remote'.

CASE 3   SEEING LIKE AN ARCHITECT: A SEARCH FOR IDENTITY

While the previous cases focused on boundaries that have already emerged or disappeared, my third and final case concerns a certain moment when the transformative potential of globalising processes is reflected upon, although not necessarily realised. On a Sunday evening in March 2000, an open meeting took place in the premises of the municipal administration in Båtsfjord. The occasion was the visit of a group of architects (a teacher from a Norwegian University and three of his graduate students) who were to report the results of studies they had undertaken during the previous months regarding *planning* how the physical environment of Båtsfjord ought to be utilised in the future.

The room was filled with rows of chairs, and more than 40 people were present, including a few local politicians, shopkeepers, people from the municipal administration and others. A local consultant and engineer (who had invited the architects to undertake this study, and paid for part of it himself), welcomed the audience, and then the senior architect took the floor. The first few minutes of his talk established a rationale for his presence. He explained that architects can be helpful in creating the 'good life' (*'det gode liv'*) in places like Båtsfjord. And a good life for people living here, he said, must include good conditions for local industrial enterprise (*næringslivet*). Then he told a story of a Russian woman he once met in Murmansk, who had been to three different places in Norway: Oslo, Bergen and Båtsfjord. He asked her what she thought about Båtsfjord, and, he went on: 'Well, she said it was like an ordinary Norwegian community ... Nothing special really.' 'And this', the architect continued, 'is the core of the problem in Båtsfjord. It has no identity.'

Then he paused and the audience was silent as he reached for a flipover marker and started to make a quick sketch, while inviting the audience to guess what he was drawing. Everyone watched carefully as he added one line after another.

'Can you see it?', he asked, but we all remained silent. He added a few more lines and all of a sudden we could see the image of a little boy peeing.

'So what is this?'

Still no answer.

'And, more important, *where* is it?'

The audience was silent. Then the word Brussels was mentioned, somewhere in the room, and the architect exclaimed: 'Yes, it's typical. We see this and we all know it's Brussels. The small famous statue gives Brussels its identity. Same with Oslo.'

Then he quickly sketched the more familiar skyline of the Oslo city hall, and everybody nodded in recognition.

'Now, what about Båtsfjord?' he asked, and continued: 'Well, the answer is obvious. Båtsfjord has nothing like this.'

Then, the architect mentioned the work of his students, and shortly afterwards returned to the question: 'What is really Båtsfjord?'

He turned a page on the flipover chart, and made a vertical line with a curve at the bottom. 'This is the road', he said. Indicating parallel axes on either side of the road, he continued:

... and these are the axes. There's the mountain range to the left, and the fiord to the right. These axes are given by the topography. But what about the road? Well, it is long, and it is really without any clear beginning and end. Just like the centre, which is also without a clear beginning and end. Our students have looked more closely at this road, and discovered that it actually consists of many different kinds of housing and other characteristics. They have, in fact, defined as much as six different *sequences*.

At this point he turned to the flip chart to draw six short horizontal lines across the vertical line and curve, indicating boundaries between the sequences, and then continued: 'I am not going to go into any more detail, but one idea would be to emphasise these sequences a bit more, to mark more clearly where one sequence ends and another begins.' He discussed different ways in which this could be done, using plants, surfaces, lights and so on.

His presentation went on for a while, and then one of the students presented her project. Afterwards, there was an open discussion which turned out to focus almost exclusively on the concept of identity. 'Identity' is a term which is seldom used in everyday speech. This evening, the concept of identity has never been really clarified by the architect; rather, it was taken for granted throughout his presentation. The comments that followed revealed quite different interpretations of what the term might mean, and how identity could be established. But there was one point around which all speakers seemed to agree, namely that *identity is important* and that *Båtsfjord doesn't really have one*. Some, however, remained silent, and some of them – I learned later – disagreed, but they never voiced any resistance at the meeting. Different suggestions regarding how to give Båtsfjord an identity were considered.[22] Throughout the discussion, speakers agreed that fish is important, and that the identity of Båtsfjord ought to reflect this. They discussed how visitors might like to learn more about the activities of the *fiskebruk*, but quickly agreed that they would have to put up a museum to show what's going on more or less 'next door', because it would not be practically possible for any outsider to enter the *fiskebruk* due to the legal regulations (see above).

In one of the studies presented, the *'fiskehjell'* – the wooden structures previously used to dry fish – was suggested as an identity marker in Båtsfjord. These rustic constructions can still be seen on the outskirts of the community as remnants of the time *before* Båtsfjord became a major fishing port, when vessels were much smaller, and drying was the chief method of conservation. However, among all the coastal communities in Finnmark, Båtsfjord is probably among those where dried fish was the *least* important, as its very establishment coincided with the development of freezing technologies.

While a notion of hybridity has been thought of as a characteristic trait of the region by people in Varanger, the term 'identity' carries no hybrid connotation. Rather, it conveys a simplified image which emphasises differentiation. Instead of being 'just another typical coastal Norwegian community', acquiring an *identity* will allegedly succeed in making Båtsfjord 'stand apart'. The emergence of a discourse of identity thus implies a potential emergence of new boundaries.

The idea that Båtsfjord ought to have an identity is not taken out of the blue. Rather it is an element of both academic and popular discourse which has had the ability lately to align a wide variety of interests and purposes in a wide range of fields (Bauman, 2001). One of the key characteristics of 'successful' concepts like identity (market and culture are other examples) is precisely that they appear to have no origin. Rather they are 'everywhere', anywhere, and come from nowhere. This feature in itself does not, however, explain their success. When a local audience in Båtsfjord appears to embrace this concept so readily, it may be because it seems to help clarify or distinguish boundaries that would otherwise remain less clear. Somehow, we may assume, this need for distinction may be felt as more urgent than before. Perhaps it is is precisely an experience of a global gaze, or globality (Beck, 2000) that fuels the urge to transform an unidentified locality into a distinct and identifiable place.[23]

MODERNITY ON THE MARGINS

In his introduction to the book *Occidentalism*, James Carrier emphasises how a Western notion of the Occident has both a spatial and a temporal component (Carrier, 1995: 18). Our idea of the 'West' tends to blur with the idea of modernity (or modernisation) to the extent that development easily becomes synonymous with Westernisation. Within this hegemonic temporal-spatial continuum, Båtsfjord is a place where collective efforts are being made to modernise. These efforts are couched in a rhetoric that reflects a desire to be part of, or prepared for, the 'inevitable' changes that the future will bring. This is particularly evident in the case of architectural planning, but is also relevant in the two previous cases, in which the future presents itself in the shape of a new trade or legal regulation that – having 'claimed' relevance on an increasing scale – is now interpreted locally as a dictum. Compliance is necessary in order to maintain traffic and trade – in other words, to partake in the transnational order of an imagined future.

According to David Harvey, a reorganisation of space is always a reorganisation of the framework through which social power is expressed (1990: 255). The first two cases demonstrate how the effort to take part in an imagined future of traffic and trade involved changes at the local level, which in turn had social implications in the sense that they partly eliminated an important signifier of the local social identity. We may refer to these changes as examples of *temporal discontinuities*. Simultaneously, the same shifts represent a move towards accountability in relation to a judgement from elsewhere. In relation to the outside world, Båtsfjord has become slightly more predictable and slightly less remote, as universal standards have replaced the particularity of what were previously highly specific local solutions. The recent changes thus erase what we may call *spatial discontinuities* between this and other localities. To modernise, in this context, thus becomes synonymous with efforts to adjust local practices in order to comply with regulative standards that apply elsewhere.

The third case, however, introduces a perspective on space that highlights, rather than erases, spatial discontinuities. The interventions suggested by the architects represent changes that will allegedly make Båtsfjord more distinct with regard to the judgement of an outsider. Instead of adjusting local practices to make Båtsfjord more predictable and less remote, the architects paradoxically call for the opposite. According to their view, Båtsfjord's problem is precisely that it lacks something that makes it stand out as different from the rest – it lacks 'identity'. This search for identity may be seen as part of a more general pattern which Zygmunt Bauman (2001) describes as a 'spectacular rise of the "identity discourse"', intimately related to the modern condition and to globalisation. One of the characterising features of this emergent identity discourse is that identity is, almost by definition, something 'incomplete', and that individuals are held responsible for its completion. Identity discourse thus represents a major shift of 'transforming human "identity" from a "given" into a "task"' (Bauman, 2001: 124). The problem with identity, as the architect expressed so precisely, was that 'Båtsfjord didn't have one'. During the discussion that followed, the responsibility for coming up with a solution to this problem was entirely interpreted as a local and collective responsibility.

The sudden emergence of a search for 'identity' in planning the coastal landscape in Båtsfjord echoes a trend in urban renewal that has placed its mark on cities in Europe and the USA for several decades. Harvey (1990: 92) identifies this epoch as one in which 'cities and places now take much more care to create a positive and high quality image of place', and describes how architecture and urban design are used to respond to such need. Harvey suggests simple market mechanisms to account for this shift. Its backgound, he maintains, is the history of 'deindustrialization and restructuring which have left most major cities in the advanced capitalist world with few options except to compete with each other, mainly as financial, consumption and entertainment centres' (Harvey, 1990: 92). In the field of architecture, this alleged 'need' appears to have gained its own momentum, making the 'search for identity' a universal aim.

Båtsfjord's main attraction has been, and still is, opportunities for unskilled and relatively well-paid employment. In this way, it differs markedly from the urban contexts that produced San Francisco's Ghirardelli Square and Boston's Faneuil Hall (see Harvey, 1990). However, through a rhetoric that literally transforms Båtsfjord to a place that is comparable to Brussels and to Oslo, the architect succeeds in convincing the audience (at least part of it) that identity is worth striving for. Presented as a characteristic which Båtsfjord simply lacks, this search for identity is instantaneously transformed with yet another stratified tournament in which Båtsfjord inevitably ends up starting from scratch. Unlike more 'famous' places like Brussels or Oslo, that possess distinguishable identity markers that people may remember them by, Båtsfjord is *not* a place to remember. Presenting this 'mnemonic deficit' as if it were a property of the place, rather than a property of the memory processes of people passing through, the architect naturalises marginality as a feature of the locality itself. In this way the urban-centred hegemonic order is reproduced. This case thus demonstrates how the construction of difference and of identity is an effect of structural relations of power, and the intertwining of power and place (Gupta and Ferguson, 1999: 14). Ironically, just as compliance with transnational regulations has made Båtsfjord more integrated and thereby less remote (see

Ardener), an emergent search for identity again re-establishes its marginal position.

GLOBALISING STRUCTURES AND THE RE-MAKING OF BOUNDARIES

Globalisation has been presented as the replacement of boundaries by global networks. My argument has been that globalisation implies enlistment into large-scale networks in which new boundaries may also emerge. I suggest that it is preciesly through localised analyses of shifting boundaries that the transformative potential of the globalising process may be understood.

There are many cases of transnational flows in which origins and biographies of the items that move are contained in, and also in fact serve to constitute, the object (e.g. the kula shells). This is often the case in consumption. The cases that I have presented in this chapter represent the other extreme. As new concepts are introduced in Båtsfjord, their 'route', origins or biographies are simultaneously erased, thereby allowing these concepts to represent eternal and universal truths. And this, I suggest, partly accounts for their trans-formative potential.

The coast of northern Norway has been characterised by extensive flows long before the issue of a distinct 'cultural identity' emerged. Like the Caribbean, it has been integrated in extensive global networks for centuries seemingly *without* being subjected to a transition to the state referred to as 'globality' (Beck, 2000). This is because, I suggest, it is perfectly possible to experience the presence of alternative categories or ways of being without being absorbed by them. In other words, the incorporation of foreign goods and the recognition of foreign quality criteria does not necessarily alter, or even challenge, the existing local categories or classifying criteria. This is because the social power to define the order of things at the local level is not fundamentally challenged. An important feature of this local order, however, is that it swiftly incorporates categories of 'the other' as part of the 'natural order of things'. Dealing with heterogeneity has become routine. In such situations, transnational flows do not necessarily bring about 'globality', as defined by Beck.

The introduction of the term 'identity' at the meeting with the architects, however, immediately led to a discussion through which an alternative set of criteria for evaluating or 'seeing' Båtsfjord was tried out. While the latter case may not bring about any physical changes at all, I maintain that it is by far the most significant, because it involves the absorption of a set of criteria for defining locality which has a transformative potential far beyond the event in question. More precisely, the introduction of identity as a 'deficiency' in Båtsfjord introduces a new kind of perspective (an identity discourse) which is, on the one hand, hegemonically urban-centred and reproduces the marginality of Båtsfjord, while on the other hand it is *simultaneously* presented as universal truth. Rather than being classified, and maybe discarded as a perspective typical of urban elites from the south, the notion of identity was embraced, at least by some, as a relevant perspective for the challenges of the future. Rather than becoming yet another 'other', the architect thus became a mediator of knowledge of universal value. There appears, in other words, to be a close connection between the fact that concepts or ideas are readily absorbed and the fact that they appear to have no origin.[24]

Seeking to understand processes commonly referred to as globalisation, we need to look beyond the most obvious traces of movement. This is because movement itself does not necessarily bring about significant changes, but also because the most significant changes may be brought about by movements, or trajectories, that appear to erase their paths as they move along. Tracing the implications of globalising processes thus requires an attention to shifting boundaries in local contexts, as the trajectories involved are not 'flagged' as globalisation. A methodological approach that literally 'follows the thing' will hardly enable the researcher to distinguish the routinised incorporation of foreign elements from those that have the potential to transform the local order. In order to understand how global connections serve to constitute localities, we need to apply a methodological approach that is sensitive towards the subtle changes that occur as one set of definitions is replaced by another. This is facilitated by paying attention to changes over time, whether through long-term involvement in the field, historicity or by means of a multi-temporal approach. It is precisely through such analyses of shifting boundaries that the transformative potential of globalising processes may be traced and understood.

NOTES

1. According to Marcus (1998), multi-sited ethnographies may focus on persons, things, metaphors, stories, allegories or biographies.
2. Similar cases would include the studies that track the movements of migrants in diaspora and exile (Marcus, 1999: 6).
3. Re-visits to the field have been practised by numerous anthropologists since the 1950s (see for instance Colson, 1984; Foster, 1979; Mead, 1970). In 1984, Elizabeth Colson, summarising her experiences from 35 years of involvement with Tonga-speaking peoples in central Africa, emphasised how the process of ageing with informants allows for

different kinds of identification and thus of different interpretations of local events. She also emphasised how engagement over time serves to shatter the misleading image of the field-site as a timeless present, as it allows the mapping of local changes.

4. A book published in Norway about the international trade of dried fish more than a century ago may serve to illustrate the way global trade brought about a certain 'globality'. The book (Wallem, 1893) is an impressive source of information on the conditions for Norwegian export of fish. It includes, along with detailed information on the different qualities of fish and quantities for export, a detailed description of the various preferences for different qualities of stockfish in different regions of the world, and the importance of considering these preferences in the production process. The author emphasises in particular the importance of the *'vraker'* the person who serves as a broker between Norwegian fishermen or local/regional buyers and the international market. Knowing the specific preferences of different markets is essential for succesful export operations, indicating the adoption (by at least some actors in the trade) of what is often referred to as a 'global gaze'.

5. According to Held, globalisation can be thought of as 'a process ... which embodies a transformation in the spatial organisation of social relations and transactions – assessed in terms of their extensity, intensity, velocity and impact – generating transcontinental or interregional flows or networks of activity, interaction and excercise of power' (Held et al., 1999: 16).

6. 2,472 inhabitants in January 1999, but the number fluctuates from year to year (SSB, 2000).

7. The municipality of Båtsfjord consists of two settlements, one in Båtsfjord and another in Syltefjord. Unlike Båtsfjord, Syltefjord has a few small farms and a pastures suitable for sheep. The population of Syltefjord has declined steadily since the 1960s, however, and numbers only a handful of all-year inhabitants. When I refer to Båtsfjord in the following, I refer to the settlement Båtsfjord, and not to the entire municipality.

8. Until recently, the continent east of the border to Russia was sometimes simply left out of such maps, or given a neutral, blank and non-informative shade.

9. Since the Second World War, and due to effective national assimilation policies, the coastal Saami in the Varanger area have increasingly identified with the Norwegian majority, and ethnicity has been 'silenced'. This was the situation until the late 1970s and 1980s, when due to processes of ethnopolitical revival, people have increasingly recognised a Saami heritage. However, the ethnopolitical pressures towards exclusive ethnic identification, 'taking sides' as it were (which is common in inland areas) tends to be resisted in the coastal communities by people who claim a mixed ethnic origin.

10. http://odin.dep.no/ud/engelsk, Map of Barents Region.

11. There has been and still is a steady export of fish (historically dried, now frozen) from this area to ports on either side of the Atlantic, including now also Japan and the rest of Western Europe. There has also been, and still is, considerable migration from inland (northern Finland) to the

coast. Since the the the early 1990s there have been a number of exchanges across the Norwegian/Russian border.

12. The story was first published in the *Ladies' Home Journal*, and later appeared in Isak Dinesen's *Skæbne-anekdoter* (*Anecdotes of Destiny*) (1958).

13. It should come as no surprise that, when the story was made into a film in 1986, the selected locality in which the narrative unfolded was no longer Berlevåg, but somewhere 'on the desolate coast of Denmark' (http://www.blixeninfo.com/babette/html).

14. Source: local school, year 2000.

15. From 1997 through 1999 more than 1,500 Russian trawlers were registered as arrivals each year in the Varanger region (source: Harald Andersen, customs director, at Troms and Finnmark customs authority, Vadsø).

16. In 1999 the percentage of net movement of people both into *and* out of the community district was 11 per cent, indicating a considerable change of personnel (SSB, 2000).

17. Several other examples could illuminate this enlistment to standards and regulations on an increasingly wide scale. For instance, according to local rumours, in the early 1980s the local ambulance driver did not have a driver's licence. He was considered a reliable driver, nevertheless. A decade later, such irregularities would have been hard to imagine, due to the effectiveness of the municipal administration's struggles to achieve a certain coherence between (national) regulations and local practice.

18. Running the risk of reifying a much too nostalgic image of the past, it is tempting to suggest that fish, in a sense, 'belonged to the community'. It was practically never sold within the community, but was integrated within a complex network of food gift-exchange. Reciprocity is still widely practised (Lien, 2001).

19. There are examples of young doctors who, during their six-month period of medical practice in the community, never managed to acquire fresh fish (Lien, 1989).

20. More precisely: the exclusion of a person from the arena where fish circulates increasingly involves formal and bureaucratic – rather than informal and social – mechanisms of exclusion. Thus the experience of finding it hard to get hold of fresh fish increasingly affects local inhabitants almost regardless of their level of integration in the local community.

21. Nor can it be replaced by the concept of marginality. While Shields (1991) discusses marginality as a relational dimension reflecting hegemonic order, remoteness relates also to inherent qualities of localities themselves (Ardener, 1987: 223).

22. A woman referred to the Finnish town of Ivalou, where she once had to make a stopover on the way north, and where a blue glass dome was lit up at night, supposedly representing the Northern lights. It could be seen from a distance, and for her, this was something that made it easier to remember Ivalou. A man complained about the lack of coherence that meets the eye of the visitor: 'You arrive at the airport, and there's one identity. Or you arrive in the harbour [*hurtigrutekaia*] and there's another identity.'

23. This, in turn, may be seen partly as a result of extended economic systems, as illustrated through the previous cases.

120   *Globalisation*

24. Once the hegemonic order is established, no further justification is needed, and the origin of certain ideas becomes irrelevant. But it may also work the other way around: revealing the origin of certain ideas may implicitly also serve to remind the audience that truth is always relative, and could thus serve to undermine the appropriation of an idea as a universal truth. What I suggest here is simply that the act of exposing or revealing origins is a sensitive issue, and closely connected to definitive power, as well as to social and spatial hierarchy.

REFERENCES

Appadurai, A. (ed.) 1986. *The Social Life of Things*. Cambridge: Cambridge University Press.
Ardener, E. 1987. *The Voice of Prophecy and Other Essays*, edited by M. Chapman. Oxford: Basil Blackwell.
Bauman, Z. 2001. Identity in the globalising world, *Social Anthropology* 9(2): 121–9.
Beck, U. 2000. *What is Globalization?* Cambridge: Polity Press.
Blixen, K. 1977. *Babettes gjestebud og andre historier (Babette's Feast and Other Stories)*. Oslo: Den norske bokklubben.
Carrier, J.G. (ed.) 1995. Introduction. In *Occidentalism: Images of the West*, pp. 1–32. Oxford: Clarendon Press.
Colson, E. 1984. The reordering of experience: anthropological involvement with time, *Journal of Anthropological Research* 40(1): 1–13.
Dinesen, I. 1958. *Skæbne-anekdoter*. København: Gyldendal.
Foster, G. 1979. Fieldwork in Tzintzuntzan: the first thirty years. In G. Foster et al. (eds) *Long-term Field Research in Social Anthropology*, pp. 165–84. New York: Academic Press.
Gupta, A. and J. Ferguson (eds) 1997. Discipline and practice: 'the field' as site, method, and location in anthropology. In A. Gupta and J. Ferguson (eds) *Anthropological Locations. Boundaries and Grounds of a Field Science*. Berkeley: University of California Press.
—— 1999. *Culture, Power and Place: Explorations in Critical Anthropology*. Durham, NC: Duke University Press
Hannerz, U. 1996. *Transnational Connections*. London, Routledge.
Harvey, D. 1990. *The Condition of Postmodernity*. Oxford: Basil Blackwell.
Hastrup, K. and K.F. Olwig (eds) 1997. *Siting Culture*. New York: Routledge.
Held, D., A. McGrew, D. Goldblatt and J. Perraton. 1999. *Global Transformations: Politics, Economics and Culture*. Cambridge: Polity Press.
Kearney, M. 1995. The local and the global: the anthropology of globalization and transnationalism, *Annual Review of Anthropology* 24: 547–65.
Lien, M.E. 1989. *Fra boknafesk til pizza; Sosiokulturelle perspektiver på matvalg og endring av spisevaner i Båtsfjord, Finnmark*. Oslo Occasional Papers in Social Anthropology, 18. Oslo: Universitetet i Oslo.
—— 2001. Likhet og verdighet: Gavebytter og integrasjon I Båtsfjord ('Equality and dignity: gift exchange and social integration in Båtsfjord'). In M.E. Lien, H. Lidén and H. Vike (eds) *Likhetens Paradokser. Antropologiske undersøkelser i det moderne Norge (Paradoxes of Equality: Anthropological Explorations of Modern Norway)*. Oslo: Scandinavian University Press.
Marcus, G.E. 1998. *Ethnography Through Thick and Thin*. Princeton, NJ: Princeton University Press.

—— 1999. What is at stake – and is not – in the idea and practice of multi-sited ethnography, *Canberra Anthropology* 22(2): 6–14.

Mead, M. 1970. Field work in the Pacific Islands 1925–1967. In P. Golde (ed.) *Women in the Field: Anthropological Experiences*, pp. 293–331. Chicago: Aldine Press.

Megard, B.O. 1999. Kvener og finskætta: En undersøkelse av betegnelsene 'kvener' og 'etterkommere av finske innvandrere' I politisk diskurs og utforming av identitetstilknytning ('Kvener' and Finnish descendants: a study of ethnic terms in political discourse and identification) Masters thesis in Social Anthropology. Oslo: Department of Social Anthropology, University of Oslo.

Mintz, S. 1985. *Sweetness and Power: The Place of Sugar in Modern History*. New York: Viking.

Nadel-Klein, J. 1995. Occidentalism as a cottage industry: representing the autochthonous 'other' in British and Irish rural studies. In J.G. Carrier (ed.) *Occidentalism: Images of the West*, pp. 109–34. Oxford: Clarendon Press.

Said, E. 1978. *Orientalism*. London: Routledge & Kegan Paul.

Shields, R. 1991. *Places on the Margin: Alternative Geographies of Modernity*. London: Routledge.

SSB. 2000. *Regionalstatistikk Finnmark* (Regional Statistics, Finnmark). Oslo: Norwegian Bureau of Statistics.

Trouillot, M.-R. 1992. The Caribbean region: an open frontier in anthropological theory, *Annual Review of Anthropology* 21: 19–42.

Wallem, F.M. 1893. *Handelen med Tørrfisk og Klipfisk (efter specielle konsulat-beretninger, flere landes officielle handelsstatistik, børsnoteringer og andre meddelelser samlede efter foranstaltning av Departmentet for det Indre.* [Trade in Dried Fish and Stockfish]. Kristiania (Oslo): W.C. Fabritius & Sønner.

7 CONSIDERING GLOBAL/LOCAL RELATIONS: BEYOND DUALISM

Knut G. Nustad

The more discretely and specifically we define and bound the units of our study, the more provocative, necessary, and difficult it becomes to account for the relationships among those units; conversely, the more effectively we are able to analyze and sum up the relationships among a set of units, the more provocative, necessary, and difficult it becomes to define the units. (Wagner, quoted in Strathern, 1991: n3)

The point of departure for this chapter is what appear to me to be some inconsistencies in the way in which the conceptual pair local and global is deployed. There are a bewildering number of definitions of globalisation and the global. A dividing line can be drawn between those, following Wallerstein, who discern an underlying force behind globalisation, such as the intensification of economic relations across national boundaries (e.g. Held, 1995; Rosenau, 1990) and those who focus on a cultural process involving homogenisation and diversification (Appadurai, 1991; Robertson, 1995). Jonathan Friedman (1994, 1995) distinguishes between the two and argues that the global system, understood as the objective forces that create centre/periphery relations, that is articulated as expansion and contraction of units, must be distinguished from globalisation, as subjective awareness of the increased interconnections and the organisation of the global system by such bodies as transnational companies and international organisations. Despite the differences, in much of this literature there seems to be an effortless shifting between a definition of globalisation as simply long connections, and globalisation as a distinct realm of reality that has agency and is thus able to interact with or transform another part of reality: the local.

Tomlinson, in a recent book (1999), defines globalisation as complex connectivity: 'the rapid developing and ever-densening network of interconnections and interdependences that characterizes modern social life' (1999: 2). We are here presented with a vision of globalisation as connections. But some 20 pages on, these connections seem to be delegated to a separate realm from that which they connect, when we are informed that 'globalisation is not a "one-way" process of the determination of events by massive global structures, but involves at least the possibility for *local intervention* in *global processes*' (1999: 26, emphasis added).

The reason for this inconsistency, I believe, must be sought in the relationship between anthropological models and that which the models are meant to explain. Roland Robertson (1995), in stressing that globality is an aspect of the local, is the author that comes closest to the argument. He argues that:

it makes no good sense to define the global as if the global excludes the local. In somewhat technical terms, defining the global in such a way suggests that the global lies beyond all localities, as having systemic properties over and beyond the attributes of units within a global system. (1995: 34)

This is very similar to my conception of the dualism. Robertson further argues that what appears to be local is 'essentially included within the global' (1995: 35). Here he has in mind such forms as nation-states, that claim legitimacy from articulations of local and specific traditions, but that nevertheless are global in their outreach. Friedman (1995), in turn, criticises this approach for being too culturalist; the similarities in forms, for him, arise out of the structurally similar conditions produced by the global system.

Even when for Robertson the local is produced by globalisation, he still retains what looks conspicuously like a causal link between the two when he states that 'globalisation – in the broadest sense, the compression of the world – has involved and increasingly involves the creation and the incorporation of locality, processes which themselves largely shape, in turn, the compression of the world as a whole' (1995: 40). Friedman, in turn, argues that 'the world investigated by anthropologists is a world already transformed by its *integration* into the global system' (1995: 74, emphasis added). Here he retains a duality by falling back on a Marxist notion of the global system as an underlying structural reality that incorporates localities. These two authors have in my view come a long way in conceiving of the categories local and global in such a way as to avoid establishing a causal relation between the two. They both explicitly state this as their aim. However, as we see, a dual conception of the local and the global creeps back into the analyses. The problem is accurately stated by Wagner in the quote above, and is probably a fault of our language as much as of analysis. I do not pretend to solve the problem here, but I want to identify it more clearly by examining its epistemological background, and suggest an alternative approach to studying local/global articulations that avoids slipping into a duality.

Ulrich Beck (2000) makes a distinction that in many way parallels Friedman's (1995) distinction between global system as objective and globalisation as an awareness produced by it. Beck, however, divides the cultural element into two sub-categories. He distinguishes between *globalism* as the ideology that a world market now has supplanted politics, and *globality*: the notion that we are living in a world society, a world without closed spaces. The objective process is for him captured by *globalisation*, the *process* through which nation-states are criss-crossed and undermined by transnational actors. Beck's introductory example of this is the transnational corporations. These actors undermine any pretence of running a national economy by their very size and their lack of containment. They locate production to those areas where the cost of labour is kept down, they pay taxes in countries that hardly tax corporate profit, and their executive staffs live in affluent welfare states, having access to all of their benefits without contributing to their maintenance.

It is of course a truism that one can apply any model one finds useful to the study of social interaction, from system to structure to individual/society, as long as one does not confuse the model itself with that which the model is meant to explain. So what I want to do in this chapter is to explore the epistemology of the conceptualisation of social processes as dual, as distinguishable into local and global, and then suggest methodological implications. A lot will be left out in the following discussion, including the transformation of the economy and the undermining of democratic control that these processes entail. What I am concerned with here is to do some conceptual tidying up. But, as I will show, more is at stake than a purely conceptual debate. How we conceive of the global and the local, also determines the scope for engaging politically with these issues.

Osvaldo de Rivero provides an example of this. In a recent book (de Rivero, 2001), he describes the predicament of Third World countries in a way that leaves little hope for a solution. The quasi-nation-states, as he terms them, are faced with an international economic order that in his rendering appears as a totalised system. Instead of functioning as a provider of productive investments, global capitalism resembles a global casino. Through a system of intellectual property rights, the transnational corporations have closed off the possibility for the copying of technology that was instrumental in developing early capitalist economies. This world order is maintained by the new aristocracy, the transnational corporations, with the aid of the new clergy, the IMF and the World Bank. His description leaves us with a rather hopeless picture of the situation, where an unholy alliance between big money and state structures creates an international system of total domination. This model that implicitly treats them as contained. Within this context, all the connections, the railroad that links our station to Berlin and Madrid, appear of a different order, as an agency that has the capacity to alter the local. This agency is then placed outside the system under study, and it thus appears as capable of influencing 'it'.

GLOBAL ACTORS

Above I concluded that the question of whether the global exists, and whether it can influence the local, is wrongly put. It is a question that appears meaningful because of the way in which we use language and models. Phenomena appeared as either local or global depending on the focus one chose. Further, this duality arose as a heuristic device to meet the shortcomings of a sociological model that tied group and social characteristics to territory. The global, then, was simply all that that model could not account for.

With this initial conception of a network as both global and local, let us turn to the global actors that are constituted through such networks. If today we have global actors, that are constituted through very long networks and can mobilise masses of people and objects in such ways as to bend the intentions of governments, how are they held together? In pushing this part of the argument, I find it useful to return to the earlier discussion of macro and micro actors. Although Robertson (1995) argues that this is a deviation from the debate, in my conception, if we want to stop conceiving of the world in terms of a global–local interaction, size is all we are left with. Callon and Latour (1981) have examined the related question of whether micro and macro actors could be said to exist, and conclude in the affirmative. Some actors, such as IBM, are macro in the sense that they control a large number of people, are able to act in many places at once, etc. But, and this is the important point, one cannot start out by looking for criteria that distinguish such actors from other actors. This for the simple reason that they shift focus from society as a given, to the processes that constitute a version of society. Thus, the fact that IBM is a macro actor is the end result, the outcome of a process. It follows that one cannot a priori distinguish between small-scale and large-scale, one will have to examine the processes that make it possible for some actors to achieve a large size. Then, after having examined the process, one can ask whether in the process of achieving size, certain other characteristics are also achieved.

How, then, does an agent become a macro actor? Their answer, in short, is by establishing associations between people and objects, by translating the will of others into a single will for which it speaks.

picture is also mirrored in Beck's opening description of globalisation. The global here appears as something almost tangible, imbued with an agency and a will to dominate the local.

There are thus both epistemological and political reasons for examining the relationship between the local and the global. In the following I will argue that the division of social phenomena into global and local rests on a fiction. The global and the local is better understood as two perspectives that are applied to the same objects: these objects, in turn, appear as either local or global, depending on the context into which they are put. This would imply that the global and the local are creations that inhabit our theories, and that the distinction finds no reflection in reality. Hence, no interaction can be said to take place between a local and global level, and the global cannot be said to influence the local in any meaningful way. I will argue that the reason why it still appears to do so is a result of the conceptual apparatus that has underpinned much of the modern social sciences, including anthropology.

I then go on to explore the global actors that Beck describes as the agents behind the break-up of nation-states. I am aware that I thereby make global actors compatible with what used to be called macro actors, and this is deliberate. Robertson (1995) argues that posing a similarity between micro/macro and local/global is one of the errors of the globalisation literature. Here I want to exploit this error for a specific purpose. Much of the debate about the local and the global follows a similar line to the discussion of micro and macro. Macro actors, as Callon and Latour (1981) use the concept, are similar to Beck's definition of global actors, but what gives the debate about globalisation a new twist is the conception of globalisation as a process that is transforming the world.

I will argue that, although I do not find it helpful to break up reality into the global and the local, global actors, in the sense of actors that transcend national boundaries and are constituted through relations that are very long, certainly do exist. An increase in their number or size can certainly be described as globalisation. The question is whether their agency is usefully explained in a 'global' realm that somehow transforms localities. I will propose a different approach, one that focuses on how these actors are held together through myriad techniques and practices. This has political implications: I will argue that an examination of the way in which global actors are screwed together also make them less threatening.

ANTHROPOLOGICAL MODELS AND DUALITIES

My initial assumption, when I began working with this material, was that the whole dualism, the conceptual pair of global and local, was a trick of perception that social scientists, and maybe especially anthropologists, were prone to make because of the history of our discipline. I will not bore you with a tour of this well-traversed territory, but as Bauman (1992), Beck (2000), Latour (2000) and others have pointed out, the social sciences have long been implicated in an epistemology that has the nation-state as its frame of reference. This epistemology starts out with society as a given, consisting of so many closed, bounded entities. Nations, of course, which Giddens described as 'the pre-eminent form of power container, as a territorially bounded ... administrative unity' (1985: 13), with policed borders, are the prime example, but also social classes, ethnic identities and individuals as contained entities in interaction with an equally contained society were modelled on the state, with its clear boundaries vis-à-vis other entities. This epistemology created a framework in which causal relationships could be examined: how society, culture, class, ethnicity influenced and shaped the individual, and how individuals modified the categories. It is within this framework that a conception of global processes as able to influence local events has its roots.

This was mirrored in both American and British anthropology. The insistence on boundaries, and the functional integration of the different elements within these boundaries, depicted the world of the primitives as nation-states in the making, without the integrating effect of a modern state, to be sure, but with the 'culture', tradition and language out of which the modern states had made their nation-states. So, as Grimshaw and Hart (1993) have pointed out, if the people of Melanesia and Africa were not seen as living in states, they certainly were analysed according to a model that implicitly depicted them as nations.

Now anthropology, because of the weight it traditionally has given to empirical studies over theoretical debates, was early in picking up some of the inadequacies of this framework. Important work was done by the associates of the Rhodes Livingstone Institute to rethink the models of earlier anthropology in the face of the empirical challenges of what they called the African industrial revolution (e.g. Epstein, 1978; Gluckman, 1958, 1961; Mitchell, 1956, 1970). Methods such as extended case studies (van Velsen, 1967), situational analyses (Mitchell, 1970) and network analyses were meant to draw attention to the complexity of the situation, the impossibility of sorting a flow of interaction into neat categories. So, in anthropology and in the other social sciences there has been an attempt to develop a new theoretical apparatus to capture a reality that seemed increasingly complex; that is, complex in relation to earlier assumptions.

But at some point in the developing complexity of our we began to confuse the models with the reality that we se describe. I tend to pinpoint the culprit as the macro/micro The concepts that were launched prior to it, such as ne tended to focus on extensions and interactions. If a dua introduced somewhere, the micro/macro distinction seems place to look for it. In that debate as well, reality was divid the conceptual and disciplinary divisions. Some disciplin concerned with the 'macro processes' of society, others micro, debates raged about their interaction, and some peo found a reality middle ground in a meso level.

This debate clearly shows a confusion of model and realit an economist studies a transaction and relates it to econor and hence to a macro level, whereas an anthropologist sees transaction as embedded in micro social relations, they studying two different phenomena. They apply different tives to the same phenomena. So one could argue for the g the local as well: they are not two processes in the world perspectives on the same point.

This is an extension of an argument made by Latour (argues that the modern associations of objects and sub enormous scaling effects; networks of associated actor: much further than they could possibly have done before. networks should not be seen as global with the conno universal. Even if they are large, they do not cover every the surface of the earth. These networks should rather be he suggests, with the analogy of railroads and pipelines i a railroad local or global? Neither. It is local at all points, because there are sleepers and stations everywhere. Yet i because it takes you from Madrid to Berlin. At the same tir universal enough to take you everywhere.

By extending this metaphor, I think we can identify sc problems we are facing. Imagine not the whole railrc station. How do you go about analysing that? The : primitive, but let us say that modernist social science tried it as a local system, sufficiently bounded and contained to to analysis. The present predicament stems from the reali much that goes on in the station has nothing to do with itself as an entity. Is it local or global? Both. And, : Strathern (1991) has argued, the realisation that the obje when it is put into a new context, also gives rise to t realisation that every perspective can only be partial. T standpoint from which a phenomenon can be grasped in

The local/global dualism arises, therefore, I would argu monsters that crowd in when one tries to fix phenomer picture is also mirrored in Beck's opening description of globalisation. The global here appears as something almost tangible, imbued with an agency and a will to dominate the local.

There are thus both epistemological and political reasons for examining the relationship between the local and the global. In the following I will argue that the division of social phenomena into global and local rests on a fiction. The global and the local is better understood as two perspectives that are applied to the same objects: these objects, in turn, appear as either local or global, depending on the context into which they are put. This would imply that the global and the local are creations that inhabit our theories, and that the distinction finds no reflection in reality. Hence, no interaction can be said to take place between a local and global level, and the global cannot be said to influence the local in any meaningful way. I will argue that the reason why it still appears to do so is a result of the conceptual apparatus that has underpinned much of the modern social sciences, including anthropology.

I then go on to explore the global actors that Beck describes as the agents behind the break-up of nation-states. I am aware that I thereby make global actors compatible with what used to be called macro actors, and this is deliberate. Robertson (1995) argues that posing a similarity between micro/macro and local/global is one of the errors of the globalisation literature. Here I want to exploit this error for a specific purpose. Much of the debate about the local and the global follows a similar line to the discussion of micro and macro. Macro actors, as Callon and Latour (1981) use the concept, are similar to Beck's definition of global actors, but what gives the debate about globalisation a new twist is the conception of globalisation as a process that is transforming the world.

I will argue that, although I do not find it helpful to break up reality into the global and the local, global actors, in the sense of actors that transcend national boundaries and are constituted through relations that are very long, certainly do exist. An increase in their number or size can certainly be described as globalisation. The question is whether their agency is usefully explained in a 'global' realm that somehow transforms localities. I will propose a different approach, one that focuses on how these actors are held together through myriad techniques and practices. This has political implications: I will argue that an examination of the way in which global actors are screwed together also make them less threatening.

ANTHROPOLOGICAL MODELS AND DUALITIES

My initial assumption, when I began working with this material, was that the whole dualism, the conceptual pair of global and local, was a trick of perception that social scientists, and maybe especially anthropologists, were prone to make because of the history of our discipline. I will not bore you with a tour of this well-traversed territory, but as Bauman (1992), Beck (2000), Latour (2000) and others have pointed out, the social sciences have long been implicated in an epistemology that has the nation-state as its frame of reference. This epistemology starts out with society as a given, consisting of so many closed, bounded entities. Nations, of course, which Giddens described as 'the pre-eminent form of power container, as a territorially bounded ... administrative unity' (1985: 13), with policed borders, are the prime example, but also social classes, ethnic identities and individuals as contained entities in interaction with an equally contained society were modelled on the state, with its clear boundaries vis-à-vis other entities. This epistemology created a framework in which causal relationships could be examined: how society, culture, class, ethnicity influenced and shaped the individual, and how individuals modified the categories. It is within this framework that a conception of global processes as able to influence local events has its roots.

This was mirrored in both American and British anthropology. The insistence on boundaries, and the functional integration of the different elements within these boundaries, depicted the world of the primitives as nation-states in the making, without the integrating effect of a modern state, to be sure, but with the 'culture', tradition and language out of which the modern states had made their nation-states. So, as Grimshaw and Hart (1993) have pointed out, if the people of Melanesia and Africa were not seen as living in states, they certainly were analysed according to a model that implicitly depicted them as nations.

Now anthropology, because of the weight it traditionally has given to empirical studies over theoretical debates, was early in picking up some of the inadequacies of this framework. Important work was done by the associates of the Rhodes Livingstone Institute to rethink the models of earlier anthropology in the face of the empirical challenges of what they called the African industrial revolution (e.g. Epstein, 1978; Gluckman, 1958, 1961; Mitchell, 1956, 1970). Methods such as extended case studies (van Velsen, 1967), situational analyses (Mitchell, 1970) and network analyses were meant to draw attention to the complexity of the situation, the impossibility of sorting a flow of interaction into neat categories. So, in anthropology and in the other social sciences there has been an attempt to develop a new theoretical apparatus to capture a reality that seemed increasingly complex; that is, complex in relation to earlier assumptions.

But at some point in the developing complexity of our models, we began to confuse the models with the reality that we set out to describe. I tend to pinpoint the culprit as the macro/micro divide. The concepts that were launched prior to it, such as networks, tended to focus on extensions and interactions. If a duality was introduced somewhere, the micro/macro distinction seems a likely place to look for it. In that debate as well, reality was divided to fit the conceptual and disciplinary divisions. Some disciplines were concerned with the 'macro processes' of society, others with the micro, debates raged about their interaction, and some people even found a reality middle ground in a meso level.

This debate clearly shows a confusion of model and reality. When an economist studies a transaction and relates it to economic laws, and hence to a macro level, whereas an anthropologist sees the same transaction as embedded in micro social relations, they are not studying two different phenomena. They apply different perspectives to the same phenomena. So one could argue for the global and the local as well: they are not two processes in the world, but two perspectives on the same point.

This is an extension of an argument made by Latour (1993): he argues that the modern associations of objects and subjects had enormous scaling effects; networks of associated actors reached much further than they could possibly have done before. But these networks should not be seen as global with the connotation of universal. Even if they are large, they do not cover every place on the surface of the earth. These networks should rather be analysed, he suggests, with the analogy of railroads and pipelines in mind. Is a railroad local or global? Neither. It is local at all points, he argues, because there are sleepers and stations everywhere. Yet it is global because it takes you from Madrid to Berlin. At the same time it is not universal enough to take you everywhere.

By extending this metaphor, I think we can identify some of the problems we are facing. Imagine not the whole railroad, but a station. How do you go about analysing that? The allegory is primitive, but let us say that modernist social science tried to explain it as a local system, sufficiently bounded and contained to lend itself to analysis. The present predicament stems from the realisation that much that goes on in the station has nothing to do with the station itself as an entity. Is it local or global? Both. And, as Marilyn Strathern (1991) has argued, the realisation that the object changes when it is put into a new context, also gives rise to the uneasy realisation that every perspective can only be partial. There is no standpoint from which a phenomenon can be grasped in its entirety.

The local/global dualism arises, therefore, I would argue, from the monsters that crowd in when one tries to fix phenomena within a model that implicitly treats them as contained. Within this context, all the connections, the railroad that links our station to Berlin and Madrid, appear of a different order, as an agency that has the capacity to alter the local. This agency is then placed outside the system under study, and it thus appears as capable of influencing 'it'.

GLOBAL ACTORS

Above I concluded that the question of whether the global exists, and whether it can influence the local, is wrongly put. It is a question that appears meaningful because of the way in which we use language and models. Phenomena appeared as either local or global depending on the focus one chose. Further, this duality arose as a heuristic device to meet the shortcomings of a sociological model that tied group and social characteristics to territory. The global, then, was simply all that that model could not account for.

With this initial conception of a network as both global and local, let us turn to the global actors that are constituted through such networks. If today we have global actors, that are constituted through very long networks and can mobilise masses of people and objects in such ways as to bend the intentions of governments, how are they held together? In pushing this part of the argument, I find it useful to return to the earlier discussion of macro and micro actors. Although Robertson (1995) argues that this is a deviation from the debate, in my conception, if we want to stop conceiving of the world in terms of a global–local interaction, size is all we are left with. Callon and Latour (1981) have examined the related question of whether micro and macro actors could be said to exist, and conclude in the affirmative. Some actors, such as IBM, are macro in the sense that they control a large number of people, are able to act in many places at once, etc. But, and this is the important point, one cannot start out by looking for criteria that distinguish such actors from other actors. This for the simple reason that they shift focus from society as a given, to the processes that constitute a version of society. Thus, the fact that IBM is a macro actor is the end result, the outcome of a process. It follows that one cannot a priori distinguish between small-scale and large-scale, one will have to examine the processes that make it possible for some actors to achieve a large size. Then, after having examined the process, one can ask whether in the process of achieving size, certain other characteristics are also achieved.

How, then, does an agent become a macro actor? Their answer, in short, is by establishing associations between people and objects, by translating the will of others into a single will for which it speaks.

This turns the successful macro actor into the centre of a web, where all communications between the different nodes have to pass through the centre. Their familiar lack of distinction between objects and people is important for their argument here. A group of baboons, they argue, is forced to shape their society in a flux of unstable social relations that have to be constantly negotiated. A collective can only reach a certain size if it is not able to attach itself to more durable objects than social relations. This, in Callon and Latour's reading, was the importance of taboos and totems in the construction of society for Durkheim; the group associated durable objects to itself, thereby giving the group itself more durability.

So instead of dividing the subject into human/non-human or micro/macro, Callon and Latour want to focus on gradients of resistance and consider variations in the relative solidity and durability of different materials. The more materials, objects, relations one is able to associate, the larger an actor can become. This is achieved through locking away, as they say, objects into black boxes. By this they mean that some elements that are used to build the association no longer need to be considered. The will that associated the different elements takes on the appearance of a force.

As an example, we are introduced to the attempt by Electricity of France to launch an electric vehicle. To do so, the company used statistics, natural sciences and public concerns about pollution and global warming, and advances in technology, to make an association of the interests of the public, the needs of nature, the technologically feasible that had only one possible conclusion: petrol engines would be impossible in the future, and all efforts needed to be put into developing the technology of electric vehicles. The black boxes here are all the things that the company tried to keep out of the discussion: natural laws, statistics, pollution, etc. But the black boxes are not completely sealed. Renault, feeling threatened by the attempt, questioned the assumptions made by Electricity of France, and was able to establish a different association that created a future place for the petrol engine. This example demonstrates that whether an actor is a macro, or global, actor or not can only be determined after the fact. Electricity of France attempted to establish itself as a global actor through the association of different discourses, technologies and interests, and had they succeeded they would have taken over much of the transnational transportation industry. They did not, however, and Renault was able to hold on to its position. This has an obvious implication for the discussion of the global and the local. The local and the global do not appear here as two different entities, qualities or sites, the relationship between which can be subject to a meaningful discussion. Instead, the global and the local appear as the same. What distinguishes a global actor and a local actor is not any innate qualitative difference, but, and here we reconnect with the standard definition of globality, simply its outreach in space. The advantage of this conception is that it avoids posing an a priori distinction between the local and the global, and hence demonstrates the futility of analysing their relationship.

GLOBAL ASSOCIATIONS

Callon and Latour therefore suggest an answer to the question with which I began: if global actors are simply actors that have established long networks, and are able to enrol many other actors (objects, relations, etc.), then we cannot speak of global forces, of globalisation as a force with the ability to transform local settings, or itself be influenced by local forces. There is no dialectic, as Beck argues, and not two entities that are able to enter into a relationship, however conceived.

I want to push this tentative conclusion further by examining some of the techniques and concepts that appear to be global, with the connotation of universal. As I argued at the beginning, it is this connotation of global that underpins the ideology of globalism. Marilyn Strathern (1995) has pointed out that culture now appears to be one such concept. From being our heuristic tool for contextualising others, culture has been recontextualised by agents, using it as a self-description. Thus transnational companies now have a culture, and they launch programmes to improve it or create a new one. I will let that lie for the moment, and instead look at another concept that in recent years seems to have become universal.

Audits have of course long been an integral part of accounting, but after Margaret Thatcher made it a part of her new administration, the concept has mutated and spread to almost all parts of the world. As Strathern (2000) points out, audits are portrayed as instruments of accountability, and as such they are almost impossible to criticise. The principles behind them are principles that most liberals subscribe to, such as openness, responsibility and the widening of access (2000: 3). Audits are launched of schools and universities, of public sector institutions, and even of whole economies. As instruments of power, they are closely related to what Foucault (1991) described as governmentality, the self-discipline achieved through creating knowledges and subject positions in such a way as to ensure that the objects of knowledge monitor themselves, without the state needing to keep an eye on day-to-day operations. This power-technique appears to be global; it has certainly spread to most sectors in most parts of the world. How are we to explain such spread? Why does it appear to us a result of a globalisation process? As long as we look at the flow of the concept itself, we will be tempted to see it as a result of a process that is independent of locality. As Appadurai (1991) has pointed out, this is a result of perspective. From the point of view of an institution such as a university, which has no prior experience of audits, suddenly being subject to such an exercise will appear as a radical break with the past, attributable to some global process. If we return to our station on the railroad, the sociologist who had attempted to make sense of it through analysing it as a contained setting would have found the men in suits who descended on it in order to audit it part of a globalising trend that transformed a local setting.

But if we treat the place as neither local nor global, and do away with the physical connection of a railroad, it can be shown that techniques such as audits are instrumental in keeping the different parts of the network associated together. Audits are tools used, among others, by global actors to create connectivity, because they can be used to associate a huge number of objects, people and processes. They are furthermore powerful; because once these entities have been associated they define the extent of the possible.

THE IMF AUDIT

Let me explain what I mean with the help of an example. The International Monetary Fund is a global actor however we choose to define the term. Most anthropologists have tended to view it in line with de Rivero's (2001) description, as a totalising force that destroys and transforms those societies that we have studied. And the IMF certainly has wreaked havoc on many people's lives through its economic policies.

From the above discussion, it is not surprising that the IMF should be seen as a global force with the capacity for transforming a local setting. But by analysing IMF as a network as it has been defined above, as neither global nor local, gives a rather different picture of the power of the IMF. Harper (2000), an anthropologist who has worked with the IMF, applies a different perspective than the one I use here. He is concerned with demonstrating how an audit mission is a deeply social process, but his case study is so detailed that it lends itself to the reconceptualisation that I will attempt here. Harper's account can be used to demonstrate the remarkably associative power of the concept of the audit. Through it, all activities of the whole population of a country appear to be representable by so many numbers. There is a massive act of translation going on here. By translating all these activities to give a coherent picture of the economy, an impression of commensurability is created. The economy of country A can be compared with the economy of country B. Through being commensurable, they also become part of the same entity, the world economy. The audit is therefore able to associate 'the world economy', decisions of government, and international institutions in such a way that it all appears to hold together.

One of the IMF's central functions is to audit national economies, and what Harper describes is one such auditing mission, to the country he anonymises as Arcadia. The IMF auditing team consisted of a chief and his deputy, an administrative assistant, the desk officer for the country, a fiscal economist and a junior economist. Harper stresses the interpretative and negotiable nature of these inquiries. The economists, contrary to other social scientists' perceptions of them, were not expecting to find clear-cut and tidy numbers, they set out to negotiate a version of the economy to which all could agree. These meetings and interviews had two purposes according to Harper: first, the mission sought advice on how to separate what they called the flotsam from the main economic facts, what signified an underlying trend and what was the result of on-off events. The second purpose was to learn from the government officials their views on what were the economic trends. The officials that they interviewed themselves represented sectors of government and the economy, so that at the end of the process, what was sought was an authoritative account of the condition of the economy, an account that all parts could ascribe to.

After the initial interviews, the mission began to achieve a higher-level picture of what was going on. Harper stresses that all the numbers, all the facts, had to be sanctioned by the chief of the IMF mission, because only he had the overall picture. Thus the chief would ask his staff how they had arrived at the numbers, and if they contradicted other findings, it was his responsibility to investigate what lay behind the discrepancy. What was clearly going on was an attempt to make all the numbers speak to each other. The mission was concerned with translating all the numbers – themselves translations of millions of minute events and interactions – into one single authoritative story. Once this had been achieved, the next task was to enrol all the different actors, to make all ministries and representatives agree to the story.

This was done in a meeting towards the end of the mission. Harper stresses how this meeting itself constitutes an arena for negotiation. The meeting took place in the Central Bank, and the dramatology of the event suggests a confrontation. First enters the chief with his cohort of advisers and they seat themselves on one side of the table, the chief with one senior economist on either side of him. In front of him he places the main charts and figures that the mission has found, on top of them some hand-written notes. An official then burst in and announced the arrival of the bank governor. The governor arrived with a cohort of economists and secretaries, and seated himself directly opposite the Chief, similarly surrounding himself with staff.

The chief began by telling the Arcadian authorities about the state of their economy, and what needs to be done in the future. He complimented them on the work that has been achieved in the past year, and the impressive performance of some sectors of the economy. He noted the practical difficulties of preparing the data during the mission with regard to such areas as collecting foreign debt figures and the totals of credits to the government, but, with hard work and the cooperation of the Arcadians, they have finally arrived at the basic features of the economy. Then he elaborated on the prospects for the economy, problems that will inevitably arise, and the policy measures that will have to be taken to avoid problems.

In Latour's terms, what the chief is doing here is outlining a problematisation. He closes off black boxes by giving a version of the reality that gives a picture of the Arcadian economy in relation to the world economy. If the Arcadians agree to the problematisation, there is little they can do but accept the conclusions. If they do not want to accept the conclusion, its premises must be challenged. After a long silence, this is exactly what the governor did. He consulted with his advisers and asked for the numbers to be read out more slowly. The Arcadian officials brought out their pocket calculators and checked the figures. After another consultation, the governor stated that the calculations were correct, but he again set out to prise open a black box by asking the chief how they had arrived at the figures. There followed a long examination of the specifics, and the changing of some variables such as projected interest rates, before all parties had agreed on the construct of the economy.

Harper stresses how the numbers now have a changed moral status. Once the individual findings of the investigation, the numbers, had been sanctioned, they had the ability to act. They could 'jostle other numbers, sometimes resulting in those other numbers being ejected or returned to a non signed-off status' (Harper, 2000: 47). The end result of the audit was a common story, where all agreed on the main parts, and the implications for Arcadia in the future. The single most important entity on which the audit acted was on future economic policy. Through this device, then, all the actions of the inhabitants that were classified as economic activities were represented in a single statement about the economy of the country, and what the relationship should be between the country and the IMF. The global power of the IMF is here seen as an outcome of a negotiation process.

The audit that the IMF produced had as its outcome a framework, and understanding of economic reality, that made the work of the IMF relevant to the country. In this way the network was established

and maintained through the device of the audit. But this conceptualisation has a number of other consequences. First, it shows that,
like Foucault's definition of power, the power of the IMF was an
effect of the relation it established with the country. Second, this
gives a rather less totalising picture of the power of a global actor
like the IMF. Its power is not inherent in its being, and it is not global
with the connotation of universal. Its power arises as an effect of the
successful associations it establishes through ideas of the economy,
negotiated through the audit.

POLITICO-METHODOLOGICAL IMPLICATIONS

Seeing the 'global' as effects of 'local' processes ensures the relevance
of traditional anthropological methods that much of the writing on
globalisation appears to have closed off. For if global processes take
place in a realm different from situated practices, then all an anthropologist can do is to study the effects of these processes on local
settings. By reversing the causation, and defining globality as a
possible outcome of such processes as described above, the focus of
analyses must also turn to situated attempts at creating global effects.
Much more is of course involved in these situations than are present
in the board room. But it is precisely the ability of the IMF audit team
to enrol all these entities that needs to be examined. The above
example pointed to several possible fields of inquiry. Why, for
instance, is economics such a successful language for relating a huge
number of actors? Surely some of the answer lies in the grammar of
that language. Economic equations, statistics (see Hacking, 1986 on
this point) and quantifications enable an actor to translate vast
numbers of phenomena into entities that can be related to each
other through comparison, evaluation and grading.

   This methodological point also has political implications: if the
power of the IMF does not reside in its global character, but rather
in its ability to create global effects by linking disparate entities, then
it is also less total and more open to influence. Anthropological
studies of globalisation, then, should study the way in which some
actors are able to produce effects on a transnational scale, rather than
taking global actors at face value, and studying the effects they have
on local settings.

CONCLUSION

So where has this left us? I began by arguing that the dichotomy
global/local was used in a way which suggested the existence of two
separate levels that stood in some sort of relationship with each

other, dialectical or otherwise. I have argued that this apparent dichotomy arises as an effect of the models we have used to study social processes. Epistemologies that treat society as a given, a contained entity, will have problems explaining the increased interconnectedness of objects and subjects. From this perspective, something external to the object studied appears to be influencing it: hence the dual conception.

If the global actors that now undermine the archetypical contained society, the nation-state, are conceived of as networks, as extensions, then each point of the network is both global and local, and hence neither. The effect arises from the context in which the point is placed. Only from within the old framework of the contained society does the duality appear as a meaningful description. This difficulty led both Roland Robertson and Jonathan Friedman to slip back into a discussion of the relationship between the global and the local: in the first case through examining how the local becomes an expression of the global, in the second through seeing the local as incorporated into the global through the workings of an underlying global system.

When this is combined with an examination of global actors and how they are held together, a peculiar twist to the local/global problematisation appears. It now seems as if the idea of the global as a distinctive sphere, in which reside such solid objects as the economy, plays an important part in holding together global actors. This is of course nothing else than saying that the ideology of globalism is an important element in the construction of global actors.

We also saw why this becomes a self-fulfilling perception of reality. That ideology universalises the networks that I modelled on the railroad, making it appear that connections were established not just between stations, but everywhere. Being able to portray oneself as part of a universal phenomenon is of course no disadvantage when one seeks to enrol others.

The focus therefore shifts from local/global interactions to how global actors are held together. Latour suggests that the answer is through problematisation and association. Myriad objects are associated through networks, and the durability of some of these objects make it possible to freeze some associations or put them in black boxes. This we clearly saw in the case of the IMF audit. The black box here was the economy, once the audit team had negotiated a common understanding of the economy; they had in effect enrolled an enormous amount of objects, subjects and relations.

The importance of this, in addition to untying a conceptual tangle, is to put global actors in their place. Beck demonstrates that one of the connotations of global – namely the universal – is tied to that term in the ideology of globalism. Transnational economic processes and the impossibility of containing capital are in this ideology presented as universal. What the IMF case demonstrates is that the relations are much more fragile than this. The IMF does not have a massive amount of power. The power it has lies in its ability to link economies to the world economy in a way that makes certain actions and policies appear as natural outcomes of objective descriptions.

But the vision of the power of global actors that I have outlined here also leaves scope for resistance. The actions on the streets in Seattle and other social movements are in effect questioning the constructions of society from which global actors such as the IMF derive their influence. I am not saying that their strategy is the most effective, but putting global actors in their place by these actions at the very least reopens a space for politics, which globalist ideology has subsumed to market forces.

REFERENCES

Appadurai, A. 1991. Global ethnoscapes: notes and queries for a transnational anthropology. In R.G. Fox (ed.) *Recapturing Anthropology*. Santa Fe, NM: School of American Research Press.

Bauman, Z. 1992. *Intimations of Postmodernity*. London: Routledge.

Beck, U. 2000. *What is Globalization?* Cambridge: Polity Press.

Callon, M. and B. Latour. 1981. Unscrewing the big Leviathan: how actors macro-structure reality and how sociologists help them do so. In K. Knorr-Cetina and A.V. Cicourel (eds) *Advances in Social Theory and Methodology: Toward an Integration of Micro- and Macro-sociologies*. Boston, MA: Routledge & Kegan Paul.

de Rivero, O. 2001. *The Myth of Development: Non-viable Economies of the 21st Century*. London: Zed Books.

Epstein, A.L. 1978. *Ethos and Identity: Three Studies in Ethnicity*. London: Tavistock.

Foucault, M. 1991. Governmentality. In G. Burchell, C. Gordon and P. Miller (eds) *The Foucault Effect: Studies in Governmentality*. Chicago: University of Chicago Press.

Friedman J. 1994. *Cultural Identity and Global Process*. London: Sage.

—— 1995. Global system, globalization and the parameters of modernity. In M. Featherstone, S. Lash and R. Robertson (eds) *Global Modernities*, pp. 69–90. London: Sage.

Giddens, A. 1985. *The Nation-state and Violence*. Cambridge: Polity Press.

Gluckman, M. 1958. *Analysis of a Social Situation in Modern Zululand*. Manchester: Manchester University Press.

—— (1961) Anthropological problems arising from the African industrial revolution. In A. Southall (ed.) *Social Change in Modern Africa: Studies Presented and Discussed at the First International African Seminar, Makerere College, Kampala, January 1959*. London: Oxford University Press.

Grimshaw, A. and K. Hart. 1993. *Anthropology and the Crisis of the Intellectuals*. Cambridge: Prickly Pear Press.

Hacking, I. 1986. Making up people. In T.C. Heller, D.E. Wellbery and M. Sosna (eds) *Reconstructing Individualism: Autonomy, Induviduality and the Self in Western Thought*. Stanford, CA: Stanford University Press.

Harper, R. 2000. The social organization of the IMF's mission work: an examination of international auditing. In M. Strathern (ed.) *Audit Cultures: Anthropological Studies in Accountability, Ethics and the Academy*. London: Routledge.

Held, D. 1995. *Democracy and the Global Order: From the Modern State to Cosmopolitan Governance*. Cambridge: Polity Press.

Latour, B. 1993. *We Have Never Been Modern*. Cambridge, MA: Harvard University Press.

—— 2000. When things strike back: a possible contribution of 'science studies' to the social sciences, *British Journal of Sociology* 51(1): 107–23.

Mitchell, J.C. 1956. *The Kalela Dance: Aspects of Social Relationships among Urban Africans in Northern Rhodesia*. Manchester: Manchester University Press.

—— 1970. Tribe and social change in South Central Africa: a situational approach, *Journal of Asian and African Studies* 5(1–2): 83–101.

Robertson, R. 1995. Globalization. In M. Featherstone, S. Lash and R. Robertson (eds) *Global Modernities*. London: Sage.

Rosenau, J.N. 1990. *Turbulence in World Politics: A Theory of Change and Continuity*. Princeton, NJ: Princeton University Press.

Strathern, M. (1991) *Partial Connections*. Savage, MD: Rowman & Littelfield.

—— 1995. Foreword: shifting contexts. In M. Strathern (ed.) *Shifting Contexts: Transformations in Anthropological Knowledge*. London: Routledge.

—— 2000. Introduction: new accountabilities, anthropological studies in audit, ethics and the academy. In M. Strathern (ed.) *Audit Cultures*. London: Routledge.

Tomlinson, J. 1999. *Globalization and Culture*. Chicago: University of Chicago Press.

van Velsen, J. 1967. The extended-case method and situational analysis. In A.L. Epstein (ed.) *The Craft of Social Anthropology*. London: Tavistock.

8 ANTHROPOLOGIES IN POLICIES, ANTHROPOLOGIES IN PLACES: REFLECTIONS ON FIELDWORK 'IN' DOCUMENTS AND POLICIES

Simone Abram

STUDYING GLOBALISATION?

Globalisation studies pose some conceptual problems for those wishing to undertake ethnographic research. While we are well aware that apparently small or remote communities have multiple points of contact with the world around them, a preference for fieldwork based in definite geographical locations, or with kin-focused locality-linked communities threatens to confine us to examining the 'impacts' of globalisation on marginalised communities. While these studies have a vitally important place in the understanding of globalisation effects, we equally need to examine the processes of globalisation. In Nader's (1972) terms, we need to 'study up' the scale to the powerful global networks that appear to orchestrate the trends toward globalisation. But how, then, do we adapt our ethnographic practices to approach global networks, rather than localised communities? Where are these networks to be studied? Do they actually exist in physical reality, or only in virtual spaces? Where do we go to do fieldwork on globalisation?

The term 'globalisation', of course, refers to many different phenomena. In the course of the Globalisation Research Programme, so far, we have grappled with the difficulties of isolating a subject for study. Globalisation can be used to refer to:

- the spread of certain cultural forms,
- the concentration of capitalist power in the hands of a few, in particular transnational corporations whose activities escape the control of states,
- the increasing speed of transport between distant places (with its corollary that those left out of the transport network are left increasingly relatively inaccessible – and marginalised),

- the growing accessibility of telecommunications across the globe, albeit unevenly,
- Increasing colonial-style relations between certain capitalist forms and many countries, nations and states.

People use the term 'globalisation' to refer to these perceived processes and more besides, and we often end up talking past each other by using one term to refer to widely differing processes. For the purposes of this discussion, I will use the term to refer to social relations built up through translocal networks. That is, associations between people and material forms that are not based in one place, but extend across distances, and the question of whether such associations are available to ethnographic research.

This chapter therefore reflects on the imagined 'place' which organises the activity of fieldwork. While a traditional model of ethnographic fieldwork used the geographical locus as synchronous with the locus of community, these two are increasingly recognised as separate spaces. As anthropologists within Europe began to acknowledge the interconnections between 'small places' and larger frameworks (state, nation, federation, etc.), the notion of the 'isolated community' began to dissolve. 'Remoteness' was recognised as 'an outsider's illusion' (Ardener, 1987). The myth of the compact, self-contained society has been dispersed (Gupta and Ferguson, 1997), and we recognise that 'isolated' or 'remote' places are still intimately connected to far-flung locations, through migrations, governance, markets and other forms of communications.

The association between place and society as the locus of research is now also challenged as ethnographers study global social organisations (Amit-Talai, 2000; Hannerz, 1996; Miller and Slater, 2000). Fieldwork can be focused, therefore, on networks, associations and objects as well as places, as the object or notion that defines a social group. The work of sociologists and anthropologists of science and technology, for example, demonstrates that there are many paths through complexity, and that the focus on 'place' as the determining factor of ethnographic inquiry is only one of many options. This is not necessarily to identify the locus of anthropological inquiry as what Augé defines as a 'non-place', 'a space which cannot be defined as relational, or historical, or concerned with identity' (1995: 77–8), but to locate it according to non-geographic criteria. Fieldwork that takes as its focus a policy document, for example, incorporates the actors assembled around that document, just as fieldwork on electronic 'virtual' networks explores the relations between people and/through technologies. This chapter therefore argues that all fieldwork is equally place-located and place-dislocated. By freeing ourselves from the insistence on place-situated fieldwork, we open a new era in the study of comparative social relations. Perhaps, though, it is not that new. Just as Latour urges us to 'follow the actor' as our path through a network, Gell also urged us to follow the art, or trace the paths of the material object through its transactions and various uses, and to consider the meanings attributed to it at various points along its journey, as though it were a form of technology (Gell, 1999).

In this chapter, I bring together two approaches to ethnographic inquiry, one place-based, the other policy-based. In this way, the relations between place and policy are explored, and the social alliances formed in the context of policy-debate are considered with reference to the notions of place that are contested during the debate.

STUDYING POLICY

In the last few years, I have found several different ways to study policy-making. All of these have been focused on the forms of communication (including non-communication) between policy-makers, that is, politicians and administrators (bureaucrats, or public servants), and members of a so-called 'public'. In each case, while there has been place-based fieldwork, there has also been policy-based fieldwork. That is, the policy has formed the focus around which fieldwork has developed. Paradoxically, the policies studies have all been place-related. That is, I have been looking at policies about land-use. The three particular cases have been as follows:

- Strategic (county) planning for housing in Buckinghamshire, in south-east England;
- Local (district) planning for housing in a part of Buckinghamshire;
- Local (district) planning and vision-setting near Oslo.

In the first case, I examined the influence of third parties on strategic planning. That is, I interviewed planners and a selection of those who had sent in letters of objection to the proposed long-term strategic plans for a county in south-east England; fieldwork also entailed attending public meetings and a three-week-long public hearing about the validity of arguments over the policies. The respondents included developers, residents' groups, voluntary workers, environmental groups, politicians, planners at different regional levels, and the Professor of Planning who chaired the hearing. The work also spread into consideration of the regional level of planning, which involved following some of the same actors into regional debates and hearings. The place under discussion throughout this process was a county, that is, a large area with many towns and villages, hundreds of community groups and a large and relatively transient population. Much of the point of the work was to examine the constructions used in arguments about the future of the county, both by central and local planners, that is, through the use of technical discourses about statistical forecasts, and by residents, through broad-ranging visions of social and environmental practices. It was only at the public hearing that most of the actors I encountered during the fieldwork actually met each other, and my work was to understand the different conceptualisations of futures held by the various actors, and how these built up in different ways into a policy. As mentioned, all the debates were, at least in principal, about places, but there was no common 'place' in which to do fieldwork, other than the three-week-long public hearing and the mental spaces created by the actors involved in the process.

While these conditions presented extraordinary opportunities to trace the passage of powerful discourses through policy-making stages, there were clearly limitations to the type of fieldwork I was able to do. There are collective representations to be found among people who belong to only imagined communities (e.g. in the study of symbols and discourses of nationalism, see Anderson, 1991/1983), but these were mainly to be found in what was not contested rather than the actual discussion that took place. A more intense kind of fieldwork was possible with the second project mentioned above. In this second case, the project followed the county plan to the district level (that is, more local level) to see whether there were differences in the public response to and influence over policy-making at the less abstract level treated in local plans. That is to say, whether geographical location brings a particular dimension to policy discourse. In this case, I chose again to focus the study on a policy, but this policy concerned a plan to locate housing on the edge of a particular settlement, and I chose this settlement as the base for the research. Having done this, though, a settlement of nearly 5,000 inhabitants from different class, regional and national backgrounds, and the related activities of politicians, planners, commercial developers, etc., represents a very varied field, and one that also constitutes very much an imagined locality-based community. Although there were undoubtedly lively social relations within the 'village' where I based the work, they were far from homogeneous or comprehensive. Furthermore, it was clear that this so-called village represented a key counter-site of globalisation, since many of its occupants formed part of a general counter-urbanising movement within Britain that has arisen in response to the centralising tendencies of the concentration of global labour-market employment in the capital, to which many residents commuted (Boyce and Halfacree, 1998).

Although the fieldwork concerned the development of a plan policy to locate a few hundred houses in a so-called 'rural village', it was not by any means a 'village study', nor was it solely occupied with the responses of villagers to governmental plans. Rather, I attempted to take what Latour calls a more 'symmetrical' approach to the work, and try to gain an understanding of the various parties to the plan debate. In effect, I investigated a small section of the lives of a wide variety of actors, rather than a wide sector of the lives of a small number of actors (although, in fact, there was a core of key informants during this fieldwork, just as in most). I had contact, therefore, with planners and other local government officers, politicians of various parties and various factions of local residents through a variety of political, activist, social and welfare organisations. What emerged was a collection of very different understandings about the meaning of a policy and of the meaning of a particular place. This place, however, was not merely the location of the fieldwork, but an apparently innocuous farmer's field nearby. Although I did look at the field in question, and walk across it, that was the extent of my own (and many of the others') direct experience of it. It took on, however, an array of symbolic meanings viewed not as an 'anthropological place' (in Augé's terms) but as the object of a policy around which people's arguments congregated.

The policy gathered around it a congregation who became the object of ethnographic investigation. Although we are aware that the 'community' in which ethnographic research is undertaken is always an illusion, since any community has constantly redrawn and redefined boundaries, in this case that illusion was less accessible than usual. A brief explanation of how the policy came into being will illustrate how it created its own social and material networks , and why the process of policy-making was intrinsically divisive and confrontational. Policies can be conceived as the making concrete of a particular instant in a history of development. Telling the story of a policy, therefore, is a plucking out of particular strings of narrative. In other words, it does not start at the beginning and end at the end, but picks up trails and gives accounts of them. In this case, we will begin with the logic of the policy, beginning with the point of view of planners.

Planners working for the local authority were obliged to advise politicians that they must comply with national and regional policy on housing provision and their interpretation of the imperatives of sustainable development. This led to the creation of a clear policy line for the district, which is to accommodate a certain level of housing, as demanded by regional government, and to locate this in existing settlements with good connections to public transport, and mostly in the more urban areas of the district, so that, as the 'official story' goes (in governmental 'planning guidance'), homes are located close to employment sites so as to minimise the likelihood of commuting. So far, few people (and none of the politicians involved) would argue with the good intentions behind these policy lines. In addition, according to a model commissioned by council planners for calculating transport movements, they will distribute housing allocations between urban and rural areas in the ratio 75 per cent to 25 per cent. All these factors point to the rural development going to one particular location, a large village with both bus and rail services. Interviews with various planners indicated that this argument formed the formal 'rationality' of the plan. However, longer informal discussions at various planning events also revealed that the planners had long seen the village as a potential location for development, and it was impossible to determine whether the rationalisation had appeared to support that 'intuition', or vice versa.

However, the residents of this location have experienced a massive expansion in the village housing stock over the past 25 years, leading to the feeling that if the village grows any more, it will lose all semblance of being a small community and become a faceless town. They also knew that there were long waiting lists for appointments at the medical clinic and that some of the classes at the village schools were oversubscribed. However, property prices in the village were extremely high, and there was very little rented accommodation available. Many villagers would have liked to see more affordable housing available in the village, particularly for the children of less wealthy residents and workers in the village's small factories. Unfortunately, they were also very aware that housing allocated through the planning process would not meet local needs, nor would it be provided through the creative re-use of sites within the village, but that planners would more likely allocate yet another outlying field for large, detached family homes for commuters. Such issues formed the daily topics of conversation at coffee mornings, badminton games in the village hall and pub conversations, as well as at meetings of village protest groups.

The planners were not interested in finding sites for anything less than 50 houses at a time, as they were allocating sites for some 7,000 houses altogether in a short space of time and with limited staff. They had neither the time nor the inclination to address issues of small sites. In fact, up to 25 houses could be built on sites not identified in the plan, sites which are known as 'windfall' sites (as if they had spontaneously fallen from the sky, like apples from a tree – an interesting metaphor in its own right). Villagers were aware, therefore, that even without a site for 300 houses allocated in the village over a 20-year period, 300 houses could well be built on a collection of small sites that might become available during that time. That would suggest that, with a planned allocation of 300 houses on new sites, up to 500 or 600 houses could actually be built.

On another level, there were villagers who were qualified planners working in other authorities, retired or working for private firms. They were aware of the judicial character of local planning, which they also advised on at parish (i.e. village) council meetings, protest group meetings and in interviews and other discussions. When the plan was finalised by the district, a public inquiry would be held, where barristers acting for developers would challenge the validity of the district's plan in the hope of having the plan overturned in favour of sites they wished to develop, rather than those the district council wished to see developed. Developers might argue, therefore, that there are reasonable grounds to build houses in the countryside, and that the district's refusal to allocate sites does not follow central government policy to provide decent homes where people want to live. By not identifying the village for any housing, there was a danger that the plan could be overturned and developers win concessions to build many more houses than the district was proposing. At the same time, this argument was used by district planners to persuade councillors to accept their proposed plans, and many villagers were sceptical, considering it a crude scare tactic.

Councillors, that is, local representative politicians, on the other hand, had different dilemmas. Although the councillor representing the village actually avoided any formal interview with me, the justifications below were used in public meetings, both in the village and at the district council. The councillor representing the village initially aimed to improve local employment opportunities and saw growth as positive. He also wished to appear 'responsible' in relation to other councillors, all of whom were struggling with the difficulties of finding sites for large amounts of new housing, but none of whom wanted to appear to be 'selfish' (these emic metaphors defined the discussion of the plan process). However, local residents made increasing objections to the plans. From discussions with other politicians, in both the same party and other parties, his position was explained as follows. The politician hoped to be re-elected, and therefore needed to demonstrate that he was 'listening' to local residents without betraying his political alliances. He also needed to maintain loyalty to a particular group of residents who said that local objections were from the rich residents and that local workers did want expansion (up to a rather undefinable limit). The political wranglings over development sites within the council committees present their own set of priorities and rationalities that are also quite divorced from either the 'technical' bureaucratic issues or the residents' concerns.

Even in this very brief outline of a scenario we can see that there are some fundamental differences in the meaning-worlds of the actors in this case, which we (Murdoch and Abram, 2002) have described as competing rationalities. Policy-makers easily perceive villagers' objections as the selfish actions of those who are defending their own privileges (property values). Planners also experience explicit racism and snobbery from residents in other parts of the district, and transfer their experiences to the anxieties of the villagers. Villagers see narrow-minded bureaucrats making decisions that are not in the best interests of the population of the village, a population that numbers nearly 5,000 people. Only by including the various sides in the conflict within the ethnographic research was it possible to see beyond the stereotypes that the groups had of each other. It was possible to trace some of the political manoeuvring that was determining policy, as well as the many internal disagreements within and between different residents' groups in the village that led to a certain form of conflict taking place. Furthermore, the broader question of governmental or state determination of the limits to local discourse were available to the study from the prior work at the county and regional level. Through discussions with a key county planner and politicians active at the regional level, the events at the local level could be contextualised in terms of the requirements of national, regional and county planning objectives. The transnational strategies of global corporations bring about planning pressures on the national scale which translate into regional and more local pressures, such that the response of villagers to plans for only 300 houses is locked into a global system, but without looking at all these aspects, we would see only a local dispute about house building.

The story I was then able to tell about the plan became (I hope) a rich tapestry of interwoven interpretations of policy proposals, various mutual interpretations of the actions of different groups, both within and outside the village, and the (Foucauldian) disciplinary conditions set by central government offices under pressure from global capital (e.g. the supposed ability of transnational corporations to move their activities between countries if appropriate conditions are not available, e.g. housing for executives) and supranational organisations (e.g. EU spatial policies). Had I only examined social relations and events in the village, I would have had little understanding of the district-level politics that were determining the village-level debates, nor would I have had any understanding of the processes of globalisation which were leading to the effects causing local conflicts, such as the concentration of population in particular places (e.g. through 're-urbanisation'). We could not 'explain' the local situation without recourse to a broader field which follows the effects of decisions in one place through their many transformations into decisions at another place. It is for this reason that locating fieldwork in the mental space of a policy, rather than the geographical space of a settlement, makes accessible processes of globalisation, flows of concepts, and networks that span the local and the global.

This sort of fieldwork allows us to relate the social actors locked into policy conflicts to the structures of governance within which they labour. It allows us both to understand the complaints of local residents about the 'incompetent bureaucrats' and to follow the paths which led bureaucrats to choose policies that appear locally to be crazy. It shows us that the different worlds in which the different sets of actors conceptualise their beliefs in the future of a locality meet at few points, and that these points of intersection represent the clashes between what anthropologists have called world-views. When bureaucrat meets resident, their frames of reference are most often at odds, so that each is reasoning according to different criteria. Within these frameworks they act as each other's 'other', whose 'otherness' serves to reinforce their own self-image and justifications. It is not surprising, then, that they so often fail to reach either understanding or agreement. It is not surprising, either, that many local politicians, whose role includes bridging the communication gap between 'government' and 'people', as well as balancing the interests of different social groups, face an almighty task, which often leads to them choosing to take sides at moments of crisis, either for or against 'the council' (as a corporate institution).

It was this specific relationship that I aimed to examine in the third project mentioned above. In this case I gained access, in a way that was never possible in Britain, to the corridors of a district council, where the relations between administrators and politicians were more available to study. In this case, the research focused internally on the council as a collection of organisations, both political and administrative. Given this focus, it was not possible, for a number of practical reasons, to include as many different actors as in the previous study, but this disadvantage was outweighed by the level of insight into internal council activities and discourses. Although the main aim of the research was to learn how local plans are made in practice, this also coincided with a major reorganisation of the administration of the council, which threw up a number of problematic questions about organisational beliefs and rituals. Most of the research was done in the physical space of the town hall, but this space had flexible conceptual boundaries, at times incorporating other council buildings, and occasionally extending to distant hotels and conference centres. Any space referred to as 'the council' must also be recognised as conceptual as much as physical. While the council owns buildings and grounds, it also has existence as a configuration of people, sometimes referring to different sectors of that population, and the council can also refer to the area within the administrative boundaries in political-geographic terms. It can also be considered to exist in the terms of the written texts that are used to codify council policy and guide practice.

In this case, though, it was the passage through the place of visitors from other places – both local organisations and foreign institutions – which constituted the perspective from which flows of concepts and global influences were perceived. Ideas, such as the forms of reorganisation (or, indeed, the very impetus to administrative reorganisation) flowed into and through the town hall, via representatives from other councils (in Norway and Denmark), via 'study tours' of town hall employees and politicians to other councils (again, in Norway, Denmark and Sweden), via 'consultants' of various kinds, and through the networks of discourse which the various individuals inhabited. The town hall, viewed in this light, became a veritable traffic flow of ideas and concepts culled and transformed into local practice. Different elements of these flows could then be 'traced', and their local manifestations compared to other versions (specifically through a comparative study of the same processes in a Scottish local authority, and in the context of political and legislative change under the newly established Scottish Parliament).

None of these projects conformed to a traditional ethnographic holistic study of a stable community. However, it is my belief that this tradition has never really existed in the terms in which it is often described but is canonised to the exclusion of a much broader variety of styles of ethnographic research. Studies of political councils in the 1970s indicate that the classic monograph was always one of a number of forms through which to represent the discipline, never the only one (as, indeed, Gupta and Ferguson, 1997, relate). It is therefore both radical and completely normal to conduct the kinds of fieldwork which I have described above. Looked at from this perspective, our qualms about examining globalising trends should not present an insurmountable barrier to ethnographic research methods. While the location of research may be idiosyncratic, the methods are not. As social anthropologists we are trained to be aware of the ways in which people construct the world through classificatory practices, we are alert to the way material facts are imbued with meaning, and the modes through which people reinterpret and re-present external and internal worlds through collectively understood modes of expression. While the diversity of these factors may be more difficult to become familiar with in disparate networks, this can become a feature of our research, rather than a drawback to it.

What this means is that we have to relinquish our more nostalgic notions about the authenticity of community. Are we prepared to admit that the collective representations that exist among fleeting networks in disparate places with little face-to-face contact are as 'authentic' for our study as those between 'indigenous' peoples with long-established common experience? Does globalisation engender new forms of society that are as 'valid' despite their newness? Can we separate ourselves from the romantic notions of 'noble savages' to the extent that we reject it completely? Or does this make us hopeless relativists with no political or moral guts?

COMPARATIVE POLICY RESEARCH

Part of the point of the third case, as mentioned above, was to compare practices in Norway with those in Scotland, specifically to examine whether there has been cross-national policy-learning in the field of social planning. Policy-learning has become a buzz-word in policy research, not least in planning studies, where it refers, broadly speaking, to processes of change. Our aim, in other words, is to study policy change, and to try to investigate where ideas for policy change come from, and how they are disseminated. Are policies or policy-themes globalising, and if so, in what directions and by what means?

I should pause here, to come back to the question of whether the spread of policy ideas can be included under the rubric of globalisation. As I suggested above, one of the problems of analysing globalisation, as with most complex forms, is a lack of clarity in the definition of what globalisation itself is, as mentioned above. Are we considering the spread of cultural forms through capitalistic relations of power, similar to processes during colonial eras, or are we concerned with the powers of transnational corporations to operate beyond the reach of national states? Are we, rather, referring to the creation of supra-national states whose policies govern vast populations, or the activities of international banking corporations that bind together the economies of distant regions? Or are we referring to the speed of telecommunications, which allow 'news' and other forms of stories to reach distant parts of the globe more or less simultaneously, or the use of electronic protocols that allow people all over the globe to watch the same television programmes? I would argue that these are rather different phenomena which deserve rather different treatments. In this case, therefore, I am referring to the spread of theories and policy ideas about social planning beyond and between regions or nations, or, for that matter, continents. In order to trace these passages, we find ourselves coming into contact with networks again. International conferences, professional networks, political alliances are nodes on the web of those interested in planning around the world. Next week, I will attend a conference of Norwegian planning academics, in February I was at a meeting of Norwegian planners addressed, as usual, by both Swedish and Danish speakers; later this month, an international conference of planning theorists will be held in Oxford, and this year's annual conference of European Schools of Planning is being held in association with the World Association of Schools of Planning, in Singapore, next year's in Greece. Many of those attending these conferences and meetings write regularly for the planning practitioners' press, and most schools of planning have 'liaison groups' to enhance the links between education and practice in planning. At such meetings, paradigms are formed and sustained, and radical changes of paradigm sometimes also occur. Notions such as 'communicative planning' have emerged over the course of several conferences as dominant themes (e.g. at the Planning Theory conference in Oxford in 1998), and then been subject to general criticism at others later. Few self-respecting planning theorists will now admit to not having read Healey's book on *Collaborative Planning* (1997) or Flyvbjerg's book on *Rationality and Power* (1998), for example, in order to have a critique of one or both, and these are also books read by practitioners (to some extent).

Such globalised academic debates may then have varied implications. On the one hand, various versions of these notions are being taught to future-professional-planners in different places. On the other, ideas filter through to policy-makers, in some cases through talks given to practitioners and policy-makers, and in others through specialist advisers to policy-makers. Equally, though, practitioners and policy-makers are also attending similar (sometimes the same, sometimes parallel) international networks and conferences where ideas are pooled and then reinterpreted. A small coterie of senior bureaucrats from Kristiansand council visited York Council in autumn 2001 and spent three days being told about York's methods for regenerating run-down areas and engaging alienated citizens. Which ideas did they take home? Probably the only thing we can say for certain is that their understanding of what they experienced in York was partial, not only given the choice of representatives and projects offered to them during their visit, but since their interpretations were based in the conceptual and political world of 'back home'. Ideas about the creation of inclusive practices towards 'alienated youths' or 'ethnic minorities' may be taken up in future activities in Kristiansand, for example, but we can be sure that what is created will not be identical to what has taken place in York, but a utilisation of selected ideas transformed during the journey between the two cities.

It is no surprise that planning in Britain and Norway share some similarities, since they have heavily influenced each other through the ideas of significant theorists on both sides of the North Sea. The spread of the utopian ideals of Ebenezer Howard and the Garden City Movement in the early twentieth century is visible in the garden suburbs of Oslo as much as in Welwyn Garden City, even if the Oslo version retains more of the social cooperative practice that was lost in the British movement. On the other hand, much of what we might call the globalisation of planning ideas can also be traced to colonial and postcolonial practices. The British planning system was exported almost wholesale to a number of countries, most notably Malaysia, complete with hierarchical policy systems and codes, and British planning schools routinely educate planners from Malaysia, China and many other countries. It seems fairly clear from the research I have done in Norway that much of the Norwegian system was similarly absorbed from Denmark. The relative porosity of Scandinavian administrative boundaries to ideas may have changed with regard to constitutional status (for example when Norway became an independent state, or when Sweden and Denmark joined the EU), but there is evidence to suggest that bureaucratic practices and policy ideas nevertheless follow long-standing routes. Administrators and politicians I worked with in Norway took fairly regular trips both to twin-districts in Denmark and Sweden, and to intra-Scandinavian colloquia to learn about new styles of administrative practice. When they were specifically on the lookout for new organisational ideas, it was no coincidence that they invited representatives of Danish districts to gain the benefit of their experience. The wisdom of Danish governmental practices was one realm I never heard criticised (this was prior to the election of a right-wing Danish government in 2001).

In Scotland, also, administrators and politicians aiming to radically change the planning system travelled to England, the Netherlands and to Denmark for examples and evidence of the workings of schemes that they could then bring back and adapt for home use. It is also known that the policy unit in the British government (in the Department of Transport, Local Government and the Regions) sends civil servants abroad to bring back 'policy lessons', although due to the closed nature of the British civil service, it has not been possible (for me) to find out where they have been, when or why. This form of learning, known as seeking 'best practice' is a well-established form of governmental learning. Otherwise understood as filching other people's ideas once they have found out where the mistakes are, it consists of drawing up a list, often self-selected, of examples of success, and then copying them elsewhere. As a methodology, it has its faults. There are many cases where the motives of those writing up supposedly successful cases are less than transparent, and where cases presented as successes are revealed, through more careful research, to have been fraught with difficulties. One example that some may recognise is the Porsgrunn model of involving young people in local democracy. The aims of the policy and the principles of the practice are widely admired and referred to among local government administrators. However, there are many critics, including anthropologists, as well as local government officers in similar fields who informed me, during fieldwork, that all was not as it seemed in the Porsgrunn programme; some claimed there have been financial irregularities associated with elements of the project. Similarly, I have a collection of student investigations which belie the sweet stories of successful participative policy-making exercises in Sheffield boasted by the City Council. As most of us will appreciate, the Vice-Chancellor's interpretation of the success of his reforms at a British university may bear little resemblance to the experiences of employees of the same institution.

Furthermore, policies that work well in one context often transfer poorly to a different set of conditions. Although policy-transfer literature is beginning to appreciate this fact, there is still little systematic consideration of what factors might be expected to affect the transfer of policies and to what degree. Notions of integration of sectors of council activity have been enacted through changes to organisational structures in Norwegian local government, but, in Scotland, they have provided a discourse that sustains a network of disparate institutions and organisations to promote common interest where little existed before (Cowell, 2002). Given the complexity of 'context' (which is what anthropologists seek to expose, above all), the mere notion that one might be able to predict how a policy would work in a different national, or even regional, context, suggests that we may need to adopt more of the practices of the shaman than of the political scientist. We can, however, through careful study of the discourses and practices of transnational networks, begin to understand the distance between these instrumental representations and conditions in any particular locality. The discursive constructions of managers, for example, in the New Managerialism, are so stylised in their form that we can relatively easily point out the stumbling blocks that policies based on their principles might meet in practice. It seems sensible to assume that these problems are common to many forms of globalisation. We now know that the very same television programmes are watched differently, as well as interpreted differently in different places (Abu-Lughod, 1994), and that cross-cultural communication is often best characterised as miscommunication (Carroll and Volk, 1988). If policy (or almost anything else) is to be transferred, then, if we can predict anything, we might expect that fundamental changes will occur that will lead to unexpected consequences. With reference to the third of the three projects mentioned above, one might well wonder how a policy on 'holistic future visions' could feasibly be copied in a country with overriding emphasis on class from a country with overriding emphasis on equality/similarity (Lidén et al., 2001).

In examining the impact of imported ideas, I draw again on fieldwork carried out in the Norwegian district council, from the third of the projects. Many interesting differences in experience of district activities were observable during this fieldwork. Working both within and outside the town hall, it was possible to examine at close quarters the representations of the council by the central management and how these were interpreted in the very different working contexts of service providers. In this case, then, it is possible to see the workings of 'global' mentalities in particular contexts. The global concept that is spreading throughout Norway, I would argue, as it has spread from California, through Britain and onwards, is the domineering ideology of government as service provider to consumers. This has profound impacts on the roles and behaviours of administrators and service-providers whose implications are rarely appreciated by those who adopt the ideology, despite years of evidence that the outcomes can often be counterproductive. While the council's administrative leaders pushed a major reorganisation through with the justification that it would enable the council to be more 'client-focused', the consequences of the reorganisation itself were ignored. 'Reorganisation for better services' was the lesson brought in by management consultants and from forums of council leaders, but the practice of reorganising was a locally contextualised process bound up in ritualised administrative practices, personal relationships and leadership styles.

Concepts such as client focus and budget discipline took on widely varying implications at the different levels of the council, and public debate about these themes was quite separate from private discussion and rumour. However, what I would like to highlight here is the way that the paradoxes, dilemmas and conflicts that exist within an organisation can be hidden by the use of concepts and roles. During this work, I was able to observe closely the ritual roles adopted by politicians and administrators in any meeting where all were involved. I was struck by the extent to which administrators, in particular, were expected to adopt certain forms of behaviour, and how these forms were both tied to a set of belief structures and interpreted as demanding a certain type of personality. (This I have also described in more detail elsewhere – Abram, forthcoming.)

In meetings of the council, or council subcommittees, a member of the administration will always be present to support the meeting with information, reference to local and central policy, and advice over the potential consequences of political decisions. In many cases, administrators are present to offer advice or opinions in addition to the papers they have prepared in advance to present a particular case to the committee. However, a clear line is drawn between the political and non-political. Committee meetings are a 'political arena', they are chaired and directed by politicians. A good working relationship is necessary between the chair of the meeting, a politician, and the administrator responsible to the committee, to ensure that the politicians receive appropriate advice. As it is a political forum, the administrator must wait to be asked for their opinion. Rather like the rituals relating to addressing the Queen of England, (one does not address the Queen unless she specifically opens a dialogue, and then as 'Your Majesty' or 'Ma'am') the administrator in the committee room is silent until invited to speak, and all utterances should be prefaced by the role-name of the chair: 'Ordfører' ('Mayor'), for example. Any additional administrators who may be present when their specialist responsibilities are to be discussed, must wait to be invited to speak by the administrator responsible to the committee, leading to a highly channelled flow of information. We could describe it as a kind of 'obligatory passage point' for all information flow during a meeting or, indeed, outside of the meeting (Callon, 1986). Politicians are also strictly disciplined in their speech, through the use of timed interjections taken in turn between parties. That is, politicians are invited to speak at a podium where are allotted a certain time limit on their speeches, and when their time is up, a red lamp lights up on the podium, and the chair may require them to return to their seat. These practices are also adopted in the youth council, where young people resident in the district are offered the opportunity to join a one-day debate and choose a project according to a budget allocated by the main council. Here, young people learn ritual behaviours and speeches as practised by their adult counterparts, under the guiding influence of the mayor who chairs their debates.

This strong discipline clearly structures the flow of information. It also impinges bodily on the behaviour of the participants, politicians and administrators. Administrators may well have to sit through a meeting where a policy is discussed that they can see may have concealed consequences, but be unable to make politicians aware of these unless the senior administrator is able to alert the chair of the meeting to the desire to add a point of clarification. Politicians can use brevity, wit or drama to make their points within their allotted times, but administrators must be able to distance themselves from the consequences of policies they personally may have recommended against (or have wished to, if they had been given appropriate opportunity) which are adopted according to the wishes of politicians. This is said to require a certain kind of personality of administrators. They must carefully separate their own political beliefs from their efficient functioning as advisers to politicians. They may argue a particular case, but once a policy is decided, they must support it wholeheartedly even if it has consequences they reject.

In Norway, this becomes particularly interesting when individuals occupy positions in both roles. An administrator (although not the most senior administrators) may also be elected to the council (in contrast to British local government where the two roles must be assumed by different persons). While they cannot make decisions that concern their own employment, they are still required to behave in different ways. They recount their ethical imperative to distance themselves from their own experiences on the one hand, and yet use that experience and local knowledge to inform their political decisions. Their politics must become general and not personal, they avoid using personal examples to support policy decisions, and declare an interest if a policy area begins to approach their own professional interests too closely. This approaches a political ideal, however, as one politician suggested that they would avoid using themselves as an example to make policy, as their political responsibility extends beyond their own experience.

Even in more informal meetings between politicians and administrators, the latter hold their tongues. One senior administrator suggested that he never spoke out at any meeting without thinking through his reactions at least three times. In that way, he could be sure that he would not be making political statements, but offering technical support to decision-makers. Political disciplining was effectively deeply internalised, and such administrators suggested that individuals who found it difficult to distance their personal or political beliefs from their role as administrators were 'unsuitable' for the work, and should find another kind of job. Given this judgement, we might reflect on the earlier example from Britain. Despite the differences in practices adopted within the councils in different countries, the basic ethos of a non-political administration is similar. We can see, then, that in the British case, administrators were not in any position to consider the local protest against political decisions, as political decisions were not theoretically theirs to alter. While there are many layers of nuance and subtlety in the actions of administrators in influencing policy (described artfully by Forester, 1989), the separation of duties between politicians and administrators itself leads to discontinuities between the individual case and the district-wide policy. It is the more fundamental and internalised beliefs and rituals within the council system that make certain kinds of policy impossible and others straightforward. The various players restrain each others' ambitions, and, although this is an expedient way to avoid extremism, it is also a recipe for problematic policies.

Although the theme of attempting to separate the political from the administrative or technical was common to both these examples, the situation in which they occur makes their implications quite different, and this became apparent in the spread of a different policy idea. As mentioned above, the notion of collaborative planning has become very widespread. In the English context, the relationship between politicians and adminsitrators is relatively informal: politicians often called into the offices of the planners in the case mentioned above, and they 'knew each other' well. Cases could be discussed informally, and planners could often reach agreements with politicians about priorities well in advance of formal meetings. Pre-meetings between chairs and sub-chairs of committees and administrative leaders preceded formal political meetings, so that administrators knew when they would be called to speak, and were sufficiently informal with politicians that they could raise issues in political meetings. However, in the Norwegian case, the split was applied much more strictly. Most administrators, including some section leaders, told me that they never spoke to politicians – since they did not have the right to initiate contact with politicians, and politicians very rarely came to see them to ask questions, they were completely reliant on good meeting-practices to ensure that mistakes were avoided.

The implications of this became most apparent in the adoption of notions of collaborative planning. In English and Scottish (and other British) planning systems, increasing emphasis is laid on the notion of 'participation' in plan-making. This means, roughly, that public forums are generated where non-members of the council can put forward their ideas and comments on council policies. This is carried out with varying levels of success through public meetings, model-making events, 'visioning' conferences, planning exhibitions, etc. it is often planners or other bureaucrats who conduct these events and try to generate public comments. However, on arriving in the Norwegian council and being told that they were about to embark on a participative planning process, I was surprised to realise that this would entail participative goal-setting between senior administrators and senior politicians. Both councils declared that they were carrying out 'participative planning', but they were describing processes with wholly different practices and conse-quences. Attempts to 'compare' participative, holistic planning in Norway and Scotland, in order to understand 'policy transfer' and to find out whether concepts were becoming global, were immediately problematised.

CONCLUSIONS: TRANSNATIONAL POLICY FLOW?

If this is what policy flow implies, then we need to assert different ethnographic methods in order to study them. Focusing on policy networks, investigating policy study tours as a kind of tourism ethnography, or following policies through different contexts are some of the possibilities that we can consider in developing ethnographic practices for these globalisation questions. The place-connections of the actual ethnographic research are clearly different for each of these forms, and the kinds of social relations that exist across distances require different ethnographic approaches.

In any kind of fieldwork, we find ourselves presented with varying interpretations of events from the viewpoints of different social actors. When these actors are well known to each other, we can begin to understand what motivates their different interpretations and draw out the layers of meanings that are attached to particular episodes. In the case of more loosely drawn networks, it can be profitable to use team-work or serial ethnographies to draw in a variety of different social and material contexts that form the background to meetings between different parties. What I hope I have shown, however, is that ethnographies of complex and loosely woven networks can lead to important and interesting insights into social processes that shed real light on policy activities and policy learning or, indeed, other flows of concepts. If we are to investigate global processes, of whatever sort, we need only to be creative with our use of ethnographic techniques to lead us to findings from under the surface of the normal reports. For example, claims about global forces of capitalism can be scrutinised as the activities of a related network of corporations locked in a competition built up of many facets, from futures trading to marketing. Rather than see a corporation of mammoth proportions, we can see 'global capitalism' as an idea built up of many smaller relations that are more accessible to in-depth research. As Nustad argues in this volume, we need not align ourselves with *either* local or global, but see them as mental constructs which we may set aside, and adopt a different construct, such as 'network' instead. In short, we need to ask what is globalising, who is globalising, where are they doing it and what is their means of communication? In answering these questions, we are making globalisation available to ethnographic research.

REFERENCES

Abram, S. forthcoming. Personality and professionalism in a Norwegian District Council. *Planning Theory*.

Abu-Lughod, L. 1994. Finding a place for Islam: Egyptian television serials and the national interest. *Public Culture* 5: 493–513.

Amit-Talai, V. 2000. *Constructing the Field: Ethnographic Fieldwork in the Contemporary World* (European Association of Social Anthropologists). London: Routledge.

Anderson, B. 1991/1983. *Imagined Communites: Reflections on the Origin and Spread of Nationalism*, revised edn. London: Verso.

Ardener, E. 1987. 'Remote areas': some theoretical considerations. In A. Jackson (ed.) *Anthropology at Home*. London: ASA.

Augé, M. 1995. *Non-places: Introduction to an Anthropology of Supermodernity*. London: Verso.

Boyle, P.J. and K. Halfacree. 1998. *Migration into Rural Areas: Theories and Issues*. Chichester: Wiley.

Callon, M. 1986. Some elements of a sociology of translation: domestication of the scallops and the fisherman of St Brieuc Bay. In J. Law (ed.) *Power, Action and Belief*. London: Routledge & Kegan Paul.

Carroll, R. and C. Volk. 1988. *Cultural Misunderstandings: The French-American Experience*. Chicago and London: University of Chicago Press.

Cowell, R. 2002. Reflexivity and reticulism: the social art of community planning. In *Papers in Environmental Planning Research*. Cardiff University: Department of City and Regional Planning.

Flyvbjerg, B. 1998. *Rationality and Power: Democracy in Practice*. Chicago and London: University of Chicago Press.

Forester, J. 1989. *Planning in the Face of Power*. Berkeley, CA and London: University of California Press.

Gell, A. 1999. *The Art of Anthropology: Essays and Diagrams*, Monographs on Social Anthropology, vol. 67. London: Athlone Press.

Gupta, A. and J. Ferguson. 1997. *Anthropological Locations: Boundaries and Grounds of a Field Science*. Berkeley and London: University of California Press.

Hannerz, U. 1996. *Transnational Connections: Culture, People, Places*. London: Routledge.

Healey, P. 1997. *Collaborative Planning: Shaping Places in Fragmented Societies*. Basingstoke: Macmillan.

Lidén, H., H. Vike and M. Lien. 2001. *Likhetens paradokser: antropologiske undersøkelser i det moderne Norge*. Oslo: Universitetsforlaget.

Miller, D. and D. Slater. 2000. *The Internet: An Ethnographic Approach*. Oxford: Berg.

Murdoch, J. and S. Abram. 2002. *Rationalities of Planning*. London: Ashgate.

Nader, L. 1972. Up the anthropologist: perspectives gained from studying up. In D. Hymes (ed.) *Reinventing Anthropology*. New York: Random House.

9 COMMEMORATING GLOBAL ACTS: A NORWEGIAN WAY OF HOLDING AN EMIGRANT WORLD TOGETHER

Sarah Lund

Part of the challenge in addressing global issues from an anthropological perspective relates to the methodological position of the ethnographic field, that is, its concreteness and the aspiration to sustain anthropological attention to micro level phenomena and processes. Engagement with the emergent nature of ethnographic localities, ones that both anchor and yet open up our perspectives on global issues, must be a preoccupation. In the light of new demands to encompass such far-flung processes, how might anthropology characterise global localities while maintaining its insistence that global factors are and always have impinged upon and been embedded in all local contexts? Given the current preoccupation with globalisation as uniquely contemporary, how does history become implicated in global issues of locality and how might this time dimension be characterised?

In this chapter I will be exploring anthropological perspectives on globalisation by presenting an ethnography that incorporates Norway and North America in a single place. Several communities in the upper Midwest are participating in a heritage project in western Norway, a project which seeks to commemorate the emigration of the approximately 850,000 Norwegians to North America between the years 1825 and 1925. By donating old pioneer buildings and actively helping in their disassembling and re-inauguration in Norway, individuals and local groups find new and meaningful ways to think about their shared emigrant/immigrant past.

Through their joint work of preserving pioneer buildings in a localised Norwegian setting, Norwegians and Norwegian-Americans seek to create a commemorative monument to Norwegian emigration. This popular exercise of constructing and representing patterns of cultural movement and interconnectedness of people across continents concretely blends American pioneer architecture with a Norwegian west-country landscape. The constructed site is a manifestation of certain kinds of limited localities cut free from their moorings in place and thus able to contribute to the immediate experience of the global as spatially unbounded. However, the creation of this rootless place stands in contrast to its surroundings in a uni-local community, a model of locality so much out of favour in anthropological discussion of the global (Mintz, 1998: 20). Indeed, the very contrast provides impact and gives meaning to the public exercise in memory work in which lost relationships of an emigrant past are re-imagined.

Perhaps global localities can best be perceived in terms of their contrast with the bounded community in which people actually do not migrate but stay put (Mintz, 1998). Given the time span we are dealing with here (1825–1925), actual family bonds are genealogically distant and spatially dispersed, even when studiously recognised and maintained by many Norwegian and Norwegian-American families. Despite intermittent revivals, the intensity of interaction and exchange between families on either side of the Atlantic is fading. The physical connections of worldwide span are transferred instead to displaced pioneer buildings built into and intertwined with the bounded locally oriented community, revealing the latter as breaking its own limitations and opening outward to difference and belonging.

All localities have within them the potential for representing themselves in terms of a global dimension, thus reflecting upon how wider connections relate to local identities (see Bahloul, 1996). The history-making endeavour under consideration here is a powerful source of such reflection, at once both intensely personalised as well as striving toward broader historical perspectives of regional, national and global dimensions. Indeed, generally speaking, mass migrations and diaspora forms of longing and memory are the potent stuff of just such kinds of global story-making. Migrant networks circulate people transnationally. Their multiple attachments of locality are constructed and maintained through the telling of global tales about how separate places become single communities over vast distances. Thus migrant history-making confronts the norm of the nation state, which is a territorialised historical story of singular attachment and restricted mobility over national borders (Torpey, 2000: 122; see Olwig, this volume).

While stories of state insist upon an exclusive place–culture relationship as natural, global story-making inverts the relation of culture to geographical and social territories (see Parkin, 1999: 309; Tomlinson, 1999: 107). Much as we see the rootless place as highlighting the contrast with the rooted community, counterpoised story-making of migration and of settlement seem to acquire greater purchase in relation to each other, the one simultaneously provides a secure leverage for commentary on the specific historical experience of the other.

GLOBAL STORYLINES: COMMEMORATING CONNECTIONS

In most cultures we find a preoccupation with commemoration as a means of collective remembrance. The act of recalling a shared event that took place at some fixed historical date (Connerton, 1989: 45) becomes a venue for exploring personal identities as well as a shared heritage. Such recollections are explicit in their emphasis on continuity and thus they come to play a significant part in shaping the performance content of commemoration acts as well as emphasising the sequential rejuvenation of communal memory (Connerton, 1989: 48).

As many authors have demonstrated in terms of the modern nation-state, national elites have been intent on making such claims to continuity with an appropriate historic past as part of the task of inventing national tradition (Anderson, 1983; Gillis, 1994; Kertzer, 1988). While rituals of nationhood may vary in the degree to which they emphasise explicit commemorative content, all such celebrations depend to some degree on collective remembrance. By means of national rituals, performers act out a relationship of continuity and identity between themselves and the shared scripts or representations of what it means to be part of the nation.

Yet such performances generate fundamental variance as well as continuity. Because a similar act of commemoration dramatically reworks the content of tradition even as it reproduces it, there is a basic bifurcation in the performance of commemorative rituals. Invariance is explicitly structured in the assumed, often hegemonic, relationship between the performance and what it is that the participants are supposedly depicting. On the other hand, variance is demonstrated through the 'reservoir of meaning' (Connerton, 1989: 56) available within the narrative content of the prototypical persons and events being remembered (see Blehr, 2000).

Traditional forms of commemoration construct singular national identity in an increasingly pluralistic world. Demands for a greater democratisation of memory are aired as official commemorations become too impersonal and totalising (Gillis, 1994: 19–20). In other words, public memory in such national rites is an area of contentious debate (Bodnar, 1992: 15–20) residing at the intersection of official and vernacular cultural expressions. Official versions of public memory promote visions of the past and present that downplay alternative interpretations. On the other hand, local performances of commemorative rites reformulate the national content into vernacular versions of the diverse and the experiential (see Bodnar, 1992). Thus, commemorative events can be seen to generate a political discussion about the nature of society from the contradictory vantage points of the local expression of lived experience and the national project of an imagined unified whole. This is particularly the case when considering commemoration of emigration that, in this Norwegian instance, is locally significant and privately maintained while simultaneously controversial and contentious when taken as part of a hegemonic tale of nationhood (see Lovoll, 2001).

Communal memory is shaped through the re-enactment of commemorative events in modernity. Such bracketing of one set of events as point of origin assumes that other occurrences are deliberately set aside in an act of silencing (see Trouillot, 1995). This pinpointing manoeuvre becomes contested through interpretations of particular local experiences of community and place. While loyalty to the national project of commemoration, located as it is in the declaring of national independence, may be implicitly retained and upheld, from a local perspective, the past is appreciated commemoratively as a vast collage of images and styles relevant to an interpretation of immediate shared experiences (Connerton, 1989: 62). Commemorating the loss through emigration of a large percentage of the local population in rural Norway over an extended period in the past (Blegen, 1931: 21; Semmingsen, 1950: 193–5) will in the following be seen as a counter-commemoration to that of nationhood.

Acts of commemoration are immediate and local as well as hegemonic. Potentially, mnemonic enactment becomes individualised and heterogeneous. Such commemoration acts are consciously lived through as personal identity, an attitude in the lives of individuals whose versions of a shared past event become a repetitive stewardship for remembering significant recurrent patterns in individuals' lives. They can provide new interpretative avenues for understanding recurrences that might otherwise be incomprehensible. Through consciously enacting repetition, an individual life experience is able to reincorporate the valued past event into the present, thus giving a fresh incarnation to the celebration of traditional values and roles.

Commemoration ceremonies provide a reservoir of performance possibilities. In the instance under discussion below, they are a resource for re-enacting the shared past event of Norwegian emigration. From the imagined nation of the distant homeland, to local experiences of shared multi-sited community, to the individualised and embodied connections of distant kin, this layered perspective on commemorative acts will provide a focus on remembrance for two sets of peripherally located communities:

Norwegian-Americans in the Midwest and Norwegians on the west coast of Norway. By constructing a deterritorialised site in their midst, an appreciation of new forms of transnational locality emerge. Shared tales of emigration from Norway and immigration to America are enacted through the construction of a building site. Individual movement is crucial to this project of memory work between Norway and America. Local communities on two continents interact through volunteer work groups in order to construct new versions of past events and by so doing national commemorative stories are questioned and to some extent revised.

A HISTORICAL BEGINNING

Between 1825 and 1920, during the zenith of organised emigration, nearly 850,000 Norwegians left their homeland for North America. This was a significant portion of the population and their departure had serious social ramifications and came to colour subsequent developments in the country during the twentieth century (Semmingsen, 1950). These were largely rural peasants drawn by the promise of fertile farming land in the prairie states of the upper Midwest and the great plains of Manitoba. The agricultural and economic conditions in both Norway and in North America had a push and pull effect on emigration from Norway. The vast displacement of people occurred in a process of ebb and flow over the 100-year span (Blegen, 1931: 18). The emigration was organised in regional groupings. Extended families, and indeed entire local communities, were displaced at times so that America Fever, as it was called, had an extremely disruptive impact on rural Norway in particular (Semmingsen, 1950: 47).

It should be kept in mind that in Norway during most of this time, there were strong nationalistic sentiments abroad calling for independence from Sweden. Nationhood was only finally attained through mutual accord in 1905, long after the major waves of migration were over. Norwegian-Americans were well informed of developments in the home country, and were both emotionally and economically involved. Thus Norwegians on both sides of the Atlantic were strongly affected by nationalism, their lives coloured by this struggle, and they had a stake in these developments.

The official view on emigration during such a period of national crisis should be noted as well. The massive scale of the emigration alone gave considerable cause for concern (Semmingsen, 1950: 425–6). Institutions such as the state church and the ruling elite made considerable efforts to stem the tide of people leaving, especially during the early period (Blegen, 1931: 149, 154–8).

Officially it was considered disloyal to leave the country. Thus emigrants were under considerable pressure to remain at home. Despite the public outcry, people left the country in droves, virtually no family being left untouched. In the poorer districts of the mountain valleys, some communities were left as seeming ghost towns, with only the old people staying behind.

While officialdom pressured people to remain in Norway, intimate family relations across the Atlantic were loyally maintained even through generations. Letter-writing was important, and returnees also served to open the flow of information and encouraged latecomers to join in by subsidising passage and promising of help (Semmingsen, 1950: 57, 75). Also, as communication improved and steamship travel replaced the dangerous crossing under sail, many immigrants began to travel back and forth simply to visit, thus revitalising family contact over the years. However, with passing generations by the end of the twentieth century much of the immediate family connectedness has dropped away. In the case of the majority of families claiming Norwegian-American ancestry, four or five generations have passed since emigration and family identity and roots are now firmly attached to the American continent.

If immediate family ties have weakened with passing generations, the sense of personal identity and interest in a sense of shared Norwegian heritage remains a dynamic force in many communities with large Norwegian-American populations and may be seen as more vibrant today than in earlier times when interest in ethnic identity seems to have been less relevant (Waters, 1990). In Norway, on the other hand, for much of the twentieth century, there is little sense of identification with those who left the homeland a hundred years before. People are aware that segments of their family emigrated and contact was lost, as if these people disappeared into the void. Some may have memories of care packages sent to their families after the Second World War. The figure of the unknown bachelor uncle in America who dies and leaves an inheritance is proverbial. Economic gain has been the consequence of a loss of family personnel in an obscured past. The unexpected appearance on the doorstep of visitors with distant family ties is frequently related, and is often a cause of considerable consternation. Many of these unannounced guests are searching for the family farm of generations past and excursions are taken into the countryside. In these visits, gifts are given, less consequential family heirlooms may be presented and photographs exchanged. Blood ties are acknowledged despite the disquiet over finding oneself related to a stranger so strikingly different. Such visits are identity encounters that explore the vast cultural dissimilarities against the perceived bedrock of blood connectedness.

SLETTA: COMMEMORATION ON A MONUMENTAL SCALE

A recent initiative has been made on the part of rural communities in Norway and the Midwest to create an interpretative centre in Norway in order to commemorate the Norwegians who emigrated during the 100 years of organised passage. The commemorative setting is in the small township of Sletta north of Bergen on an island called Radøy. Under the inspiring leadership of Asbjørn Ystebo, this small community has instigated the transport, reassembling and restoration of various pioneer buildings from western Minnesota and eastern North Dakota. A schoolhouse, a pioneer log cabin, the jail, a doctor's office and the town hall, all have been donated from various small Midwestern towns. They have been brought to Radøy where they cling together at the bottom of the field donated by Rune Meldingen for the project. These buildings stand in the shadow of the largest relocated building of all, the First Lutheran Church from Brampton, North Dakota that stands just across the road from the simulated 'Main Street'.

Transported Midwestern buildings form the core of a project that intends to create an interpretative facility for the mutual exploration of a historical moment, one in which Norwegians joined the vast tide of European emigration to America. In addition to the imported buildings, a modern learning facility is planned where visitors from both Norway and America can meet to consider the emigrant/immigrant experience. Library facilities, an auditorium, workshops for learning crafts, and archives of genealogical materials all will be housed in the projected interpretative centre. Through the contemplation of buildings, some complete with their authentic inventory brought from the Midwest, Norwegians will be provided with an imaginative authentic example of the fate of past relatives and of so many of their countrymen and women. Norwegian Americans in turn can visit Sletta as an avenue to reflective learning about family heritage and roots without necessarily arriving at this understanding through the fading kinship ties that are all but vanished at this late stage. They may consult the genealogical archive that is housed here in preparation for further travels to locate the family farm, place of departure for grandparents or even earlier generations. However, actually visiting immediate relatives is becoming a less frequent experience for many, simply because contact over generations has not been maintained.

Even at this early phase, when much of the project remains on the drawing board, the setting at Sletta presents an evocative opportunity for Norwegians and Norwegian-Americans to meet and interact during summer festivals organised yearly around the Fourth of July. Sletta has become a central meeting place to celebrate

American Independence Day for all of the western counties of Norway, particularly the city of Bergen. During several of these festival occasions, select honorary guests from the Midwest have been invited, as when the Brampton Church was inaugurated. On that occasion, the remaining congregation of 15 people who had officially given the church to Sletta the previous year made the trip from North Dakota to Norway to be present at the church inauguration. The congregation returned to the church that had figured so prominently in their community life on the prairie and, at the same time, they travelled far from home in order to do so. Ruth, the organist, took her place at the organ as she had through decades before to accompany the hymns during the service. Church keys were handed over by the president of the church board and church dignitaries from both Bergen and Fargo gave commemorative sermons on the life of the church as pioneer building and as worshipping community.

During the festival in another year, the doctor's office was opened to the public. The grandson of the rural physician who had practised for years in the small office was present to open the building. He could relate many anecdotes from his grandfather's practice, as he had been partially raised in Rothsay, Minnesota and had spent many hours helping out in the office. This man and his extended family were central in tracking down and donating some of the original inventory in the clinic and this was presented as a gift to the project at Sletta when the building was inaugurated.

Norwegian-Americans with special attachment to the buildings at Sletta are actively incorporated into the local Norwegian celebrations on the Fourth of July. They have been assigned the role of an essential relatedness with the buildings reassembled there, and they provide these houses from Main Street with a particular historical voice. From a different angle, the local Norwegians hosting the festivals have a sense of relatedness to the buildings as well, because they have spent years of free time working on the reconstruction in the centre of their village. The preservation and authentic reassembling of buildings that otherwise are removed from indigenous building styles and techniques have claimed their diligence and attention. Through rebuilding pioneer houses, they reoccupy them and claim them for the community.

Even during these early stages, Norwegians and Norwegian Americans coalesce at Sletta. In popular festivals at a place in Norway, they gather together to construct a mutual ritual space defined through architecture, through shared work, and through geography to represent authentic pioneer America rooted in the rural landscape of a homeland left behind 150 years ago. Participants agree that the setting at Sletta provides them with a meaningful context for the performing of commemorative rituals in which themes of continuity are explored by means of an assumed mutual past. Commemoration is both the original motivation for the concept of the project and the ongoing dynamic force in gathering people and eliciting contributions in terms of the buildings, their inventories and long hours of work needed to reassemble and restore them on the field at Sletta. The continuity of commemoration however, is sought from different sources and with differing emphasis.

DWELLING IN TRAVELLING/TRAVELLING IN DWELLING

Sletta is like a hinge, enabling us to look back at the past. It provides us with a means of reflecting upon the inconsistencies in the opposition between dwelling and travelling (Urry, 1997: 75). In this constructed setting, buildings – to which we tend to ascribe fixity – are in this case continental travellers. They are dwelling places on the move. Thereby the fixity and privileging of dwelling is given an unusual twist through monumental displacement.

On the other hand, travels undertaken by people seem to return them to their dwelling places. Travel to complete voluntary projects of disassembling buildings is undertaken by Norwegians to the Midwest and Norwegian-Americans to Norway in order to enable the movement of buildings. In doing so, the two groups mirror themselves in the trajectory of the other. Norwegians from the western counties travel to small Midwestern towns in order to disassemble buildings and pack them for shipment. They work together with local people to accomplish the task. Many Norwegians express relief in the fact that their families did not emigrate to such desolate places.

Norwegian-Americans travel to Norway and visit their own hometown buildings at Sletta. They are visiting the buildings of their American past, built by immigrant Norwegians during the first generation of their settling in America. Undoubtedly their main motives for travel are to tour Norway and to become familiar with the authentic places from times prior to the starting point of embarkation of their forebears. In their connections with buildings at Sletta, they are confronted with American times and places that jar – that bring them up short with the backward glance. Instead the images elicited there call upon other experiences of origin. The juxtaposed hometown buildings and authentic rural Norwegian setting evoke conflicting images that involuntarily disrupt temporal linearity (see Leslie, 1999: 117). The jarring is part of enacting commemoration at Sletta for these visitors.

COMMEMORATION IN A ROOTLESS PLACE

Commemorative practices at Sletta tell us about creating and sustaining links between diaspora communities in a global world. This is not a contiguous world but rather one in which localities are stretched out both in terms of time and of space. Through a call to commemorate, bits and pieces from widely disparate worlds are brought together and given a joint relevance based in an idea of origins. However, differences tantalise beyond the diaphanous veil of similarity, as social memory reformulates what has gone before in particular local terms and through new individual experiences of displacement.

Each person participating at Sletta addresses a common version of a shared past that relates to historical facts about proportions. Of all the European countries of the period, Norway had the largest number of emigrants to America in proportion to its population of any nation apart from Ireland (Blegen, 1931: 22). Emigration and its commemoration is part of a national appreciation of Norwegian history during a period when Norway struggled to achieve independence from Sweden and finally succeeded.

In immigrant America, the Norwegian-American community retains a seemingly great degree of cultural ties and material sense of community with Norway, more so than many other immigrant groups (Nelson, 1994: 5). They celebrate their distinctness in a national atmosphere of ethnic revivalism. From such a vantage point, Norway as nation or origin is part of the American narrative of nation.

At Sletta both Norwegians and Norwegian-Americans proclaim shared substance with the emigrating peasantry, but each does so in relation to quite contrary stories about nationhood. The communal project of sharing similarity through commemoration in an uprooted place like Sletta is superimposed over disparate concerns about inclusion in nation-specific loyalties. Organisers at Sletta would contest the public official version of Norwegian nation-building as incomplete. They would harness commemorative fervour from both sides of the Atlantic in order to reformulate national narrative to include the peasant emigrant to America, recognising the error of their subsequent obliteration from a national identity.

Norwegian-American communities of the Midwest respond to the 'call to remember' originating from a dimly perceived homeland by giving their old buildings. However, the generalised figure central to Midwestern social memories is the American pioneer and the monumental efforts made by ordinary people to build the frontier (Bodner, 1992: 121). Through the joint work of recalling that which is shared, the migrant and the non-migrant mutually enlighten each other. Through this kind of global commemorative exchange, a placeless space of remembrance is created which reflects back upon and deepens national certainties: stretching, exploring and reconfiguring them.

Commemoration provides an imaginative bridge compelling local communities in two different parts of the world to fill in the gaps in what is known about each other. The imaginative work within a place like Sletta is facilitated and authenticated by the tangible. The work of disassembling and restoring pioneer buildings provides a compressed site for interaction. Pioneer buildings pinpoint commemoration at Sletta and enable the disassociation from place. The assumed permanence of architecture and its unusual displacement lifts the interpretative centre site unto a level free from locality and the bonds of Norway as nation. Conventional distinctions between home and abroad are dissolved and memories are freed to spin beyond the known. This freeing from place characteristic of global phenomena allows and mediates a co-presence between communities of difference.

At Sletta, commemoration must transcend the paradoxes of global spaces and discontinuous times in order to recreate the interlinks between such far-flung communities with such disparate historical experiences. Enacting the criss-crossing of space and place, of movement and fixity, creates the continuity that commemoration demands. Interacting with the setting at Sletta becomes a global act of tying the world together.

REFERENCES

Anderson, B. 1983. *Imagined Communities: Reflections on the Origin and Spread of Nationalism.* London: Verso.
Bahloul, J. 1996. *The Architecture of Memory: A Jewish-Muslim Household in Colonial Algeria, 1937–1962.* Cambridge: Cambridge University Press.
Blegen, T. 1931. *Norwegian Migration to America 1825–1860.* Northfield, MN: The Norwegian-American Historical Association.
Blehr, B. 2000. *En norsk besvärelse; 17 maj-firande vid 1900-talets slut.* Falum, Sweden: Nya Doxa.
Bodnar, J. 1992. *Remaking America: Public Memory, Commemoration, and Patriotism in the Twentieth Century.* Princeton, NJ: Princeton University Press.
Connerton, P. 1989. *How Societies Remember.* Cambridge: Cambridge University Press.
Gillis, J. (ed.) 1994. *Commemorations: The Politics of National Identity.* Princeton, NJ: Princeton University Press.
Hegard, T. 1998. Trekk av den norske friluftsmuseumsbeveglesens historie. In M. Skougaard and J. Nielsen (eds) *Bondegård og Museum: Frilandsmuseernes teori og praksis.* Øster Gøinge Herred: Landbohistorisk selskab.

Kertzer, D. 1988. *Ritual Politics and Power*. New Haven, CT: Yale University Press.

Leslie, E. 1999. Souvenirs and forgetting: Walter Benjamin's memory-work. In M. Kwint, C. Breward and J. Aynsley (eds) *Material Memories: Design and Evocation*. Oxford: Berg.

Lovoll, O. 2001. The creation of historical memory in a multicultural society. In *Norwegian-American Essays – 2001*, pp. 27–40. Oslo: NAHA-Norway.

Mintz, S. 1998. The localization of anthropological practice: from area studies to transnationalism, *Critique of Anthropology* 18(2): 117–33.

Nelson, M. 1994. Material culture and ethnicity: collecting and preserving Norwegian Americana before World War II. In *Material Culture and People's Art Among the Norwegians in America*, pp. 3–72. Northfield, MN: The Norwegian-American Historical Association.

Parkin, D. 1999. Mementoes as transitional objects in human displacement, *Journal of Material Culture* 4(3): 303–20.

Semmingsen, I. 1950. *Veien mot Vest: Utvandringen fra Norge 1865–1915*. Oslo: Aschehoug.

Tomlinson, J. 1999. *Globalization and Culture*. London: Polity Press.

Torpey, J. 2000. *The Invention of the Passport: Surveillance, Citizenship and the State*. Cambridge: Cambridge University Press.

Trouillot, M.-R. 1995. *Silencing the Past: Power and the Production of History*. Boston, MA: Beacon.

Urry, J. 1995. *Consuming Places*. London: Routledge.

Waters, M. 1990. The costs of a costless community. In M. Waters (ed.) *Ethnic Options: Choosing Identities in America*, pp. 147–68. Berkeley: University of California Press.

10 EXCHANGE MATTERS: ISSUES OF LAW AND THE FLOW OF HUMAN SUBSTANCES[1]

Marit Melhuus

In this chapter, I raise questions pertaining to the movement and transnational flow of biogenetic substances derived from human beings. I will explore social phenomena, which in a particular context, serve to facilitate or impede the movement of specific substances. The setting is Norway and the substances are ova and sperm.

My overall research has been concerned with meanings of kinship in Norway and my approach to the topic has been through the many social arenas of assisted procreation. In what follows, I will not address the disparate empirical processes and articulations of assisted procreation (but see Melhuus 2000, 2001). Rather, I have chosen to concentrate on one aspect of this procreative universe: the law that regulates infertility treatment in Norway.[2] This law is one of the most restrictive in Europe. This deliberate limitation allows me to focus on those issues of legislation which highlight the shifting morality underpinning social processes; what the law implies for social actors and how it impinges on social practices and representations. It allows for a cultural reading of a specific state intervention, which has implications for questions of globalisation, while at the same time addressing broader sociocultural matters.

A specific focus on law and legislation not only discloses local particularities, but also serves to reveal an interface between the national and the global. The Norwegian law regulating fertility treatment is an explicit response to a transnational phenomenon: the accessibility of knowledges and technologies that can be made to act on human reproduction. In fact, the law can be seen as a local, morally embedded reaction to a globally available science or knowledge system. It is an attempt to control, place and hence contextualise phenomena that are perceived as free, and virtually independent of context. In fact, I suggest that the specific law that regulates infertility treatment is an example of a localising strategy. It inscribes and is inscribed in a narrative of the nation, articulating its borders, both morally and territorially, and reflecting central cultural values. These become all the more evident in those areas which raise dispute. The law, inevitably, entails room for discrepancies, creating moral predicaments for social actors by the mere fact that it forbids 'actions which for the people concerned are acceptable or desirable within their own moral code' (Harris, 1996; see also Humphreys, 1985). One of the intentions of this chapter is to illustrate areas of moral ambiguity.

If this law is understood as an attempt at fixity and closure, I hope to indicate the contrary: how the law, in practice, opens up a world, setting persons and things in motion and thereby laying the basis for new social relations. It is, nevertheless, important to keep in mind that although for the task at hand I choose to limit my focus, the particular codification of this – or any – law is a historical product. The most recent of these historical processes with respect to the Act relating to the application of biotechnology in medicine will be accounted for, albeit it briefly. The account will necessarily be simplified, an extraction of a very complicated field. The number of peoples, documents, debates as well as issues, media coverage and positions that can be linked to the formulation of this one Act are almost limitless, and point in many directions. Moreover, in order to adequately fill out a global picture, this particular Act should be viewed in relation to other parts of Norwegian law and the Norwegian legal tradition compared to other legal traditions.[3]

NEW DISCOVERIES SET NEW THINGS IN MOTION

The potentials embedded in the new reproductive technologies, in particular *in vitro* fertilisation (IVF), have unleashed unprecedented imaginings. These technologies make possible the fertilisation of ova *ex utero*, representing a radical breach in the Anglo-European understanding of procreation. The most unsettling element of IVF is the possible separation of social and biological motherhood. These technologies not only render the procreative universe more open, they also raise fundamental uncertainties regarding questions of relatedness. On the one hand, more relations are implicated in the creation of the child; on the other hand, more women are given the opportunity to have a child. Our conventional notions of kinship and what constitutes kin-relations are fundamentally challenged, as are notions of property and property relations (see e.g. Edwards et al., 1993; Franklin, 1997; Lundin, 1997; Simpson, 2001; Strathern, 1992, 1999). Not least, these technologies rekindle debates about what life is – as well as when life is.[4] Developments in science and technology are inevitably conducive to processes of cultural production.

The rapid developments and innovations within biomedical technologies have also shaped the imaging of the deconstructed body.
The body is no longer – and only – the locus for an individual, whole
and singular, but also represents its potentially detachable parts
(heart, kidneys, sperm, ova, fetus, blood – and their derivatives, stem
cells, plasma, etc.).[5] And vice versa: any single body may potentially
be made up of components extraneous to the 'original' body.[6] In
some contexts, the boundaries of the body appear fluid, flexible and
malleable. As such, the images of the fragmented body run parallel
to images of the fragmented state, so much so that body fragmenta-
tion and globalisation can be seen as mutually reinforcing processes
(Sharp, 2000). However, in order that such parts be detached and
reassembled, they must first be made available. In what follows, what
interests me is not only the fact that certain substances are available
(technically), but rather *how* they are made available (socially), that
is, the social circumstances which mediate between available and
obtainable. In Norway, legislation is one such mediating process.

The circulation of bodily substances is an international – global –
phenomenon, as are the technologies which make them available
and the knowledge of how to make use of them. As with all other
globe-trotting artefacts, these substances, their accompanying technologies and knowledges are transformed once they become
localised. They are appropriated and written into local discourse and
practices. Norway is no exception. Morever, the specificities of the
circulation of bodily substances make them particularly interesting
in a context of globalisation as these substances are inevitably
endowed with moral connotations. Issues pertaining to the removal
and transfer of human substances invariably cause commotion.
Emotions are mobilised – and no wonder: the issues concern matters
of life and death; they also challenge established perceptions of what
is natural, right and good. The potential (re)movement of substances
through acts of detachment and attachment raise crucial ethical
questions about accepted limits to human manipulation, choice,
ownership and power.

Making genetic matter available, then, inspires a consciousness
about such substances. Once confronted with the substances, we are
also confronted with notions of their essence. The substances are
attributed meaning while at the same time becoming bearers of
meaning. Moreover, availability – or making something available –
is a precondition for transfer and exchangeability. The fact that
something is capable of being transferred – or transferable – can be
seen as a quality (innate or potential) of that object. In certain
situations the object is attributed characteristics which permit
exchange. However, the kind of exchange that flows from the object

will necessarily be determined by the types of relationships that contain the exchange. With respect to human substances, the issue of commodification and the efforts to restrict the influence of the market, represent an important nexus of contestation.

The fact that genetic substances are available for exchange and hence on the move does not necessarily make them commodities. However, the commodification of objects tends to emerge as a result of the very tranformative processes that sets them in motion. Nevertheless, in Norway (as in many other places, but in contrast to the USA) there is a strong moral resistance to including human matter in a regular market economy. This resistance is seldom questioned; it is taken for granted and any violation of this unstated principle would be considered an ethical breach. This attitude was reflected in my interviews with politicians and is mirrored in the laws, rules and regulations that are applied to the movement of human substances.

Below, I will explore cultural factors that restrain or facilitate the availability of ova and sperm. In this endeavour the differing articulations of origin, boundaries and border crossings are important. I also wish to grasp the meanings that these phenomena generate as well as those with which they are endowed. Among other things, this has to do with processes of classification and reclassification, the relation between public and private, natural and unnatural, and matters of value. In addition to legislation, this exercise will involve a focus on the properties of the substances ova and sperm as represented and articulated by various actors and implicated parties in the Norwegian public sphere ('*norsk offentlighet*').

It is my contention that specific properties surface once the objects become subjects of exchange, thereby making the implicit explicit. In other words, exchange serves as a lens through which the cultural production of meaning becomes visible. At the core of any exchange nest the troublesome questions of equivalence. Hence, it is crucial to explore not only what is exchanged but also what underpins the exchange in terms of value. This includes both the object of exchange and the relationships through which the object moves.

Before I embark on this venture, a word of caution: the substances I am dealing with are not generally visible; I cannot trace them literally. In many respects, they pass incognito, their social lives not readily available for inspection (see Appadurai, 1992). At an individual level ova and sperm (and their functions) are generally taken for granted, are considered very personal and normally pertain to the most intimate spheres of our lives. They are, almost by definition, hard to grasp. Publicly, however, they become emblems of dense moral discourses. Egg donation and sperm donation are cases in point.

MATTERS OF LEGISLATION

As mentioned, the Norwegian law regulating assisted procreation is one of the most restrictive in Europe. It permits sperm donation by anonymous donor, but does not permit the donation of ova; it only permits treatment of heterosexual couples (married or cohabiting); it does not permit the combination of IVF with donor sperm. The Act states:

The medical staff are under an obligation to ensure that the sperm donor's identity is kept secret.
   A sperm donor shall not be given information concerning the identity of the couple or the child. (section 2 - 7)

In vitro fertilisation may only take place in cases where the woman or her husband or partner is infertile or in cases of infertility for which no cause has been identified. Such treatment may only be carried out with the couple's own oocytes and sperm. (section 2 - 10)

Embryos may only be used for transferring into the woman from whom the oocytes originate. (section 2 - 11)

Embryos may not be stored for more than three years. Storage of oocytes is prohibited. (section 2 - 12)

Only clinics authorised by the government may give treatment of assisted procreation. Only two private clinics have been granted such authorisation in Norway (in 1986 and 1999).

This Act was passed in 1994, replacing the Act No. 68 passed in 1987.[7] The 1987 Act was the first Act passed to regulate practices of assisted procreation in Norway. It was also one of the first in the world. Attempts to regulate such practices had been made already in the early 1950s, when there was a Nordic effort to coordinate legislation.

In 1950, the Norwegian government appointed a committee to review the questions tied to artificial insemination.[8] It was known that artifical insemination was being practised (Løvset, 1951) and the committee was asked to evaluate the need and conditions for articifical insemination as well as the legal status of the child. The committee was to cooperate with similar committees in the other Nordic countries. The committee submitted its report in 1953, the majority suggesting that legislation be passed permitting artificial insemination with anonymous donor semen. However, no legislation was passed until 1987. The reasons for this have been difficult to ascertain. Our research revealed that politicians and medical personnel are only vaguely (or not at all) aware of the attempt made in the 1950s. However, one medical doctor, a veteran in the field, suggested that it was most likely the fear that legislation might result in forbidding AID that stopped any further attempts at making a law.

The 1953 report opens with a discussion of the legal grounds for AID, and especially important were questions pertaining to the legal status of the child (is this a legitimate child?); whether artificial insemination by donor could be considered a sexual offence; whether AID could be considered a case of adultery; whether the practice of AID would fall under the law of quackery (*'kvakksalverloven'*); the significance of consent; whether the registration of children born through AID would amount to forgery. These questions are more or less resolved in the report. The committee takes for granted the institution of marriage and, moreover, it assumes the rule of *pater est*[9] (that the father of the child is the one who is married to the mother). In fact, this was the moral ground upon which the rest was drawn. The most controvertial issue was that of anonymity for the donor.

The debates for and against AID in the 1950s shifted between biological and psychological arguments, between nature and nurture (*'arv og miljø'*) and the moral connotations these evoked with respect to what is natural, good and right. Arguments on both sides centred on the institution of marriage, the home and love, on the one hand, and women's natural desire to have children and the significance of infertility for masculine identity, on the other. Lying and the introduction of a third party in marriage are themes constantly reiterated. Not surprisingly, those persons who are for regulation of AID are also the ones who give weight to nurture over nature. Their main argument is that what is important for a child's psychological development is not its biological origins but its home environment. A good home, moreover, was seen as consonant with a good marriage. The main point was to stress that relatedness is not necessarily born of biological bonds. Adoption and the role of the stepfather was used as an exemplary case.

Those who were against AID turned the arguments around, insisting that homes were not harmonious, divorce was increasing, that a child biologically linked to its mother and not its father could create tensions and, most significantly, that introducing a third party into a marriage was equivalent to undermining that very institution. As we shall see, later debates shift the grounds on which arguments are based. The institution of marriage is no longer the nexus around which the arguments revolve, although the heterosexual stable couple is important (but as a marker against homosexual couples). The introduction of a third party also loses ground (except for spokesmen for the Church). In the case of both AID and egg donation, it is the significance of knowing one's biological (genetic) origin that becomes paramount. In addition, with respect to egg donation, arguments grounded in natural notions of motherhood prevail, as do those pertaining to certainty.

The legislation for assisted procreation is likely to be revised again soon. A White Paper was submitted to Parliament in March 2002 recommending that the principle of anonymity be repealed, and that the freezing of oocytes be permitted while upholding the restrictions on donor oocytes.[10] According to most doctors and experts who work within this field, rescinding the anonymity of the donor will result in termination of this treatment, as it is assumed to be very difficult, if not impossible, to find suitable, known donors.[11] However, the successful development of new techniques such as ICSI[12] might radically reduce the need for donor sperm for heterosexual couples. However, single women and lesbian couples will still need donor sperm. In so far as they wish to be impregnated under secure conditions (i.e. with sperm that has been screened), they will have to travel abroad. At present, most clinics in Norway which offer donor insemination as one possibility in the treatment of infertile couples, import the semen they use from Denmark.[13]

The recent revision of the legislation in Norway is not just a reflection of a peculiar Norwegian drive to regulate through laws. The need to revise reflects the continual state of flux of the particular social arena which the law seeks to address. In fact, it would be difficult for any law-making agency to keep pace with advances in biomedicine. Being well aware of this, Norwegian law-makers prefer to apply a precautionary principle in the field of biomedicine, reflecting the uncertainty and perceived risk that these technologies are seen to represent.[14] This attitude was made very evident in discussions with politicians who have sat on the select committee for health issues. It became particularily salient with respect to research (and research was in that context assumed to be research in the field of hard sciences). Several of those interviewed revealed a scepticism to science and research, even while recognising its beneficial aspects. This scepticism was reflected in a lack of confidence in the ethical judgement of scientists. It was implied that if left to their own devices, they would not know where to draw the line.[15] It is therefore worthwhile noting that Norwegian legislation forbids research on embryos (Act No. 56, section 3 - 1). The issues pertaining to research have been a particularly sensitive point. The policy-makers argue for the precautionary principle whereas medical expertise finds that position hypocritical.[16] As one doctor said, referring to the regulation of assisted reproduction: 'Norway exports its ethical dilemmas. The same can also be said for the Norwegian position on biomedical research' (see Hazekamp and Hamberger, 1999).

What is evident is that Norwegian legislation with respect to assisted procreation restricts certain practices. These restrictions have several implications. On the one hand, they impede the circulation of ova and sperm by attempting to enforce limits to movement. On the other hand, they induce a particular flow of these genetic substances, but in a different circuit altogether: one which is transnational. This tendency might be exacerbated with the recent move by Parliament to demand payment for infertility treatment.

Until 2002, infertility treatment was considered part of the health care system. Those granted the right to such treatment did not have to pay clinical expenses, although they did have to cover costs of medicine. The conservative coalition government (consisting of the Right Party, the Christian People's Party and the Left Party) which came into power after the 2000 election proposed that infertility treatment be dropped from the health budget. The reasons given were matters of priority in the health sector. The proposal nevertheless reflects the government's view that infertility is not to be classified as an illness. Our conversations with politicians revealed also an alternative position: that adoption is viewed as preferable to IVF treatments; enforcing payment for infertility treatment would render this alternative on a par with adoption and hence perhaps encourage people to adopt rather than go through IVF. Adoption expenses are not covered by the public welfare system, although tax deductible.

MATTERS OF EXCHANGE

There are many good reasons for grounding an analysis of the flow of biogenetic substances in exchange theory. Not only do exchange relations permeate soical life but, as Thomas reminds us: 'exchange is always, in the first instance, a *political process*, one in which wider relationships are expressed and negotiated in a personal encounter' (Thomas, 1991: 7, my emphasis; see also Appadurai, 1992; Carrier, 1996). Thomas also stresses the importance of recognising that particular features of exchange relations are derived from a much broader set of premises which include asymmetries and differences between people in their access to resources. Such a broader set of principles can, for example, be embedded in legislative documents and practices. Moreover, exchange works so as to mediate conditions and relations which are not constituted within the immediate framework of exchange; hence 'many of the factors which make a particular exchange relation distinctive are not visible in its enactment but must be traced through the longer-term dynamics of the social situation' (Appadurai, 1992: 9). Thus, a historical contextualisation is necessary in order to gain a political understanding of different forms of exchange, as well a more specific focus on the cultural forms of value. Exchange relations are always morally embedded.

However, Thomas also reminds us that we are all mutually entangled through international relations of production and appropriation which bind us together directly or indirectly in time and space. In this geo-political landscape, it is the movement of objects which most clearly make visible the features as well as the effects of such relations. He pursues his discussion of objects to include questions of disposal and, more importantly, what it is that makes an object inalienable. Such questions concern how things are differentiated and how that differentiation is reflected in exchange relations. The point is that certain objects have certain qualities which influence their exchangeability, and hence their availability. Hence, the focus should be directed towards grasping what these qualities are, what they mean and how they come about. In other words, we need to focus on the significance of the object in different contexts. What makes an object a subject of exchange, or, vice versa, what impedes an object from entering exchange relations? How do 'cultures ensure that some things remain unambiguously singular' (Kopytoff, 1986: 73)? In my understanding, a central characteristic of such unambiguously singular objects is that they have no equivalents or equivalence; they are objects which are restricted in their movements, even immobile. They are not commodified and resist commodification.

Although the qualitative distinction between gift and commodities lays the basis for much theorising about exchange, it is generally recognised that both forms of exchange exist simultaneously in all societies. Moroever, it is assumed that the same object may move between these two forms of exchange; and that the moment the object is put in motion it lives different lives, is transformed, and thereby serves to punctuate different relationships. In other words, many objects have some commodity-like characteristics. Human substances are no exception.

Nevertheless, in the case of biogenetic substances, it is the notion of gift that prevails to describe the transaction where transfer of such substances is involved (e.g. Ragoné, 1994; Sharp, 2000; see also Starr, 1999). Whether this usage is deliberate or not, the effect is to evoke images of altruism and obfuscate those aspects that are associated with commercialism, profit, money, bureaucracy, thereby making the act of relinquishing human substance – a part of oneself – uncontaminated and uncontaminating. Hence, the ethnography itself invites us to examine this flow in terms of exchange.

Much of the rhetoric surrounding the provision of various substances (blood, organs, semen, ova, surrogacy) is couched in terms of giving. This benevolent discourse provokes the culturally correct emotional reactions, in Norway, as elsewhere. In Norway people who provide these substances are called donors – blood donor, organ donor, semen donor, etc. (*'blodgiver'*, *'sædgiver'*, *'organdonor'*). In a discussion on organ transplants, Sharp states that this realm of medicine is 'rife with potent forms of mystified commodification' suggesting that the 'rhetoric of gift exchange disguises the origins of commercialized body parts, silencing in turn any discussion of the commodification process' (2000: 13). Both Sharp and Daniels (1998: 96ff., citing Fox and Swazey, 1992) refer to the effects of 'the tyranny of the gift' and Daniels, in his discussion of artificial insemination by donor, points out how the theory of 'gift dynamics' is highly relevant to the understanding of what he calls 'semen provision'. However, he cautions against the 'tyranny of the gift' which is prompted by siutations where the obligation to return cannot be met and indebtedness occurs. This applies particularily to modern medicine, he says, which has made possible 'gifts' which are inherently non-reciprocal. This situation was recognised by medical practitioners (in connection with the early organ transplants) and efforts were made to put in place procedures that anticipate and prevent the feelings of obligation tied to the return gift. With respect to donor insemination, Daniel argues that this was achieved by 'denying the existence of the gift in two ways: by making a gift not a gift, i.e. by paying for it and through the tight control of information, i.e. anonymity and secrecy' (Daniels, 1998: 97).

Daniels also discusses two models of providers: the commercial and the non-commercial. He in fact suggests that the commercial model (implying a commodification of semen) may be a better one for recruiting providers (granted that they are in need of money!) 'because payment may be seen to finalise the transaction and remove the idea that providers are owed anything further, such as information about outcomes, counselling or social recognition' (1998: 83). The interesting thing to note is that this model has not gained ground internationally. On the contrary, in many countries payment (for sperm) has been prohibited, and donors with altruistic motives are preferred.

There exists a market – a world market – for human substances. Much of the trafficking in such substances is illicit. In the Norwegian context, human substances are withheld from the logic of the market. It is considered unethical to traffic in such goods. Human substances are not – and should not be – freely available. Access to such substances is regulated by law, as are the rights to handle and mediate them. Only those publicly authorised are granted such permission.

IN PRACTICE

Notions of exchange or ideas about the gift are not articulated in the Norwegian law. However, the law is conducive in these regards. It regulates which exchanges can take place; it specifies who can benefit; it also both directly and indirectly specifies which relations are privileged. To name a few: heterosexual couples are privileged, as neither lesbian nor gay couples are even considered; men's infertility is in one sense privileged over women's – as donor sperm is permitted but not donor egg, and surrogacy is not permitted at all; social fatherhood is indirectly acknowledged (by the very fact that sperm donation is permitted), whereas social motherhood is not recognised at all;[17] publicly recognised clinics are privileged over those not recognised; national clinics are privileged over international ones (as, until recently, treatment at public clinics was free of charge); sperm is privileged over eggs in that the freezing of sperm is permitted whereas the freezing of oocytes is not (this may change if the suggested amendment to the law is passed). These tensions created in and through the law generate conflicts; but as long as the law is perceived as clear and unequivocal, these conflicts are not taken to court.

In other countries, with different legal traditions from Norway, cases involving rights to surrogate babies, embryos, frozen sperm have all been tried in court (see e.g. Dalton, 2000; Fox, 1997/1993; Simpson, 2001; Strathern, 1999). These cases have provided interesting food for thought, not least comparatively. However, in Norway even the question of who owns – or has the right to – a frozen embryo in case of divorce has yet to be tried, despite the fact that this area of the law is not all together clear. However, a person interviwed at the National Council on Biotechnology (Bioteknologi nemda) told us that 'according to Norwegian law the couple does not own the fertilised egg or frozen embryo. They [the couple] cannot take the egg somewhere else to be fertilsed nor can they take a fertilised egg in order to bury it.' In her understanding, the couple does not have the right of diposal over the embryo. Our further queries directed to a person working at the Ministry of Health revealed that there is no law directly regulating property relations in such cases 'but that there are regulations and limitations in the law' – for example, the three-year time limit on frozen embryos which would, according to the person spoken to, have consequences for decisions pertaining to moving the substance. The same person also said that with the introduction of payment for infertility treatment in public infertility clinics, the chances are that these types of issues will become more prevalent. Her argument was that the mere fact that couples now had to pay would influence their feelings of loyalty to the hospital or clinic. If the service is bad, they might want to take their egg and go somewhere else for treatment. In theory this could imply taking the egg to a clinic outside Norway. Thus, it seems that the introduction of money and fees for a public service is seen to possibly upset established practices, perhaps prompting new attitudes and hence new ways of doing things. Whatever the case, future discussions will surely centre around the status of the embryo (see Sirnes, 1987) and not just the issue of property relations and ownership.

DONOR SPERM – A FIRST APPROXIMATION

What is interesting in the Norwegian context are the differing views of ova and sperm. In some situations sperm and ova are considered as qualitatively different matters. This qualitative difference is expressed, for example, in the fact that Norway permits sperm donation but not egg donation. This implies that the availability of sperm and egg is different – not just physiologically or technically, but also socially and culturally.

Sperm donation is used for what is called artificial insemination by donor (AID). Strictly speaking, AID is not considered part of the new reproductive technologies; these technologies belong to IVF and associated treatments. However, AID is part of what we understand as assisted conception and is offered at infertility clinics. The sperm used may be given by a known donor or anonymously. Norwegian law states that only anonymous sperm may be used. Insemination by anonymous donor sperm – as a way of treating infertile couples – has been practised in Norway since the 1930s (Løvset, 1951). However, it was only in the 1970s that AID was incorporated systematically and offered as a treatment at one of the major infertility clinics (Molne, 1976, 1996). Artificial insemination is a relatively simple method and does not normally involve hormone stimulation of the woman.

Until 1995, sperm was obtained from Norwegian donors. Donors were mainly recruited among medical students, although there were also campaigns to recruit donors from the general public. Announcements were placed in university student newspapers, on campus, as well as at blood donor clinics, the assumption being that blood donors might also be willing to give sperm. However, with the spread of AIDS and other infectious diseases (hepatitis) the need to screen sperm was imperative. The procedures became much more cumbersome. The donor had to be tested; blood samples were needed; a quarantine period of six months for the sperm was necessary, which in turn implied freezing it (cryopreservation); new screening and testing of the donor and general quality of the sperm, before the sperm could be used. At this point, Norwegian clinical practitioners decided to import sperm from Denmark.

The decision to import sperm from Denmark is grounded in several arguments. One of the main arguments has to do with costs:

to run a sperm bank is a question of capacity; it is also expensive. The sperm bank in Denmark is well run, it is efficient and they do a good job, we were told. Moreover, health personnel in Norway report that it was (and still is) difficult to recruit reliable sperm donors in Norway and, with the new procedures, it was becoming even more complicated. They had trouble obtaining enough sperm; there was a lot of administrative work and the results were not satisfactory. With the transition to employing frozen sperm it was easier to get it from Denmark. They could guarantee good sperm, as one clinician put it.[18] One doctor suggested that the public debates which drew attention to the unethical aspects of being a sperm donor contributed towards the decline in suitable donors. Another stated that the debates about the possible rescinding of the anonymity of the donor resulted in a drastic decrease in the number of willing sperm donors.

Even though the arguments are mainly pragmatic, it remains a fact that there is a perception among some clinicians that Norwegian men are reluctant to donate sperm. In fact, one person stated (with no prompting on my part) that there were cultural differences between countries in this regard. France was held up as an example of a country where it is easy to recruit donors and, taking into account the success of the Danish sperm bank, it seems that Danish men also have less inhibitions on this score. However, Daniels (1998) in his discussion of the issue of cultural differences with respect to semen providers, as he prefers to call them, suggests that differences in the success of obtaining donor sperm are not related to culture, but rather reflect differences in recruitment, demand and policies of different clinics.[19] This view was echoed by one of the clinicians I talked to. She said that she was not so sure that the Danes are more donor-willing ('*har mer giverglede*') than Norwegians. It could just as well have to do with the fact that they have carried on longer, have in place better routines; that their system works.

The very practice of anonymity makes it extremely difficult to obtain information from sperm donors about their motivations, attitudes, etc. Underlying cultural ideas must be gleaned from other sources. In the Norwegian case, it seems that the practice of anonymity rests on particular notions of paternity, which have intrinsically been tied to paternal uncertainty as a fact of life. The possibility of DNA testing radically challenges this attitude, and Norwegian law-makers have seized the opportunity that determining paternity presents. The suggested amendments to the Children Act with respect to determining and establishing legal paternity will make it easier for a man who has reasonable grounds to believe that he is the biological father of the child unilaterally to have this determined by a DNA test; it will also make it possible for the legal father, if he doubts he is the biological father, to have his case tried, likewise the mother and the child.[20]

The proposed amendment is grounded in a desire to eradicate all doubt about paternity: 'Children must know the truth about who their parents are.... Doubts about paternity can cause unease and conflict in families', says Laila Dåvøy, Minister for Children and Families. Moreover, the amendments are based on an assumption:

that there is a general agreement [in Norwegian society] that knowledge of biological origin has enormous emotional significance for individual persons. ... Many feel that it is important for children to know their biological origins as early as possible.... The secure technological methods for determining paternity imply that an increasing number of people feel it should be an overriding goal that legal paternity be determined in concordance with biological paternity.

The suggested amendments effectively undermine the rule of *pater est*. If passed, these amendments articulate the biological bond as the meaningful parental bond, thereby subverting the notion of the heterosexual couple as the parental unit which encompasses the child. It will make paternity 'certain', although questions of fatherhood remain unresolved.

Whatever the reason, the fact that clinics in Norway do not make extensive use of Norwegian men's sperm works so as to make it less available and therefore less 'exchangeable'. The paradox is that this very practice serves to increase the exchangeability of the sperm of other (read foreign) men. Using Kopytoff's (1986) words, we could say that the sperm of Norwegian men can be classified as singular in at least one sense: it escapes circulation outside of very explicit and concrete relationships. Granting men the legal right to DNA testing in cases of contested paternity may express more than the desire for certainty; it may also reflect a notion that sperm should not go astray (be unaccounted for); it should rather confirm (or not) a specific relationship: the biological bonding between a man and his offspring.

Of all the different forms of assisted conception permitted in Norway, artificial insemination is the one that is simplest to perform and has (medically speaking) the least side effects.[21] Nevertheless, the *practice* of AID is the one surrounded by most silence. This silence is first and foremost a result of the principle of the anonymity of the donor. This *principle*, however, has been the subject of much discussion and controversy, not only in Norway but also elsewhere (see Daniels and Haimes, 1998; Haimes, 1998). Despite its limited application, AID continues to provoke heated discussions. The various positions about anonymity can be culled from official documents, many of which have been elaborated in preparation for the law and its amendments. These are in turn sent out at a hearing, and these hearings voice public opinion, along with media coverage. In addition there are the debates in Parliament which are referred to verbatim. Together, these sources give a cross-section of opinions on the question of anonymity as well as egg donation.

ANONYMOUS SPERM

In order to understand the complexity of the phenomenon of anonymous sperm donation, it is necessary to examine its composite elements: the sperm, the exchange and the anonymity. To start with the latter: anonymity implies that the recipient does not know who the donor is and the donor is ignorant of the recipient. In terms of a transaction this is very similar to a commodity exchange. Yet, as the term 'sperm donation' (in Norwegian '*sæd donasjon*') indicates, the sperm is presented as a gift and and the provider as a donor. In Norway, sperm was not bought from donors, although a nominal fee was given (NOK 250; but this was not defined as payment for sperm but rather to cover expenses).

An anonymous sperm donor, then, is a man who gives sperm to a clinic, doctor or sperm bank in order that it may be used to impregnate a woman who has a relationship with another man. Some might say that the donor 'covers' for another man by concealing his infertility and that the fundamental relationship in this exchange is between two men. The donor gives away something that is his and the gift carries, literally, something vital from the donor. The conditions for giving the sperm are neverthless such that they appear as a negation of the gift (see Daniels, 1998, who argues the same in a somewhat different vein). The terms are such that the donor is excluded from – in fact free from – any future obligations with respect to this gift, including the recipient's obligation of reciprocity. He (at least in theory) is to remain ignorant. These are the terms of the exchange. This is regulated by law, and the recipients receive the sperm on these conditions. The law works so as to create a maximum distance between donor and recipient and it is the anonymity that ensures this distance. One way to understand this is that, precisely because the sperm is to enter into a very special and concrete relation, and because it is to be used for a unique purpose, its origins must be denied; and therefore it must be untraceable. Otherwise confusion might arise. Anonymity ensures that any potential meaning (which information about the donor would imply) is avoided. Anonymity is a way of precluding excessive meaning, by containing information, as a secret. Secrecy not only hides meanings, it is also a way of getting rid of – even anticipating – unwanted images. Ignorance is bliss. The silence surrounding the phenomenon is in itself meaningful. It is – or at least has been – the whole point.[22]

The issue of rescinding the anonymity clause is rarely discussed in these terms, however, although the problem of recruitment is addressed. On the contrary, a totally new argument is introduced, where the reasoning is taken from another discursive sphere all together. The arguments are not so much based on the moral issue of secrecy and lies, which prevailed in the debates in the 1950s,[23] but are rather concerned with the child's right to know its biological origins (and not just its form of conception). The arguments put forth are parallel to the ones that have been used in the case of an adoptive child, and adoption is also used as a reason to repeal anonymity in the case of donor semen. The argument is that there should be no differential treatment of children; all children have the right to know their biological (genetic) origin, and reference is made to the United Nations Convention on the Rights of the Child (Article 7; ratified by Norway in 1991). However, this is stated without taking into account the differences between adoption and artificial insemination. These are very different ways of becoming – or being created as – someone's child.

It was in relation to the preparation of the law of 1987 that the public debates surfaced once again. Some of the arguments reiterated earlier views. Many Church representatives and Christian organisations have been – and are – against AID on the grounds that it undermines the institution of marriage. One typical comment is that of the Bishop of South-Hålogaland. He says:

This bishop must as a matter of principle reject donor insemination AID, because it breaks fundamentally with the aspect of 'one body' which is fundamental for the biblical view on marriage.... A literally 'foreign body' will 'break into' that which should be whole and inseparable. (Ot.prp. nr. 25, 1986–87, p. 15; my translation)

In the same vein, the Norwegian Lutheran School of Theology (Menighetsfakultetet) stresses that AID brings a third party into marriage as a participant in the creation of the child. 'The child will thus have two fathers, one social and legal father and one biological.' According to them, this problem has not been given its due weight. They also insist that 'based on Christian ethics it would be natural to stress the marriage relation between man and woman as both the social and biological framework for reproduction and upbringing' (Ot.prp. nr. 25, 1986–87, p. 15).

However, there were also voices in the Church which based their arguments on human rights. As the Bishop of Møre says:

I agree with the ... committee that proposes to repeal the principle of anonymity on the basis that it is a human right to know how one has been conceived, and that it is important for people to know their roots. Here the parallels to adoption are clear. (Ot.prp. nr. 25, 1986–87, p. 32).

The Norwegian Christian Doctors Association states: 'In our opinion ... it should be considered a human right to be able to obtain knowledge of one's own biological origin' (Ot.prp. nr. 25, 1986–87, p. 32). These human rights arguments are voiced by many others and represent the major reason for repealing the principle of anonymity (see, e.g., Tranøy, 1989, for a discussion of reproductive technologies and rights). The appeal of this argument was confirmed in many of our interviews with politicians, so much so that even those who had earlier voted for anonymity said that they would vote otherwise today. In fact, when asked whether they had changed their opinions on any major issue, the principle of anonymity was the one that would be named.

Those who still defend anonymity will stress either the significance of social paternity or the fact that known donors will be hard to recruit. Thus, the Chief Adminstrative Officer (Fylkesmannen) of Troms, arguing for anonymity, says:

it cannot be said that our legislation has as a major goal to assess biological paternity. This is reflected in the rule of *pater est*.... It would be more correct to say that our regulations seek to ensure that the child has a legal father, and in that light an insemination child would not be any worse off. (Ot.prp. nr. 25, 1986–87, p. 33)

Kjell Bohlin argued the following in Parliament:

It is strange that so many seem to place more ... weight on the biological relationship to a person who for the child is a stranger than the close relationship of a secure social father. Feelings of paternity do not come with an ejaculation. It is the warm, close relation between father and child living together which creates the bond that binds.[24]

These arguments resemble those put forth in the 1950s.

There appears to be a marked shift in the grounding of the arguments. The reasoning (now so prevalent) is based on an assumption that origins – who you are – are the same as biogenetic origin. Hence, biogenetic origins are automatically given precedence over sociocultural ones, denying (in the context of these arguments) the significance of sociocultural factors in identity construction. A person's genetic origin is perceived as equal to his or her identity, who he or she *is*. To deny a person this knowledge is to deny her herself. The strongest advocates of this position will claim that this knowledge is fundamental; equivalent to a basic human right, it is unjust to not allow this information to flow freely. In this way, the substance sperm is attributed a quality: it not only creates identity, it is synonymous with it. (This position takes for granted that the ova come from a known woman.)

Granted that sperm is attributed such a singular trait, it may imply that its circulation is hampered, either through the fact that fewer men are willing to give sperm or that fewer couples are willing to receive donor sperm under these conditions (where the anonymity is repealed). The introduction of named donor sperm in such transactions changes the nature of the relationships of the involved parties; in fact it creates relations hitherto unacknowledged. The silent yet tacit understanding of ignorance contained in anonymity is transformed: it becomes explicit and available. The involved people know of each other, and this creates a connection, a form of relatedness. Whether this knowledge necessarily implies getting to know each other is another question. Nevertheless, the relations can be potentially activated. In one sense, the sphere of relationships is more open – as more information flows within it; in another sense, it is more closed, in that the distance between donor and recipients is wiped out. The named sperm creates a different circuit in so far as the relationships it moves between become mutually visible. Not least, the donor child becomes visible in a different way and becomes, perhaps, a different child.

THE SINGULAR EGG

The situation with respect to egg donation is different. Despite the fact that the new reproductive technologies also make eggs available, in the Norwegian context eggs cannot be made to move between women. Egg donation is – and will probably continue to be – prohibited. Fertilised eggs must be returned to the woman from whom they were taken. In other words, an egg can only move in and out of the same body. It is also forbidden to combine IVF with donor sperm. This is indeed a closed circuit. Those who are in need of either of these treatments must travel abroad. It is not possible to know how many couples seek this kind of treatment in other countries. However, the couples I have talked to indicate that, if necessary, this is a viable option. There does not seem to be more resistance to accepting a donor egg than there is to accepting donor sperm. In fact, there are some arguments which may indicate that the resistance is less.[25] However, the priority is given to having a baby which stems, genetically, from both of them. Yet, if this is not possible, the desire to have a child of one's own (*'et eget barn'*), in whatever form that may take, overrides any biogenetic consideration. Adoption is then considered as a possible option.

One of the interesting aspects with respect to the law is why egg and sperm are not classified as the same type of substance. Why are eggs withheld, so to speak, while sperm can be made to move? That sperm in many contexts is considered a life-giving substance and ritually transferred between men has been documented (e.g. Herdt, 1984). Little is known about the cultural meanings attributed to sperm in Norway (with respect to masculinity, sexuality, etc.) excepting its quality as being constitutive of identity. What we do know is that sperm, in contrast to eggs, is a renewable substance. It is also (and again in contrast to eggs) easily available, it is visible and it is abundant. In many respects, sperm is like blood, which is also considered a vital substance (but see Daniels, 1998, who argues the opposite). Eggs, on the other hand, are limited; they are not renewable; on the contrary, their quality diminishes with the woman's age. They are (for most of us) invisible; and they are (at least in Norway) non-obtainable. Egg and sperm, then, have some characteristics which make them qualitatively different. However, the question is whether it is these qualities that guide their availability for exchange? Or, is the case rather that each substance is embedded in separate chains of meaning (for example, differing attitudes to maternity and paternity) and it is these chains of meaning which determine their varying signifcance, and hence value?

The arguments go both ways. One example, which I cite at length because it echoes and condenses views held more generally, is that put forward by the Ministry of Health in its proposition to Parliament:

There are those who argue that egg donation is in principle not different from sperm donation.... This is a view the Ministry rejects. Women's and men's reproductive functions are different – seen both from the donor's and the recipient's point of view.

The Ministry concurs with the working group's proposal that:

In contrast to sperm donation egg donation requires medical surgery.... Donation of egg has more similarities with transplantation than it has with sperm donation.... In contrast to sperm donation, egg donation does not create a situation different from natural reproduction. Donor insemination does not break fundamentally with what occurs in natural reproduction. Whether conception occurs artificially or naturally, the sperm is something which comes from the outside. This implies that there will always be some uncertainty as to who is the father of the child. With natural conception it is not unusual that there is a discrepancy between legal/social paternity and biological paternity.... With natural reproduction the uterus and the egg constitute a natural unity. Conception, pregnancy and birth is a unified ['*helhetlig*'] process which occurs within the woman. With egg donation this unity is broken ... with egg donation physical motherhood is split ... there is reason to believe that this lack of clarity will cause insecurity with regard to the identity of the child ... (Ot.prp. nr 25, 1986–87, p. 19).

A well known politician, Grete Knudsen, following this train of thought, says:

That women give birth has been so taken for granted that in Norway there are no rules of law for who is the child's mother. Conception, pregnancy, birth have been a unified process. It is not that simple any more. And this separation – that conception occurs outside the body – *implies that mother becomes more like father*. Until now we have considered mother and the unborn child as one. This has also been decisive for the right to self-determination in the question of abortion. (my emphasis)[26]

In a later debate, the following is stated: 'With regard to the order of nature, egg donation is a significantly larger interference than sperm donation. Egg donation would be a breach of the inviolability and unity of pregnancy.' And: 'We do not know the consequences of introducing a notion of "the strange/unknown mother" [*"fremmed mor"*]. The feeling of belonging to mother [*"morstilhørighet"*] is the most fundamental of human [emotions].' Or in the words of a female Labour Party politician:

It is wrong that the mother of a child should be unknown. The belonging to mother [*'morstilhørigheten'*] is inviolable. For me this is not a question of gender equality, but respect for the order of nature. To permit sperm donation is less problematical than egg donation, first and foremost because sperm is easily available and cannot be regulated by law [sic] so that we can hinder a child from having an unknown father.[27]

As is evident, the mother is given a unique status with respect to reproduction and this status determines what is right with respect to egg donation. Recognising the implication of the technology, Knudsen acknowledges that mother becomes more like father. Eggs, like sperm, are now available 'outside' (of the body) and this shared quality has significant implications: maternity and paternity may become equally uncertain. This shared quality feeds into another one: their equal contribution to create life. In this sense, ova and sperm are the same; they have equal value. It is this biogenetic sameness – in terms of equal function – that medical personnel and the involuntary childless themselves choose to stress when arguing for the permission of egg donation. They will say that it is illogical to permit the donation of sperm and not eggs. Others have gone so far as to say that the law as practised today (permitting the freezing of sperm but not of oocytes) is discriminatory, and appeal to laws of gender equality. If the suggested amendments to the law are followed, it will imply that sperm and egg are treated the same on this count.

EQUAL – BUT NOT THE SAME?

It could be (and is) argued that it is precisely this quality (equal contribution to create life) that is the most essential one and therefore represents an adequate denominator in order to create a form of equivalence between ova and sperm (which would in turn result in equal practice). As of yet, this same essence is clearly not enough – or at least not *good* enough. Hence, the question still remains: what is it that makes ova inalienable, and as a consequence not available for circulation? Why do eggs not have the same degree of exchange-ability as sperm? What makes an ovum singular, but in a manner different from sperm?

Such questions point beyond circulation as such and have to do with fundamental issues such as gender and meanings of masculinity, femininity, fatherhood and motherhood. The questions also point more generally to the specific traits pertaining to those groups of objects that must remain separate and apart; those objects that are withheld from any form of exchange. These are objects that in some way are perceived as invaluable. They are priceless and by definition non-commodities, and their potential commodification must not be realised as this would represent a fundamental moral breach. Such things are either so trivial that there is no point (or even possibility) of putting a price on them (air has that quality, as does sand and mud) or they are so unique that they are inestimable. It seems that in a Norwegian context, ova and sperm fall into this category, but in different ways.

The Norwegian state, through its policy-making, ensures that some things remain 'unambiguously singular'. Eggs are withheld from any form of exchange; they 'belong' where they come from. There is an inner connection between a woman and her ova which is (still perceived as) qualitatively different from the connectedness between a man and his sperm. These appear as different forms of relatedness. There is no room for doubt about who is the mother of the child. In contrast, fatherhood has been constructed upon the possibility of doubt (*pater est*). However, the tendency (in law) is to contribute toward the construction of certainties. Biogenetics serve such a purpose well. The law works so as to create certain (in both senses of the word) relations which appear to be the same in one crucial aspect: the biological linking between mother and child and between father and child (irrespective of the relation between mother and father). So even though men and women are different, maternity and paternity need not be. The focus is by law on the child; the law determines the child's identity by determining the child's right to know who she is. This move rests on the premise that biogenetic origin is fundamentally clarifying.

Even so, these efforts are almost at cross-purposes with the group of people (the involuntary childless and the medical practitioners) towards whom the laws are directed. The laws are made on their behalf (but not in the sense that the law is *for* them). Those in need of such treatment are recognised, but not accommodated. What they want is a child they can call their own; preferably of their own genes, but not necessarily. Therefore they also want a choice: it should be left for them to decide the potential genetic mix of their child. If their choice falls outside the law, their option is to travel abroad.

EVERY BLOCKAGE CREATES A FLOW

There is no doubt that state policies impinge on people's lives and the choices they are allowed to make with respect to procreation. Through its policies and legislation, the state is instrumental in creating relations and new forms of relatedness. The Norwegian laws regulating infertility treatment (and biomedicine more generally, including research) appear as a concerted effort to make both objects and relations concrete and particular, even certain. These government policies imply a (re)classification of objects (human substances, rights to treatment, rights to DNA testing, etc.), in an attempt to regulate what is to be made publicly available.

However, these efforts at containment are not successful. In practice, the involuntary childless circumvent the law. Those who need an egg pay no heed to a perception of an ovum as unambiguously singular, or motherhood as an inviolable unity. They travel abroad and obtain the substances they need, paying for these treatments themselves. They will set themselves in motion and make themselves available for an exchange, trangressing certain limits that others have tried to impose. It is a matter of money and contacts. Norwegian doctors collaborate with clinics abroad, sending their patients to neighbouring countries for treatment. Moreover, medical doctors who need updating on research or practices not permitted in Norway will travel to a clinic abroad to train there.

One way of phrasing this is to say that there is a resistance (in the sense of restriction) in the law which is met by a resistance (in the sense of being against) by particular groups of people. It is precisely at this interface that a power struggle (and a paradox) is disclosed – between the state and its welfare policies and particular groups of people and their will. One issue which is at stake is the difference between sperm and egg and who defines it (the difference, that is). The question of definitional power in this context has also to do with what infertility is (i.e. the classification of infertility – as an illness or fate); who has the right to treatment; and, significantly, what treatments are to be offered (both in kind and in number) under which conditions. The recent move by Parliament to demand payment for infertility treatment at public clinics is a decision that has provoked many, not least the involuntarily childless themselves.

There is no doubt that entering money into the equation will affect the choices people make. More people may choose to travel abroad to be treated; more people may choose to adopt. Either way, various substances will be crossing borders, and these substances cannot be stopped. In contrast to illicit flows across borders (such as alcohol, arms, illegal immigrants) a pregnancy cannot be arrested any more than a person's acquired knowledge. This is the crux of the matter. Norway is a small country in a large cultural area. This geo-political position may be ideal for exporting its ethical dilemmas, while letting the implications (literally) pass. Seen from this perspective, it could be argued that the permeability of borders is a precondition for the restrictions made. The law is relative and other countries make a profit on Norwegian reticence.

Different states avail themselves of global technologies and knowledge in different ways. The legislative process is one way that the state can incorporate such knowledge systems. I have suggested that acts of legislation can be fruitfully viewed as a localising strategy, reflecting not only a global/local interface, but also disclosing the ambiguous nature of borders, be they moral or territorial. An examination of the law that regulates infertility treatment is revealing in many ways. Most significantly, it illustrates the efforts and value placed on maintaining what is perceived as a high moral ground (re precautionary principle). It also discloses a perceived social need for certainty, for unambiguousness. The restrictions in the law are not only grounded in perceptions of specific essences, but are themselves conducive to producing a certain essentialism. This is done by limiting the circulation of ova and sperm, reducing their commodity-like attributes, in an attempt to retain their singularity, their exclusiveness. They are constructed as crucial identity markers, and as such relegated to the realm of the unique. The law and the processes that have led to its formulation articulate values in Norwegian society that go beyond the questions of infertility treatment, permitting an expression of moral values and ethical reflections. Thus, infertility treatments represent a potent vehicle for sounding significant cultural meanings.

NOTES

1. This chapter is based on a collaborative research project 'The transnational flow of concepts and substances' funded by the Norwegian Research Council (NFR). I wish to thank Thomas Hylland Eriksen, Christian Krohn-Hansen, Signe Howell, Sarah Lund and James Scott for incisive comments on a first version of this chapter. The project represents a continuation of another NFR-funded project 'The meanings of kinship in Norway and beyond' carried out in conjunction with Signe Howell. It is based on interviews with Norwegian politicians, medical

and clinical personnel and bureaucrats as well as fieldwork and interviews among the involuntary childless. Many of the interviews have been carried out together with research assistant Kari Anne Ulfnes; most of the interviews with the medical doctors she carried out alone. She was also responsible for collecting and systematising the extensive documentation. Her careful work and continued assistance on the projects has been an invaluable contribution.

2. Act No. 56 of 5 August 1994. The act relating to the application of biotechnology in medicine.

3. For example, Acts relating to marriage, to children, to personal names, to inheritance, to termination of pregnancy, etc. Such an exercise, however, is beyond the scope of this chapter. See Halvorsen (1988), Aasen (1998), Michaelsen (2001).

4. See Sirnes (1987) and his discussion about the status of the embryo, also Mulkay (1997); see also the Warnock Committee (1985), Rivière (1985), Shore (1992), Strathern (1992), Malhuus (1992).

5. Blood and sperm have been objects of transfer for a much longer time; see Starr (1991) on the history of blood transfusions.

6. Even this particular phrasing belies the processes that may occur – as 'parts' may be subtracted and added at early stages of human development, before what we perceive as bodies are present.

7. The Act was passed on the basis of a bill relating to the application of biotechnology in medicine presented to the Storting (Norwegian parliament) in 1994. The bill was based on Report No. 25 (1992–93) to the Storting entitled 'Biotechnology related to human beings'.

8. See *Innstilling fra Inseminasjonslovkomitéen* (1953). The committee was split in its recommendation, three to two; the majority recommended legislation on artificial insemination by donor (AID), the minority was against and each submitted his or her own dissent. At that time no other country had passed legislation on AID.

9. *Pater est quem nuptiae demonstrant.* Marriage indicates whom the father is.

10. The White Paper (presented while this chapter was being written) is an evaluation of the Act relating to the application of biotechnology in medicine. See Stortingsmelding nr. 14 (2001–02) *Evaluering av lov om medisinsk bruk av bioteknologi.*

11. This was also the immediate reaction of the head of the infertility clinic at Rikshospitalet, Thomas Åbyholm, when interviewed regarding the proposed changes to the law (*Dagsnytt 1800* (radio programme) 22 March 2002); the comparison to Sweden was also made. In 1986 Sweden passed a law which gives a 'donor-child' the right to know its biological origins at the age of 18. However, the parents are not obliged to tell the child about the way it has been conceived. It is said that Sweden has difficulties recruiting the right donors and that Swedish couples in need of sperm prefer to travel to Denmark, where donor sperm is still anonymous.

12. ICSI – intracytoplasmic sperm injections – is a method that has been developed to help men with poor sperm quality. The method consists of selecting one sperm cell and injecting it into the egg. Although this method is permitted in Norway, it has been contested on the grounds that it subverts the natural competition (and hence selection) between sperm cells with respect to fertilisation.

13. The sperm bank used is Cryos International Sperm Bank Ltd. See http://www.cryos.dk. for further information, price lists, delivery, etc. The reasons for this practice will be elaborated below.

14. The reasons given for the need to legislate in 1987 were the fear of selective human breeding and commercialisation. There was a wish to be ahead of developments and thereby to curb potential abuse. The application of the precautionary principle in Norway is summed up in a much-quoted expression '*Bedre føre var enn etter snar*', which translates as 'Better safe than sorry'.

15. The case is not all that clear-cut; there are important nuances. Representatives of the Labour Party, in particular, have a much more optimistic view with respect to the development of science and its significance for social development. This attitude finds an echo also on the right. One of the most interesting aspects with respect to this issue is that positions cut across all traditional party lines. Granted the ethical nature of the decsions to be made, all parties let their Members of Parliament vote according to their conscience. For further discussion on ethics in Norwegian Parliamentary debates on these issues, see Brekke (1995).

16. One argument is that Norwegian knowledge – and hence practice – is parasitical on research and experiments done elsewhere. In other words, Norwegians are happy to apply what has already been tried somewhere else, but not willing to contribute to this research.

17. I am here confining myself to what the law on biomedicine articulates. It is important to note that these provisions are completely overturned by the adoption law, where obviously social fatherhood and motherhood are recognised. See Howell (2001, 2002; Chapter 11 in this volume).

18. Sperm donor and recipient are matched for eye colour, hair colour and height; there is also a category 'ethnic sperm' for those of different physical appearance than ethnic Norwegians. The same donor is not used for more than ten inseminations.

19. This has to do with the age group recruited from, their marital status, the significance of payment, etc.

20. See press release nr. 02005 of 11 February 2002 from the Ministry for Children and Families. The quotations in the next paragraph are also from this press release.

21. It has been extremely hard to obtain accurate figures, both with respect to IVF and AID. According to Dag Inge Våge at the Health Authority (Helsetilsynet), in 1998, 314 couples were treated, resulting in 99 births. See Haimes (1998) for an interesting discussion about why numbers matter.

22. See Strathern (1999: 77ff.) for an interesting discussion about the value of secrecy vs the value of a child's right to know; about the practices in different countries with respect to donor insemination and what information is made available. See also Daniels (1998), Edwards (1998), Haimes (1998).

23. See Sandemose (1952), Rønne-Pettersen (1951), *Innstilling fra Inseminasjonslorkomitéen* (1953).

24. From the debates in Parliament: O.tidene 25.5 Sak nr. 2: Innstilling fra sosial komiteen om lov om kunstig befruktnning (Innst. O. nr 60) *Stortingsforhandlinger sesjon* 1986–87, pp. 308–45.

25. There are several reasons for this, which partially have to do with notions of 'fairness' ('*rettferdighet*') and participation. For example, if the sperm

belongs to the husband/male partner and the egg is foreign, they are nevertheless equally 'present' in so far as it is the wife/female partner that carries the baby. Thus, taken together the child becomes equally theirs.

26. The debate in Parliament on biotechnology, 1989. *Stortingsforhandlinger sesjon* 1988–89 nr. 41, p. 4004.

27. These quotes are taken from Parliamentary debates and stated by Magnar Sortåsløkken (Socialist Left Party), Ole Johs. Brunæs (the Right Party), and Kirsti Kolle Grøndahl (Labour Party) respectively. See Stortingstidende 10.6.1993: Sak 1. *Stortingsforhandlinger sesjon* 1992–93, pp. 4346–87. All translations are mine.

REFERENCES

Aasen, H.S. 1998. Da mor var mor og far var far: Noen betraktninger om forplantningsteknologi, verdivalg og jus. In *Stat, Politikk of Folkestyre: Festskrift til Per Stavang på 70 årsdagen*. Bergen: Alma Mater.

Appadurai, A. 1992. Introduction: commodities and the politics of value. In A. Appadurai (ed.) *The Social Life of Things: Commodities in Cultural Perspective*. Cambridge: Cambridge University Press.

Brekke, O.A. 1995. *Differensiering og integrasjon: Debatten om bioteknologi og etikk i Norge*. Report nr. 9509. Bergen: LOS Senter.

Carrier, J. 1996. Exchange. In A. Barnard and J. Spencer (eds) *Encyclopedia of Social and Cultural Anthropology*. London: Routledge.

Dalton, S. 2000. Nonbiological mothers and the legal boundaries of motherhood: an analysis of California law. In H. Ragoné and F.W. Twine (eds) *Ideologies and Technologies of Motherhood: Race, Class, Sexuality, Nationalism*. New York: Routledge.

Daniels, K. 1998. The semen providers. In K. Daniels and E. Haimes (eds) *Donor Insemination: International Social Science Perspectives*. Cambridge: Cambridge University Press.

Daniels, K. and E. Haimes (eds). 1998. *Donor Insemination: International Social Science Perspectives*. Cambridge: Cambridge University Press.

Edwards, J. 1998. Donor insemination and 'public opinion'. In K. Daniels and E. Haimes (eds) *Donor Insemination: International Social Science Perspectives*. Cambridge: Cambridge University Press.

Edwards, J., S. Franklin, E. Hirsch, F. Price and M. Strathern (eds). 1993. *Technologies of Procreation: Kinship in the Age of Assisted Conception*. Manchester: Manchester University Press.

Fox, R. 1997/1993. *Reproduction and Succession: Studies in Anthropology, Law, and Society*. New Brunswick, NJ: Transaction Publishers.

Franklin, S. 1997. *Embodied Progress: A Cultural Account of Assisted Conception*. London: Routledge.

Haimes, E. 1998. The making of 'the DI child': changing representations of people conceived through donor insemination. In K. Daniels and E. Haimes (eds) *Donor Insemination: International Social Science Perspectives*. Cambridge: Cambridge University Press.

Halvorsen, M. 1998. The act relating to the application of biotechnology in medicine with particular regard to questions in family law. In A. Bainham (ed.) *The International Survey of Family Law*, 1966, pp. 323–3. The Netherlands.

Harris, O. 1996. 'Introduction: inside and outside the law. In O. Harris (ed.) *Inside and Outside the Law: Anthropological Studies of Authority and Ambiguity.* London: Routledge.

Hazekamp, J.Th. and L. Hamberger. 1999. The Nordic experience. In P. Brindsen (ed.) *A Textbook of In Vitro Fertilization and Assisted Reproduction: The Bourn Hall Guide to Clinical and Laboratory Practice.* New York: Parthenon Publishing Group.

Herdt, G.H. (ed.). 1984. *Ritualized Homosexuality in Melanesia.* Berkeley: University of California Press.

Howell, S. 2001. Self-conscious kinship: some contested values in Norwegian transnational adoption. In S. Franklin and S. McKinnon (eds) *Relative Values: Reconfiguring Kinship Studies.* Durham, NC: Duke University Press.

—— 2002. Community beyond place: adoptive families in Norway. In V. Amit (ed.) *Realizing Community: Concepts, Social Relationships and Sentiments.* London: Routledge.

Humphreys, S. 1985. Law as discourse, *History and Anthropology* 1(2): 241–64.

Kopytoff, I. 1986. The cultural biography of things: commoditization as process. In A. Appadurai (ed.) *The Social Life of Things: Commodities in Cultural Perspective,* pp. 64–94. Cambridge: Cambridge University Press.

Lundin, S. 1997. *Guldägget: Foreldreskap i biomedicinens tid.* Lund: Historiska Media.

Løvset, Jørgen. 1951. Artificial insemination: the attitude of patients in Norway, *Fertility and Sterility* 2(5): 414–29.

Melhuus, M. 1992. Comment on Cris Shore's 'Virgin births and sterile debates: anthropology and the new reproductive technologies', *Current Anthropology* 33(3): 295–314.

Melhuus, M. 2000. Kultur, bytte og makt: sæd og egg – på norsk, *Norsk Antropologisk Tidsskrift* 11: 161–81.

—— 2001. Kan skinnet bedra? Noen meninger om assistert befruktning. In S. Howell and M. Melhuus (eds) *Blod – tykkere enn vann? Betydninger av slektskap i Norge.* Bergen: Fagbokforlaget.

Michaelsen, D. 2001. Internasjonaliseringens historie i norsk rett, *Lov og Rett. Norsk Juridisk Tidsskrift* 40(8): 451–73.

Molne, K. 1976. Donorinseminasjon: en oversikt og et materiale, *Tidsskrift for Den Norske Lægeforening* 17–18: 982–6.

—— 1996. Slekters gang: moderne infertilitetsbehandling. In P. Børdahl (ed.) *Midt i livet: Festskrift til Norsk gynekologisk forening 1946–1996.* Trondheim: Tapir.

Mulkay, M. 1997. *The Embryo Research Debate. Science and the Politics of Reproduction.* Cambridge: Cambridge University Press.

Ragoné, H. 1994. *Surrogate Motherhood: Conception in the Heart.* Boulder, CO: Westview Press.

Rivière, P. 1985. Unscrambling parenthood. The Warnock Report, *Anthropology Today* 1(4): 2–7.

Rønne-Pettersen, E. 1951. *Provrörsmänniskan: En studie i moderne magi.* Stockholm: Bokförlaget biopsykologi.

Sandemose, A. 1952. Unnfanget i løgn, *Årstidene* 2.

Sharp, L.A. 2000. The commodification of the body and its parts, *Annual Review of Anthropology* 29: 287–328 (http://anthro.annualreviews.org/cgi/content/full/29/1/287)

Shore, C. 1992. Virgin births and sterile debates: anthropology and the new reproductive technologies, *Current Anthropology* 33(3): 295–314.

Simpson, B. 2001. Making 'bad' deaths 'good': the kinship consequences of posthumous conception, *Journal of the Royal Anthropological Institute* 7(1): 1–18.

Sirnes, T. 1987. *Risiko og mening: mentale brot og meiningsdimensjonar i industri og politikk.* Rapport nr. 55. University of Bergen: Institutt for administrasjon og organisasjonsvitenskap.

Starr, D. 1999. *Blood: An Epic History of Medicine and Commerce.* New York: Alfred A. Knopf.

Strathern, M. 1992. *Reproducing the Future: Anthropology, Kinship and the New Reproductive Technologies.* Manchester: Manchester University Press.

—— 1999. *Property, Substance, Effect: Anthropological Essays on Persons and Things.* London: Athlone.

Thomas, N. 1991. *Entangled Objects: Exchange, Material Culture, and Colonialism in the Pacific.* Cambridge, MA: Harvard University Press.

Warnock Committee. 1985. *A Question of Life: The Warnock Report on Human Fertilisation and Embryology.* Oxford: Blackwell.

Public Documents

Innstilling fra inseminasjonslovkomitéen, March 1953.

Ot.prp. (Odelstingsproposisjon) nr 25. 1986–87. *Om lov om kunstig befrukntning.*

Innstilling O. nr 60, 1986–87. *Innstilling fra sosialkomitéen om lov om kunstig befruknting.* (Ot.prp. nr 25)

Ot.prp. nr 37, 1993–94. *Om lov om medisinsk bruk av bioteknologi.*

Innst. O. nr 67, 1993–94. *Innstilling fra sosialkomitéen om lov om medisinsk bruk av bioteknologi.* (Ot.prp. nr 37)

Innst. S. nr 214, 1992–93. *Innstilling fra sosialkomitéen om mennesker og bioteknologi.* (St.meld. nr 25) (English version: *Biotechnology related to Human Beings,* Report No. 25, 1992–93, to Parliament, submitted by the Ministry of Health and Social Affairs).

O.tidene 25.5.1987: Sak nr 2. Innstilling fra sosialkomitéen om lov om kusntig befruktning (Innst. O. nr. 60) *Stortingsforhandlinger sesjon* 1986–87, ss 308–45.

L. tidene 29.5.1987: Sak nr 10. Odelstingets vedtak til lov om kusntig befruktning (Besl. O. nr 61). *Stortingsforhandlinger sesjon* 1986–87, pp. 48–73.

S.tidene 23.5.1989: Sak nr 1. Statsminsiteren redegjør i Stortinget for regjernings arbied med bioteknologi/genteknologi. *Stortingsforhandlinger sesjon* 1988–89, pp. 3696–703.

S.tidene 2.6.1989: Sak nr 1: Statsmininsterens redegjørelse for Stortingets møte 23. mai om gen-/bioteknologi. Debatt i stortinget. *Stortingsforhandlinger sesjon* 1988–89, pp. 3987–4023.

S.tidene 10.6.1993: Sak nr 1. Instilling fra sosialkomitéen om mennesker og bioteknologi (Innst. S nr. 214). *Stortingsforhandlinger sesjon* 1992–92, pp. 4346–87.

O.tidene 13.6.1994: Sak nr 1. Innstilling fra sosialkomitéen om lov om medisinsk bruk av bioteknologi (Innst. O. nr 67). *Stortingsforhandlinger sesjon* 1993–94, pp. 513–70.

St.meld. nr 14, 2001–02. *Evaluering av lov om medisinsk bruk av bioteknologi* (electronic edition).

Høringsbrev 2002. Forslag til endringer i barneloven om fastsettelse og endring av farskap (electronic version). Barne og familiedepartementet.

11 THE DIFFUSION OF MORAL VALUES IN A GLOBAL PERSPECTIVE

Signe Howell

Ethics are in the spotlight just now. Since September 11, politicians have taken to discoursing on the 'evil' and 'wickedness' that threaten us. But what the twin-towers tragedy brought home was something still more alarming – the stark relativism of moral viewpoints. An act that seemed almost unthinkably cruel and vile was evidently, for other human beings, an occasion for laughter and celebration. (From a book review by John Carey, *Sunday Times*, 6 January 2002, of *A Short Treatise on the Great Virtues: The Uses of Philosophy in Everyday Life* by André Comte-Sponville)

This chapter is not a defence or attack on cultural or moral relativism. That debate as it has been conducted in social anthropology has reached an impasse (see Cowan et al., 2001). My aim, however, is to examine some effects upon moral discourses in non-Western parts of the world that result from the Western Christian intellectual tradition that disregards cultural differences and imagines the world and humanity as one.[1] Bearing in mind the above quotation, I wish in this chapter to adopt a rather specific usage of the term 'globalisation' which I shall use to mean the normative goal that seeks to impose one moral universe. Viewed in this perspective, globalisation gives rise to discourses that ultimately ignore sociocultural differences and presuppose, at a macro-level, a single moral universe. Integral to such perception is the epistemological and moral centrality of the bounded autonomous individual as a reference point and dominant value. As Dumont has pointed out, the flip side of such an analytic centrality of the individual is the universal (1979: 729). Regardless of social and cultural origins and belongings, human beings are viewed as manifestations of universal man. A side-effect of such a presupposition is that culture almost invariably becomes reified and epiphenomenal. In my usage of globalisation, the fact that encounters between individuals or groups from different parts of the world have wide-reaching effects is not in itself sufficient to characterise them as manifestations of globalisation unless there is some form of intentionality on the part of the outsider. This intentionality, moreover, must be implicitly or explicitly normative, be this within economic and industrial spheres (transnational companies taking over local ones and reorganising them according to a liberal market economy); or political spheres (democratic institutions taking over other forms of political organisation); or religious and moral spheres (Christianity and human rights taking over other cosmologies and moralities). This means in effect that people are exposed to political, economic and cultural values and cultural processes which emanate from a few centres, whether institutions or companies, which correspondingly exercise, or seek to exercise, global dominance.

In order to explore some of these ideas, a focus will be placed on international treaties concerning children and childhood, such as the UN Convention on the Rights of the Child (1989) and the Hague Convention on Protection of Children and Co-operation in Respect of Intercountry Adoption (1993). These will be examined from the empirical perspective of the ever-growing fact of transnational adoption, whereby children from the poor South (and Eastern Europe) are adopted by parents from the rich North. Questions will be raised concerning the moral dilemmas that those concerned with transnational adoptions are facing, and the various attempted solutions that are placed within a legal framework.[2] Underlying the discussion will be a concern with the choice of methodologies that anthropologists can usefully employ.

COLONIALISM AND GLOBALISATION

Underlying my exposition will be an argument that compares and contrasts old-style colonialism with new-style globalisation that runs something like this. Colonialism was driven by the hope of economic gains. Political suzerainty over vast non-European areas was sought in order to safeguard economic expansion, and was a means to ensure the continued national interests of the European colonial nations. Accompanying the colonial expansion, and to some extent legitimising it, were the missionary efforts on behalf of the Christian churches. It was generally accepted that the various 'primitive' peoples of Asia, Africa, South America and the Pacific islands, in various ways, needed to receive the Christian message in order to 'advance' and put behind them superstitions, and a- and immoral behaviour. From such a perspective, colonialism thus took on the flavour of a moral crusade, and 'the white man's burden' (Cecil Rhodes) was to civilise the natives.[3] There is little doubt about the far-reaching and profound effects on indigenous ideas and practices in the previously non-Christian social worlds of Africa, the Americas, Oceania and parts of Asia. Even those areas where old religions have withstood the pressure of Christianity, like India, China, Japan and the Muslim world, ideas about democracy and the inalienable rights of the individual, whose roots can be traced to Christianity, are strongly felt today – even when not adhered to.

Globalisation is probably a much more complex process than that of colonialism and I do not agree with those who argue that it is nothing but old wine in new bottles. However, we can also observe here a mixture of economic, political and moral consequences – though the goals are less specific. This chapter will examine the growth of human rights that, I shall argue, have replaced the Christian proselytising message and zeal as part of a general Western understanding of its moral duty. Can one still discern a notion of the white man's burden which consist of civilising (democratising, individualising) the natives?

I am concerned here with questions pertaining to the indirect mechanisms of rule that, according to Miller and Rose, are of such importance in liberal democratic societies, namely 'those that have enabled, or have sought to enable, government at a distance' (1990: 83). Miller and Rose build their argument upon Latour's notion of 'action at a distance' (Latour, 1987: 219) whereby 'domination involves the exercise of a form of intellectual mastery made possible by those at a centre having information about persons and events distant from them' (Miller and Rose, 1990: 83). More interesting for my purposes is the suggestion concerning the functioning of networks which, according to Miller and Rose, involve:

> alliances formed not only because one agent is dependent upon another for funds, legitimacy or some other resource which can be used for persuasion or compulsion,[4] but also because one actor comes to convince another that their problems and goals are intrinsically linked, and that their interests are consonant, that each can solve their difficulties or achieve their ends by joining forces or working along the same lines. (1990: 84)

Such networks or alliances may give an appearance of being made up by equal partners. The chances are, however, that some are more influential in defining the discourses and courses of actions than others. I therefore wish to link this understanding of alliances to Foucault's ideas concerning what he calls governmentality (Foucault, 1991: chapter 4). Although his definition of the concept is far from illuminating, his discursive analysis of European political theory and the exercise of power from the Middle Ages to the present day are of interest. This has inspired others to develop further the notion of governmentality that is grounded in Foucault's 'triangle [of] sovereignty-discipline-government' (1991: 102) and to arrive at (in my view) more fruitful explications than those offered by Foucault. According to Miller and Rose, 'Governmentality is embodied in innumerable deliberate attempts to invent, promote, install and operate mechanisms of rule that will shape the investment decisions of managers or *the child care decisions of parents* in accordance with programmatic aspirations' (1990: 83, my emphasis). This supports my usage of the term 'globalisation' as inherently normative in my study of universal (global) human rights discourses.

Limiting myself to children and children's rights, the normative and universalistic ambition of the operative discourses in this field are clearly apparent. Some degree of attention is at times given to the significance of local ontologies and epistemologies, but in practice such differences are largely ignored. These discourses, moreover, rely on what one might call 'expert knowledge';[5] a tradition of knowledge developed, by and large, without taking account of non-Western traditions. Regardless of country of origin, influential non-Western intellectuals such as, for example, the Indian economist and Nobel laureate Amartya Sen, do not bring the specific local traditions of knowledge to bear on the debates, since the sources of their intellectual training emanate from within the same global (Western) academic traditions. In a background document presented to UNESCO's Division of Philosophy and Ethics in 1999, the author (a South Korean) is explicitly clear on this point. 'Global problems require global values', he states, and

[This is] the impetus behind the present articulation of ethical values and principles viable and needed across cultures and societies. Its task is to identify and forge ethical values and principles into a coherent and dynamic whole adequate to deal with the problems facing humanity. (Kim, 1999: 40)

In other words, local ethical values or morally informed practices are not regarded as relevant for present-day problems. It seems important to explore the ways in which expert knowledge is used, absorbed and transformed as it travels along the networks and alliances established between the centres (UNESCO, UNICEF and The Hague in this case) and the representatives from countries with non-Western cosmologies.[6]

CHALLENGES OF METHODOLOGY

A project such as this raises issues of methodology. How can we as anthropologists contribute to the study of globalisation, which is different from those other disciplines that hitherto have been active in delineating the issues and theories? Much of this literature displays a worrying disregard for empirical realities and leaps all too readily to global explanations – explanations that emanate in an unreflective manner from the same Western intellectual traditions that I am critiquing in this chapter. The anthropological study of international conventions demands a methodological approach that deviates from the traditional ones of long-term fieldwork and participant-observation. Nevertheless, this does not mean that we should abandon all our hard-earned analytical and theoretical insights gained precisely through confronting and dealing with the challenges of long-term fieldwork. Precisely because this material is derived from unconventional sources, I agree with Krohn-Hansen (Chapter 5, this volume) that we 'still need many of the insights developed by the classic anthropology of the twentieth century ... [in particular] we need many of the central ideas of mainstream symbolic anthropology'. But for symbolic analysis to contribute to the study of globalisation, it must be coupled to an historical approach that allows researchers to take account of the changes in the multi-directional flow of ideas and practices. Only history can help a globalised world to emerge. In my own work on transnational adoption, the theoretical anthropological tradition of kinship studies and the more recent developments towards the study of personhood and relatedness have also proving useful. The moral and symbolic universe of procreation – which includes adoption – fits comfortably with such theoretical insights. Our discipline is constituted upon a comparative dimension. The comparative study of the meaning of children and childhood, concepts of personhood, the processes of kinning, and significance attributed to flesh and blood in creating relatedness are all issues that can find useful concepts from within intellectual domain of kinship.[7] We are experienced in delving behind the utterances, seeking patterns in symbols and actions, and identifying the significant in the apparently trivial, in order to construct 'thick descriptions'. Just because this particular project needs to employ unconventional methods, there is no reason to abandon our general expertise.

Apart from concepts and approaches already developed in kinship and symbolic anthropology, the anthropological study of globalisa-tion should seek to elicit meanings from a focus on intentionality within interactive relations, the functions of networks, action at distance and governmentality. In order to do so, in my particular case, it will be necessary to follow some of the paths that necessarily go in both directions – between central legislative bodies and the many organisations charged with executing the codified demands in various countries. The power to verbalise and encode (and instigate measures to enforce) remains at the centre. According to Bauman (1998), in the new global world there is no global power that has replaced that previously exercised by the nation-state, no universal organisation with political and economic authority to counteract the encroachment of private multinational interest. While there is no political or economic global authority, this does not necessarily mean that there may not be – or come into being – moral authorities. Certainly, the increasing support given (in the West) to institutions concerned with diffusing the message of democracy and human rights, and the degree of apparent agreement displayed in most countries – at least at the level of international meetings – would support such an idea. The formulation of rights is integral to a legal process, and invariably legal officials claim a universal status for legal rules. Moreover, 'law essentialises social categories and identities' (Cowan et al., 2001: 6). The extent to which the legislative process in international fora that develop treaties takes account of alternative views of reality will always be an empirical question, but the signs are that, within the two treaties examined in this chapter, the hegemony of Western-derived understandings (with some notable exceptions, see below) went unchallenged.

CHILDREN AND CHILDHOOD: UNIVERSAL OR LOCAL?

Unlike issues pertaining to the preservation of the environment, that of children and their welfare is relatively uncontroversial. Attempts to encode global policies to ensure their quality of life and to legislate for their implementation may represent a starting-point for establishing the indirect mechanisms of rule mentioned above. Just as happened in Europe during the nineteenth century, when a shift occurred in the locus of control over children from the family to public authorities (Cunningham, 1995), so is this happening today on a global scale. Global law now defines the 'best interest of the child'. This was done at the initiative of central Western nation-states, deriving its impetus from Western family laws, and enforced by local public agencies under the beady eyes of the centres. This transfer of authority from family to government is very explicit in the case of transnational adoption. The Hague Convention displays a clear abhorrence (e.g. Article 22) towards so-called private adoptions, that is, those that are carried out without the involvement of various publicly endorsed bodies in either donor or recipient country. A point to note in this connection is that the USA, an active participant in all these fora and the self-appointed guardian of world-wide democracy – has refused to sign both the UN Convention on Children's Rights and the Hague Convention on Intercountry Adoption on the grounds that there is no national support in the country for the involvement of public bodies in matters pertaining to the family.

With the exception of the USA and Somalia, all members of the UN have signed the UN Convention on Children's Rights. The Hague Convention on Intercountry Adoption has been signed by fewer states. While most of the countries who receive children – with the exception of the USA – have signed and ratified the Convention, many of the key providers of children for adoption such as China, South Korea, Ethiopia, Colombia, Guatemala (see below) have not signed it. This convention provoked much more debate than did the UN one, but compromises were found in most instances. Reasons given by Western bureaucrats for the failure of donor countries to sign, namely that this is only a matter of time, or that a particular country has no tradition on signing international treaties, may not be the whole truth. In many countries, transnational adoption is a highly sensitive issue and there is not always consensus within the country as to the practice.

In his erudite study entitled *The History of Children and Childhood in Western Europe since 1500*, the social historian Cunningham makes the point that it is much easier to write a history of childhood than of children for the simple reason that there exists a plethora of literature and pictorial material, such as advice books, fiction and portraiture, philosophy and legislation, which makes it possible to piece together ideas and values amongst particular social groups at different times. It is much more difficult to find out about the actual life being led by children (1995: 2). This point can equally well be applied to the cross-cultural comparative study of childhood and children. But as far as my project is concerned, this does not present a major problem as I am interested in ascertaining social values about children and childhood in different parts of the world and try to contrast these to the humanitarian effort on the part of dominant Western powers in formulating international legislation pertaining to children's rights.

Any definition of rights must necessarily be based on more general notions and values concerning personhood, citizenship, family and state. In order to ascertain the degree of encompassment of Western values it is necessary to conduct comparative studies from selected countries regarding definitions of, and attitudes towards, children. To appreciate the variety in social understandings of children and childhood, one must not only conduct cross-cultural studies, but also set these within a historical frame. I am particularly interested in eliciting differences, both in time and space, in attitudes to the relationship between biological and social explanations of relatedness.

It appears, however, that the extent to which alternative cultural understandings are made relevant in the drafting of international legislation is minimal. It is not controversial to state that political discourses on rights can be traced to the eighteenth century and the work by French and English philosophers. In this chapter I cannot consider the origin and development of these ideas, but I shall discuss how the values that came to the forefront in the UN Declaration on Children's Rights from 1989 and the later Hague Convention on International Adoption express the values currently reigning on the topic of humans, personhood and human rights in general, and children and their rights in particular, among influential groups in the Western world. The logic of universalism is the law. The relationship between morality and law is far from arbitrary. Laws may more or less reflect established moral values and practices, or they may be normative, seeking to change practice and attitudes in the areas to which they apply. In the case of the two conventions considered here, my argument is that they reflect predominant Western values and practices, and that they are normative and they seek to influence the rest of the world to adopt them. At the root of the enterprise lies the unquestioned idea of the unsocial universal man.

My argument will be that this fact in itself can be said to be an expression of the global flow of concepts, which – in this as in many other fields – tend to emanate from the West to be presented to the rest of the world as indisputably good and right. To what extent and in what ways Western values on these matters have been received and contested in the different fora debating the formation of the conventions will be examined in future research. I will further question the role of relative power in the diffusion (globalising) of universal ideas of children's (human) rights. With this in mind I now wish to examine the two international conventions that seek regulate attitudes to, and practices concerning, children.

UN CONVENTION ON THE RIGHTS OF THE CHILD

A watershed in international relations was reached with the UN Convention on Human Rights of 1948. From that time onwards, we have seen a proliferation of charters specifying a number of rights with an increasingly narrow focus. The rights of children was a relatively latecomer, but the UN Convention on the Rights of the Child was adopted in November 1989, and since that time has 'dwarfed all previous international human rights treaties' because the rate of ratification was unprecedented and the Convention could enter into force the following year (Franklin, 1995: ix). According to Franklin, the reason for this acceptance is not difficult to find. It is, he says, because 'it has *a vision*. It expresses some basic values about the treatment of children, their protection and participation in society' (1995: ix, original emphasis). As stated above, only the USA and Somalia have not signed it. In my view, however, to suggest that the Convention expresses some basic values about the treatment of children is highly questionable. Recent work on the history of childhood has shown that the current idea of childhood that stresses domesticity and dependence and tends to romanticise childhood as a time of innocence is largely a recent Western definition (Boyden, 1997: 191; Cunningham, 1995: chapter 7) and one that is not shared by people in many other parts of the world. The Convention came about largely as a result of the UN Year of the Child, which took place in 1979, to be followed by the International Youth Year in the mid-1980s.

Active participants during the Year of the Child were particularly concerned about child labour and the growth in number of street children, and a focus was put on questions about children's rights. Media paid a new attention to concrete cases where, it began to be argued, the interests of children were ignored and questions concerning children's rights were raised. According to Franklin, children's rights were put on the agenda in many fora and achieved 'respectability'. In Britain, children's rights became a politically contested territory where the manifestos of both the Labour and Liberal Democrat parties of 1992 contained proposals for a Ministry of Children, a Children's Rights Commissioner and proposals to reduce the voting age (Franklin, 1995: 3). Similar proposals were discussed in other northern European countries. In 1981, Norway was the first Scandinavian country to establish an ombudsman for Children (Grude Flekkøy, 1995: 176). More recently the key concepts that are advocated globally are those that encourage children's empowerment and agency.

According to Ennew, Western thinking (derived in my argumentation in various ways from changes in and developments of expert knowledge) holds strongly that childhood should take place inside a home, inside a family, a private dwelling, and those that do not conform to this do literally fall outside – outside society, outside childhood (Ennew, 1995: chapter 15). One of the most provoking aspects of childhood to many engaged in work in connection with the Year of the Child were the street children. Ennew argues that they represented the starkest challenge to the Western notion of modern childhood, which, she states, has been globalised through colonialism and later through 'the imperialism of international aid' (1995: 202; see also Boyden, 1997: chapter 9).

In the Preamble to the actual articles of the Convention on the Rights of the Child, we can read some unquestioned assumptions upon which the articles were formulated. Some of the relevant ones in the present context are:

- Recalling that in the Universal Declaration of Human Rights, the UN has proclaimed that childhood is entitled to special care and assistance.
- Convinced that the family, as the fundamental group of society and the natural environment for the growth and well-being of all its members and particularly children ...
- Recognising that the child, for a full and harmonious development of his and her personality, should grow up in a family environment ...
- Considering that the child should be fully prepared to live an *individual* life in society. (my emphasis)

In a somewhat different direction, one that is not pursued in the actual articles of the final Convention, it is stated that there is a need to: 'Tak[e] due account of the importance of the traditions and cultural values of each people for the protection and harmonious development of the child.'

The possible diversity in meaning of the overarching aim expressed in Article 3 of the Convention, 'the best interest of the child shall be a primary consideration' receives no discussion. This same aim is expressed in the Hague Convention on Intercountry Adoption, and in various European national adoption laws, such as the Norwegian one. How actually to interpret what is the best interest of a child has turned out to be problematic at a national level many places. It might therefore be thought that such interpretation would be even more so on an international level. However, I have not found any critical literature that debates the point. Nor have I come across any deliberations as to what the family might be.

Anthropologists researching children and attitudes to children from a comparative point of view tend to agree on an interpretation of the facts and processes that argue for a colonisation by Western concepts and values, that, in effect, has set a universal standard of childhood (Ennew, 1995; James and Prout, 1995). To this I wish to add that, by making the bounded individual the basic unit at the expense of an analytic understanding that persons are constituted through the particularity of their sociality – in turn derived from local cultural and social ideas and practices – a conceptual leap is made from the individual to the universal and the global. In effect, humans are desocialised and deculturised. The most serious effect of such a globalising view necessarily plays down the constituting role of cultural and social understandings and values in the formation of institutions, legal provisions, and social and medical services. This fact is acknowledged to some extent in most circles that are actively engaged in such work. It frequently appears, however, that this knowledge is separated from practice. It continues to be ignored when it comes to actual formulation of bi- or multilateral conventions and in the implementation of them. It is perhaps less acknowledged that, given the fact that the various human rights conventions are thus predicated upon the unquestioned supremacy of the bounded individual, it follows that diagnoses of breaches and suggestions for their handling, invariably are sought in individuals, not in indigenous notions concerning personhood and relatedness. Issues that people in other places might regard as profoundly social in their very nature are not treated as such by people with power to help. I regard this point as particularly significant, especially in light of much current development jargon which stresses the need to be 'recipient oriented'.

THE HAGUE CONVENTION ON PROTECTION OF CHILDREN AND CO-OPERATION IN RESPECT OF INTERCOUNTRY ADOPTION 1993 (IN FORCE FROM 1995)

Having discussed the background to and some relevant points of the UN Declaration on Children's Rights, I now turn to a consideration of the Hague Convention on Intercountry Adoption that was finalised in 1993 and has been in force from 1995. The background to the work on the Convention can be traced back to 1988, when it was first proposed to the permanent Bureau of the Hague Convention to establish a committee to 'prepare a convention on adoption of children coming from abroad ... because substantial numbers of children from economically developing countries are being placed for adoption with families in industrialised countries' (Van Loon, 1994: 15, 17). Article 21 of the UN Convention deals with adoption, both national and transnational. The main point that is reiterated is that adoption shall ensure the best interest of the child, and that 'competent authorities' must take charge of the process. A major concern is to prevent the practice of 'improper financial gain for those involved'. The Hague Convention builds on Article 21, and elaborates the implications of it.

A general survey of the history of the Convention is provided in the introduction to the published proceedings of the Hague Convention (Van Loon, 1994). This includes a consideration of some theoretical issues connected to adoption which show a sensitivity to cultural variation in attitudes, values and practices of the participating countries. In light of this, it is interesting to note that these insights are seemingly forgotten when it comes to formulating the actual provisions, rules for conduct, etc. When disagreements about provisions arose they were primarily between donor countries on the one side and recipient countries on the other. By and large it seems that the values of the recipient countries prevailed. Nevertheless, due to the seriousness of some conflicts of interest, certain compromises were reached on the most controversial points. One of the Norwegian delegates to the conference told me that he attributes the success of the Convention to the fact that controversial issues are left open-ended. There are five main principles that form the basis upon which the Hague Convention is developed:

1. Adoption must be in the best interest of the child.
2. Central authorities and accredited bodies only shall control all intercountry adoption.
3. The subsidiary principle, i.e. adoption can only take place when efforts have been made to place a child with close family or in a family-like environment in the country of origin must be adhered to. But 'intercountry adoption may offer the advantage of a permanent family to a child for whom a suitable family cannot be found in his or her state of origin'.
4. The need to establish cooperation between the countries in order to ensure that children's best interests are looked after and that their basic rights are not violated.
5. Ensure proper procedures in both donor and recipient countries.

BONES OF CONTENTION

Adoption practices exist in some form or another in most societies and are firmly entrenched in the whole social fabric of a society, being integral to the kinship system in each case. It is not surprising therefore that when Western-style written adoption laws have been introduced into non-Western countries, or to sub-groups within a Western country, customary adoption and fostering practices have not easily been straitjacketed into Western models and have, in many instances, continued despite Western-inspired laws. This became clear at the first Australian Conference on Adoption held in 1976. The representatives from Papua New Guinea, from various Pacific islands, from Maori in New Zealand and Aborigine groups in Australia voiced dismay at the thought that adoption would entail permanent alienation not just from the 'immediate family, but from the wider kinship network, as adoption of the child diminishes the family group and is a loss for the wider society' (Van Loon, 1994: 24). In the former French colonies of West Africa, on the other hand, the introduction of the Code Napoléon during colonial times with its provision of a so-called 'simple adoption' (*adoption simple*) that does not lead to a complete severance of bonds with the biological family, and which may also be revoked, corresponds more easily with local practices of fostering (see Bledsoe, 1980; Goody, 1982).

Similarly, in Latin America, where local legal codes were based on the Spanish counterpart of the Code Napoléon, simple adoption, which is in line with many local practices, eased the transfer from customary law to the judicial system. However, this is an option that the Hague Convention has rejected, insisting on the strong version of alienation from biological ties in favour of adoptive ones. As a result, many of the countries which practice some form of 'simple adoption' have declined to ratify the treaty.

Islam further presents an obstacle to strong adoption since the practice is not recognised and therefore most, but not all, Muslim countries forbid it and Muslim children cannot be adopted trans-nationally. Exceptions to this are Tunisia, which changed to secular law in 1958, Turkey, which adheres to a secular legal system, and Indonesia which, strictly speaking, is not a Muslim country. Indonesia, however, made it difficult for foreign couples to adopt by insisting on a previous three-year residence in the country. Other Muslim countries such as Egypt and Syria do not extend their family law provisions to members of other religions. This means that Christians may adopt, but only children born of Christian parents. This insistence on strong adoption was perceived as problematic by several Muslim states when it came to ratifying the Convention. The Kuwaiti representative, for example, stated that:

While some features of adoption are to be found in our laws, they are included in the system of foster care (*kafallah*) which performs its role in the psychological, health, social and educational care of the child. ... In compliance with the koranic injunction 'Call them after their true fathers', a child cannot change its name while in foster care. (Van Loon, 1994: 27)

In other words, artificial filiation bonds are not tolerated. It follows from this that full adoption is not permissible within the Muslim legal system. Strong adoption was hotly debated during the formulation of the text, but the majority went in for no exception, resulting in the Muslim countries remaining outside.

Other difficulties that arose during the debating stage originated from countries like the Philippines that wanted a trial period before the adoption was finalised. Again, this was not acceptable. Furthermore, much debate arose between the needs of recipient and donor countries concerning the information about the child's biological background. Adoption laws in most European countries and in Canada and the USA state the legal right for a child to know his or her biological parentage upon reaching the age of maturity. This is constructed within a human rights mode of argumentation and is viewed as central to one's identity. However, many of the donor countries did not agree – primarily out of a concern with protecting the child's biological mother, but also because this knowledge was not regarded as particularly important. Article 16 is a compromise solution. It states that '1. The Central Authority of the State of origin shall ... prepare a report including information about his or her identity, adoptability, background, social environment, family history, medical history including that of the child's family', but '2. ... taking care not to reveal the identity of the mother and the father if, in the State of origin, these identities may not be disclosed.' In other words, in this case, the attempt to establish hegemony of Western values was defeated.

These two conventions are interesting to compare. Both are idealistic in their aims, both are conceived and formulated out of a Western political philosophy tradition that emphasises the centrality of the bounded individual and his or her rights. But whereas the UN Convention is necessarily very general in its domain of concern, the Hague Convention focuses on one particular limited activity, namely transnational adoption. The Hague Convention is therefore more specific in its background statement of intent, activating as it were the intentions of the UN Convention, and it is highly specific about procedure.

As was the case with the UN Declaration on Children's Rights, the Hague Convention is formulated on an unproblematised 'best interest of the child'. Both conventions endorse the idea that the best environment for the 'full and harmonious development of his or her personality, [the child] should grow up in a family environment, in an atmosphere of happiness, love and understand-ing'. Furthermore, the responsibility to ensure such conditions for every child is placed upon the state.

THE IMMORALITY OF MONEY

The background to the Hague Convention was an acknowledgement of the rapid increase in transnational adoption from the South to the North. The initiators expressed a desire to regulate the practice, so that abduction of, and trafficking in, children for economic gain could be controlled. In light of the overall argument of this chapter that, despite many avowals to the contrary, Western moral ideas continue to dictate international treaties, this abhorrence of monetary transactions in domains characterised as belonging outside economic considerations is of interest.

The exchange of children for money is regarded as particularly morally reprehensible. This runs as a thread through the Hague Convention and is a major reason for the continued surveillance of those countries that supply children for transnational adoption. A good example of attempts to control the buying and selling of children is the Convention's actions with regard to Guatemala. Guatemala has not signed the Convention, but was present at its inception. Reports sent to headquarters in The Hague indicate that the situation in Guatemala is far from satisfactory. Corrupt agents and lawyers, together with eager prospective adoptive parents, bring about the transfer of large sums of money in exchange for adoptees. The Hague has asked recipient member countries to put pressure on the Guatemalan authorities to improve their ways by refusing to adopt children from the country. The Norwegian government has listened to the appeal and, as of 2001, has imposed a moratorium on adoptions from Guatemala.

While I have no wish to endorse the buying and selling children, I wish to reiterate a point forcefully made by Bloch and Parry in the introduction to the volume *Money and the Morality of Exchange* (1989). They emphasise the not unfamiliar point that there exists enormous cultural variation in the way that money is symbolised and the way in which this symbolism relates to culturally constructed notions of production, circulation and exchange (Bloch and Parry, 1989: 1). There is no doubt that money is symbolically represented differently in different countries and the moral weight attributed to money and monetary transactions – or transactions that include, *inter alia*, money – as opposed to other exchanges, also varies. According to Bloch and Parry, one may discern a prominent strand in Western discourse that can be traced back to Aristotle – a general condemnation of money and trade compared with household self-sufficiency and production for use (1989: 2, see also Hart, 2001). The introduction of money can be said to represent a kind of watershed, but rather than arguing (like Simmel) that money gives rise to a particular world-view, I agree with Bloch and Parry when they state that 'an existing world view gives rise to particular ways of representing money' (1989: 19). Despite the fact that money is usually described as all-purpose abstract money, as opposed to various manifestations of so-called 'primitive' money, which are linked to spheres of exchange, the transfer of money is not regarded as appropriate in certain social encounters, particularly where people are involved.

Having made the distinction between gifts and commodities which perhaps may be analogous to the Christian distinction between that which is God's ('gifts') and that which is Caesar's ('commodities'), Western thinking on the matter has continued in this vein. People are not commodities to be bought and sold. Such dichotomous thinking underpins much development aid as well as international treaties and conventions that have human rights intent. It is certainly very much present in the treaties concerning children's rights and transnational adoption.[8] In the debates leading up to the Hague Convention, one contested point became how to define necessary expenses in the donor country. To what extent recipient countries may give gifts to institutions in donor countries without this becoming corruption continues to be a bone of contention. The situation with regard to human rights is very different. There is no disagreement between the various globalising agencies over the meaning and usage of alternative interpretations.[9] Human rights sprang out of a political philosophical discourse and their present formulations are the result of debate from the start. Today, only mad dogs and (some) anthropologists question the *inherent* rightness of the various declarations on rights.

TO CONCLUDE

The argument of this chapter, which future research will explore further, has been that the global humanitarians today, like the Christian missionaries before them, do not question the moral rightness of their activities. Regarding the human world as one made up of x number of individuals and disregarding the multiplicity of cosmologically constructed human solutions to existential questions, their agenda is normative. However benevolent their motives might be, the Western Christian missionaries and the Western humanitarian bureaucrats and activists work towards the global enforcement of Western ideas and values.

I wish to conclude by summing up some of my concerns and some of my tentative arguments regarding the topic at hand, namely the codification of global (one-world) regulations that pertain to the universal rights of children and the methodological approach that may be pursued in studying this as part of globalisation. From my examination of the final versions of the UN Convention on Children's Rights and the Hague Convention on Intercountry Adoption, as well as the reports of debates preceding the formulations and the subsequent reports on success or otherwise submitted by countries that ratified them, I suggest that things have not always been running as smoothly as some would like us to think. There is no doubt that the instigators in both cases are people from the rich, developed North whose moral commitment is to safeguard what they regard as children's interests. What constitutes children, childhood, and the best interest of the child are all defined according to contemporary Western ideology, derived to a large extent from current psychological thinking. Those involved have chosen to disregard the variety of moralities and cosmologies in favour of assumed universal values, something that often results in ontological incompatibilities (see the epigraph to the chapter).

My main purpose has been to identify and disentangle some of the paradoxes that necessarily arise in the processes of the diffusion of global values, and to identify the anthropological contribution towards a different understanding of the issues. The challenge is to avoid cultural fundamentalism (see Krohn-Hansen, Chapter 5 in this volume) while at the same time insisting that proper account is taken of alternative cosmologies and moralities. This means that the study of globalisation (however defined) should be undertaken with proper recognition of the analytic significance of kinship, history and symbolic anthropology. In my particular study of international conventions on children, the concept of governmentality, understood as a process by which ideas and values are diffused through alliances formed between powers at the centre and the less-powerful elsewhere, is helpful in analysing the processes. Governmentality helps construct a perception of the goals of actions as intrinsically linked and mutually supportive. Understood in this way, governmentality becomes then an integral effect of liberal democratic governing processes. However, for it to be usefully employed analytically, it seems to me that we must hold on to an understanding of it as being 'embodied in innumerable deliberate attempts to invent, promote, install and operate mechanisms of rules that will shape ... aspirations ... in accordance with programmatic aspirations' (Miller and Rose, 1999: 84). Such a view supports my contention, made at the outset, that discourses on rights applied globally today may be regarded as equivalent to the Christian sense of duty to educate and convert during colonial times. However, the group carrying the white man's burden has been extended to incorporate selected non-whites and non-Christians who have come to share the vision that continues to emanate from the West.

NOTES

1. I am fully aware of the justified critique of separating the world into 'the West and the rest' (see Krohn-Hansen, Chapter 5 in this volume). However, for my present purposes it makes sense to maintain such a division since my argument rests upon a constituting dominance of a Western (European and North American) intellectual tradition. My point is that while this tradition was developed in the West, its ambitions have become global.

2. This focus is chosen because I have been conducting research on trans-national adoption in Norway. In per capita terms, Norway adopts more children from poor countries in Africa, Asia, Latin America and Eastern Europe than any other country.

3. 'Strictly speaking, missionaries are people sent to other countries to extend religious teaching and institutions.... [T]he term can also refer to prose-lytisers ... who work on behalf of humanitarian as well as religious causes' (Taylor, 1996: 373). Since the beginning of Western expansion, Christian

missionaries have been important parties in the encounter between the West and people in all other parts of the world. From an early conversion by force to a perception of missionary work as inseparable from humanitarian and educational work, Christianity has become a global religion. Mission schools, clinics, transportation, water supply and economic development projects have been initiated under the aegis of missionary groups, and have resulted in transformed way of life throughout the world and profound changes in conceptions about reality, sociality and personhood. Moreover, missionaries have acted as a kind of two-way filter for understanding the unknown others. Through this filter 'heathens' everywhere have come to understand Western ideas and way of life, and people in the West were given their understanding of non-Christian peoples through the eyes of the missionaries. In both instances, Western ideas, values and practices became the norm and local ones were subjected to a moral critique and, usually, rejected.

4. Though in my dealing with conventions on human and children's rights, this is clearly an important aspect.

5. As ordained priests, the missionaries were, in a sense, their own sources for expert knowledge. Human rights activists or bureaucrats are, in most cases, dependent on others in the formulation of their arguments, primarily philosophers, political scientists and psychologists – disciplines that are not well-known for their sympathy towards cultural relativism.

6. A research project which explores some of these issues (the CANDID Project) is currently under way at the Centre for Development and Environment, University of Oslo under the direction of D. McNeill and M. Bøås.

7. In this project I rely heavily on texts. My main sources in this project are the conventions themselves. Of more interest still are transcripts of hearings from debates about the formation of the wording of the treaties or conventions, the background notes and follow-up documents, media commentary, subsequent reports on the application of the rulings in different countries as well as documents that highlight different aspects of the implementation – or lack of implementation – of the rulings in various countries. These are only some of the sources of knowledge

8. An ethnographic example from my own research among the Lio of eastern Indonesia demonstrates some of the moral conflicts that may arise when Westerners encounter alien symbolisation of the meaning of money. Dutch Catholic missionaries strongly disapproved of the Lio bride-wealth system that quickly included money into the category of wealth to be transferred from wife-receivers to wife-givers – the indigenous practice of *belis*. Lio kinship represents a fairly classic example of a matrilateral cross-cousin prescriptive alliance system. Women move in one direction, wealth and services in the other. In this the Dutch missionaries saw a system of men buying wives. Despite the fact that the majority of the population today has been converted to Catholicism, people continue to practice *belis* and money, due to a shortage of gold and buffaloes, is becoming the main part of *belis*. Missionaries fail to understand the wider implications of the system, which gives rise to alliance exchanges of goods and services that stretch far beyond the actual marriage itself, and is not thought of as a commercial transaction. The example demonstrated the way Western thinking constructs money as inherently immoral and the need to separate it from domains that must be kept morally pure.

9. A possible contestant to the human rights agenda may be the proposition of 'Asian values' that was developed in the 1980s in Singapore, Malaysia, and other South-East Asian nation-states in direct confrontation with what was presented by heads of state as a hegemonising effort on the part of former colonial powers.

REFERENCES

Bauman, Z. 1998. *Globalization: The Human Consequences*. New York: Columbia University Press.

Bledsoe, C. 1980. *Women and Marriage in Kpelle Society*. Stanford, CA: Stanford University Press.

Bloch, M. and J. Parry. 1989. *Money and the Morality of Exchange*. Cambridge: Cambridge University Press.

Boyden, J. 1997. Childhood and the policy makers: a comparative perspective on the Globalisation of childhood. In A. James and A. Prout (eds) *Constructing and Reconstructing Childhood*. London: Falmer Press.

Cowan, J.K., M.-B. Dembour and R.A. Wilson (eds). 2001. *Culture and Rights: Anthropological Perspectives*. Cambrdige: Cambridge University Press.

Cunningham, H. 1995 *Children and Childhood in Western Society since 1500*. London: Longman.

Dumont, L. 1979. The anthropological community and ideology, *Social Science Information* 18(6): 785–817.

Ennew, J. 1995. Outside childhood: street children's rights. In B. Franklin (ed.) *Childrens Rights: Comparative Policy and Practice*. London: Routledge.

Foucault, M. 1991. Governmentality. In G. Burchell, C. Gordon and P. Miller (eds) *The Foucault Effect: Studies in Governmentality*. London: Harvester Wheatsheaf.

Franklin, B. 1995. *Children's Rights: Comparative Policy and Practice*. London: Routledge.

Hart, K. 2001. *Money in an Unequal World*. New York: Texere.

Goody, E. 1982. *Parenthood and Social Reproduction: Fostering and Occupational Roles in West Africa*. Cambridge: Cambridge University Press.

Grude Flekkøy, M. 1995. The Scandinavian experience of childhood. In B. Franklin (ed.) *Children's Rights: Comparative Policy and Practice*. London: Routledge.

James, A. and A. Prout (eds). 1997. *Constructing and Reconstructing Childhood*. London: Falmer Press.

Kim, Y. 1999. *A Common Framework for the Ethics of the 21st Century*. Paris: UNESCO.

Latour, B. 1987. *Science in Action: How to Follow Scientists and Engineers through Society*. Milton Keynes: Open University Press.

Miller, P. and N. Rose 1990. Governing economic life. In G. Burchell, C. Gordon and P. Miller (eds) *The Foucault Effect: Studies in Governmentality*. London: Harvester Wheatsheaf.

Taylor, H. 1996 Missionaries. In A. Barnard and J. Spencer (eds) *Encyclopedia of Social Anthropology*. London: Routledge.

Van Loon, J.H.A. 1994. Report on intercountry adoption. *Proceedings of the Seventeenth Session, 10 to 29 May 1993*. Hague Conference on Private International Law. The Hague: SDU Publishers.

12 EPILOGUE: STUDYING WORLD SOCIETY

Keith Hart

Cosmopolitan Right shall be limited to Conditions of Universal Hospitality [the right of a stranger not to be treated with hostility when he arrives on someone else's territory]....

The peoples of the earth have entered in varying degree into a universal community, and it has developed to the point where a violation of rights in *one* part of the world is felt *everywhere*. The idea of a cosmopolitan right is not fantastic and overstrained; it is a necessary complement to the unwritten code of political and international right, transforming it into a universal right of humanity. (Immanuel Kant, *Perpetual Peace: A Philosophical Sketch*, 1795)

Anthropologists are now studying transnational society, as this volume demonstrates admirably. For some time now I have been wondering what it would be like to study *world society* (see the Appendix on Terms of Association). These brief concluding notes point to some of the methods we might adopt to that end. Method comes from Greek *meta-hodos*, meaning before (or after) the road, preparation for a journey or perhaps its destination. Each of us makes an idiosyncratic journey through life and absorbs a personal version of society in the process. The life journeys of anthropologists are more varied than most. So, what version of society do we end up with and how? Could it be improved upon if some of us made it an explicit vocation to study world society as such?

Our journey is both outward into the world and inward into the self. Each of us, as Durkheim (1965/1912) said, is at once collective and individual. Society is mysterious to us because we have lived in it and it now dwells inside us at a level that is not ordinarily visible from the perspective of everyday life. Writing is one way we try to bring the two into some mutual understanding that we can share with others. Ethnographic fieldwork, requiring us to participate in local society as we observe it, adds to our range of social experience, becomes an aspect of our socialisation, brings lived society into our sources of introspection. Now it is feasible for some individuals to leave different social experiences in separate compartments; but one method for understanding world society would be to make an ongoing practice of trying to synthesise these varied experiences. If a person would have an identity, would be one thing, oneself, this entails an attempt to integrate all the fragments of social experience into a more coherent whole, a world in other words, as singular as the self.

So there are as many worlds as there are individuals and their journeys; and, even if there were only one out there, each of us changes it whenever we make a move. This model of Kantian subjectivity, at once personal and cosmopolitan, should be our starting-point; but it will not do for the study of world society. For much of my professional life, I have shadowed the African diaspora through an Atlantic world whose defining moment was slavery: England, Ghana, the Cayman islands, Liberia, the USA, Canada, Jamaica, South Africa, France, Scotland, Brazil, Norway. At some point – it was actually in Jamaica in 1986–88 – I realised that what I was learning in the Caribbean helped me to integrate the other three legs of my journey to date (Europe, West Africa and North America), to see a pattern of relations. I saw how America was 'new', Europe and Africa 'old' and the Caribbean somehow both; and my guide was C.L.R. James who had travelled between all four points himself, leaving behind a series of books that were a revelation to me (Grimshaw, 1992).

I was sitting on a beach in Jamaica reading a collection of C.L.R. James's occasional writings on cricket. The place had once belonged to Errol Flynn. My daughter was playing at the edge of the sea. James had been Neville Cardus's deputy as the *Manchester Guardian*'s cricket correspondent in the 1930s. I found myself reading about my father's heroes in the Lancashire cricket team of that period as if it was today's sports news. I had been devouring everything I could by James since I had arrived in Jamaica to help establish a new graduate school for social science research. I knew that he had lived in Lancashire when he left Trinidad for Britain. It occurred to me that we had lived in the same places – the Caribbean, Britain, America, Africa – in a different sequence, at different times and with very different trajectories. Now, watching my daughter play on that exotic beach, with my father's stories from childhood coming alive again, the gap between this old black man and myself was collapsed into a single moment by the compelling immediacy of James's prose. Generation and racial difference were erased in an epiphany of timeless connection. I felt compelled to meet him and so I wrote the first and only fan letter of my life.

I trace my self-reinvention as an anthropologist, the origin of this short chapter, to that moment. Later, I was able to place myself at different points in this journey by an act of the imagination, even in several places at once. I think of this visualising process as 'cubist', the ability to see the picture from several perspectives at once (Berger, 1992). Caribbean people, whose history of movement has never given them the security of viewing the world from one place, developed this capacity without benefit of art or anthropology. I have long felt that the collective slogans under which my anthropologist colleagues make professional claims on the public are much less rich and interesting that their individual lives. And, if we look at the chapters in this volume, it is not obvious that 'ethnography' is their common source. Marianne Lien's chapter is methodologically very coherent and makes the case for repeated fieldwork visits over time to the same heterogeneous and globally connected place. But, although Christian Krohn-Hansen refers to two books by anthropologists and indirectly to his own Caribbean research, his chapter is a complex rumination on national identity that smacks more of the study than the field. Signe Howell reflects on her personal and professional concern with adoption, on missionaries, colonialism and human rights, the Hague Convention, etc. Sarah Lund lived in the United States as a Norwegian-American and was still planning to do fieldwork there when she wrote her chapter. And so on. This is not to say that I or any of these authors don't have a complex relationship to the ethnographic tradition, just that our methods and sources are much broader and more idiosyncratic than we often let on.

Atlantic history has some claim to being the crucible of modern world history; but it is not the world. Nor is movement in the world – transnational flows or whatever – the world itself. How can we approach world society as a whole? Well, we can give it a singular name. Bush the Elder announced, after the fall of the Berlin Wall, that we now live in a New World Order. Later, in their bestseller of that name, Michael Hardt and Antonio Negri announced the arrival of *Empire* (2000), a united form of global sovereignty meant to supervise a neo-liberal world economy. Almost immediately, the destruction of the World Trade Center played on television screens everywhere and we learnt that we were all to be part of Bush the Younger's 'war on terrorism', even if this hardly seemed to be the denationalised version of universal sovereignty that Hardt and Negri had in mind. It does not pay to confuse social reality with simple ideas; and I for one can only think of the unity of world society as more potential than factual.

We tend to think and talk of society as an economy these days. Globalisation is usually taken to refer to the reduction of political barriers to trade and the consequent freedom of capital to move where it will. Certainly networks established through buying and selling are more far-reaching than ever before, lending some credibility to the idea of a 'world market'. And money itself, increasingly detached from any objective form, circulates the globe without territorial restriction, a rising tide capable of swamping national economies at any time (Hart, 2001). This apotheosis of capital is closely tied to the development of global communications. The convergence of telephones, television and computers into a single digital technology has already produced as its great symbol the Internet, the network of networks, expanding faster than any previous innovation in this field. Mobile telephones have brought instant communication to places where expensive landlines were underdeveloped. And global TV audiences for major sporting events are well over the 2 billion mark, meaning that as many people now sometimes watch the same thing at once as were alive on the planet in 1945.

Mention of the population explosion should remind us that statistics were invented to allow states to count their people. It would have seemed odd in 1861 to generalise in quantitative terms about some feature of the Italian people as a whole; but we now easily absorb the information that Italian women have the lowest fertility rate in the world. United Nations organisations have been collecting statistics about world population for some time; but we are not yet habituated to think in terms of them, except perhaps for the total (6 billion and climbing ...). Quantity has been made social in some areas more than others. Counting heads, money, time or energy is more plausible than measuring the quality of life, for example, although this has not prevented many from attempting the latter task.

When it comes to saying something about world society using these indicators, there is much controversy concerning the measures used. But the real issue is whether we think the present condition of humanity is scandalous or not. Thus Robert Wade (2001), against the prevailing orthodoxy that the liberalisation of markets is the best antidote to poverty, has attempted to establish that world society is growing more unequal. I have suggested (Hart, 2002) that the world is divided into a club of rich countries (the OECD), constituting about 15 per cent of the global population, and the rest, the poor masses who have hardly any money to spend (45 per cent have less than $2 a day to live on). Moreover, this division is marked by race, region, age and gender as well as by wealth, leading me to argue that contemporary world society resembles nothing so much as the old regime of pre-revolutionary France.

We can say something about the changing morphology of human society too. Anthropologists have known about social networks at least since the Manchester School (Bott, 1954). But the idea that social relations are now more readily constituted as open-ended networks than as closed corporate hierarchies (see the Appendix under 'society') is more recent. No one has done more to argue the case than Manuel Castells (2001: 1–2):

A network is a set of interconnected nodes. Networks are very old forms of human practice, but they have taken on a new life in our time by becoming information networks, powered by the Internet. Networks have extraordinary advantages as organizing tools because of their inherent flexibility and adaptability, critical features in order to survive and prosper in a fast-changing environment. This is why networks are proliferating in all domains of the economy and society, outcompeting and outperforming vertically organized corporations and centralized bureaucracies.... Networks were primarily the reserve of private life; centralized hierarchies were the fiefdoms of power and production. Now, however, the introduction of computer-based information and communications technologies, and particularly the Internet, enables networks to deploy their flexibility and adaptability, thus asserting their evolutionary nature. At the same time, these technologies allow the coordination of tasks, and the management of complexity. This results in an unprecedented combination of flexibility and task performance, of coordinated decision-making and decentralized execution, of individualized expression and global, horizontal communication, which provide a superior organizational form for human action.

The implications of this idea for the study of world society are profound, even if its premises may be challenged. Is this the catalyst inaugurating Kant's Perpetual Peace, the cosmopolitan society whose human preconditions he explored in his *Anthropology* (1977/1798), for the sake of which he invented the name of our discipline? Are we reaching the end of a world system of territorial states? If so, how will the law be administered? One way would be for networks to constitute themselves as self-regulating clubs. Notions of justice can be disseminated without a centralised administration. Nor should we imagine that network society is necessarily non-hierarchical or open, for that matter. A recent popular science text, *Linked: The New Science of Networks* (Barabasi, 2002) claims that 'scaled networks' in a wide range of fields – social, technological and biological – conform to a mathematical model known as a power rule in which a few nodes (hubs) are highly connected and most are only weakly so. Think of the air transport network of the United States, for example, with its O'Hares and thousands of small airports. Such a model would explain why, left to its own devices, a world economy made up of unregulated market networks is becoming more connected and more unequal at the same time (Hart, 2001).

It is not as if the problem of managing the infrastructure of world society would be entirely new. We already have the precedent of global institutions devised in the twentieth century, after the First and Second World Wars. But there are others too. Several countries or federations of states are so large, so diverse and so self-contained as to constitute worlds in their own right. The United States, Russia, China, India and Brazil come to mind, while the European Union is the most dynamic political experiment on the planet. We could add to these examples some of the larger states formed in temperate zones by the British and Spanish empires or indeed any polity predicated on combining diversity. If we want to imagine what a world society might look like, we could examine these cases and ask which features should be adopted on a more inclusive scale. For our task is to make a better world society than the one we have, defined as it is by the myopia of national consciousness (Fanon, 1970/1959). We will discover that the modern principle of federalism is as old as that of the nation-state and much better suited to wide political association. The original word for society itself, *societas*, was for the Latins a loose-knit federal network, much less centralised than the federations of the United States or Switzerland.

Making a better society means using the imagination for purposes of *fiction*, the construction of possible worlds out of actual experience. And this should remind us that thinking about the macrocosm is made easier through contemplation of microcosms. Alienation is an inability to make a meaningful link between ourselves and the world; and we need symbolic devices to bridge that gap. Works of fiction provide us with such devices. Novels and movies compress the world into a narrow stereotyped format that we enter subjectively on our own terms. In doing so, we encounter history without that crushing sense of being overwhelmed by remote forces. Whereas old versions of the universal (the Catholic Church, European empires, economics) sought to dominate and replace particular varieties, the new universal will only be reproduced through cultural particulars. Great works of fiction show us this new concept of the universal, becoming more general as they plunge deeper into the circumstances of particular times and places. I have long thought that an anthropology of fiction would ask, not how specific works represent real societies, but how they construct convincing worlds of their own. The same question could be posed of the best ethnographies. And as a precedent for such an inquiry we could turn to Rousseau's extraordinary inventions of the 1760s: the *Social Contract*, *Émile*, the *New Heloïse* and the *Confessions*, through which he revolutionised European thinking about politics, education, sexuality and the self, each time with a new genre of fiction and each time pointing to a better world.

If society is hard to imagine, because it is inside us, not out there as we often believe, then we can follow Durkheim's prescription and make an external object of it, as nature (Durkheim, 1965/1912). The world may be considered scientifically as an ecology, a biological system, our habitat and home; and humanity is that part of life on earth that can think, the frontal lobes of the biomass. This confers on our species a certain duty of stewardship (Rappaport, 1999). And it does seem that a green political agenda is more likely to mobilise humanity to do something about worsening world conditions than any attempt to address global social problems directly. I like to pose the following hypothetical question. Which news item is more likely to provoke the public's moral indignation: grey seals dying of oil pollution in the North Sea or a Mozambican killed by skinheads in East Germany? It is really no contest, since nature is out there and racism is inside all of us. Again, if global warming does melt the ice caps, the fate of coastal cities will be urgent enough perhaps to provoke some sort of global framework for collective action to materialise eventually. Humanity has apparently survived the threat of nuclear holocaust, for now, in part because it provoked a substantial international peace movement. Here then is one likely focus for a world society animated by activist networks – the mitigation of global risks (Beck, 1992).

At another level, the last half century saw us leave the planet's surface for the first time and generated concrete images of how the earth looks from outer space, a powerful symbol of human unity indeed. And natural science locates that unity in an intellectual vision that has given us, among other things, the machine revolution whose uneven development is the underlying fact of the last two centuries, drawing humanity into ever closer association. There are those (e.g. Latour, 2002) who would assimilate this 'mononaturalism' and its twin, a condescending multiculturalism (we understand the unity of nature, so they can have their little cultures) to a vision of Western imperialism. Certainly there are few anthropologists today ready to sign up for the hegemony of natural science. So here too we have a pressing topic for discussion when we study world society.

What has anthropology been until now and what might it become? It began in the eighteenth century as a philosophy of human nature, asking what humanity has in common that might replace the arbitrary social differences of the old regime as a basis for living together. This Enlightenment vision underpinned the democratic revolutions of the period. The dominant paradigm shifted in the nineteenth century in order to explain a Western imperialism fuelled by machines. The Victorians found the world to be constituted as a racial hierarchy and they studied it by means of evolutionary history. After the First World War, the principle of nationalism was established everywhere and anthropology's chief method shifted as a result to ethnography, to writing about peoples considered to be naturally bounded units, symbolic microcosms of the nation-state. There was no world society as such in the twentieth century, just the wars of nations and their subsequent attempts to form associations with themselves as principal actors.

So what might anthropology become in the twenty-first century? My guess is that the general premise of universal movement will lead people to seek stable order in the least and most inclusive levels of human existence, that is the self as an identity and the world as a unity; and especially in the construction of a meaningful relationship between the two. This is close to Durkheim's idea of religion as a bridge between the known and the unknown. We are each unique personalities and the world is, at least potentially, composed of humanity as a whole. We have hitherto put an enormous effort into exploring the varieties of classification and association that mediate these extremes. This was not the priority of the liberal founders of anthropology and it may not be the priority of students in future. If I were to name what the focus of a future anthropology might be, I would choose 'subjects in history' or perhaps 'self-in-the-world'.

There would be plenty of scope in such an anthropology for a world history whose antecedents cross-cut the discipline's previous periods and paradigms. Rousseau's *Discourse on the Origins and Foundations of Inequality among Men* (1984/1754) could well be taken as the basic text for an historical anthropology of unequal world society, with Morgan (1964/1877) and Engels (1968/1884) providing nineteenth-century versions of the same and Jack Goody, among others, updating the project for late twentieth-century audiences (see Hart, 2003). But our contemporary concern with subjectivity will require such grand narratives to be accompanied by individual and collective life histories of the sort pioneered by Sidney Mintz in *Worker in the Cane* (1960) and Richard Werbner in *Tears of the Dead* (1991). Or they could be expressed in the form of novels and movies, of course.

Finally, one might ask what anthropologists would actually do when they study world society. Let us assume that ethnographic fieldwork of the kind with which we are now familiar will remain an important source of professional knowledge. But this practice is coming under considerable political pressure. Each us of us will try to resolve this problem in our own way. In my own case, I restricted the method of prolonged fieldwork to one stay in Ghana of two and half years, when I started out. Since then, I have preferred to visit new places under the auspices of a job rather than as a researcher. People expect visitors to do something for them these days and I would rather struggle with the bias of a known public position than try to explain that I am not a CIA spy. I have been most often a teacher or a development consultant in the employ of governments or international agencies. For the last five years, I have lived in Paris without either a job there or any pretension of carrying out local research. Wherever I am, I read a lot and I write. In recent years, I have begun to explore the possibilities of the Internet, of web searches and email. It is becoming ever more feasible to make universal connection without physical movement, without leaving home. All of this adds up to social experience. I make an anthropology out of that. Fortunately, I have had institutional support for this pretension. As Meyer Fortes said, after he helped to set up his trade union, the Association of Social Anthropologists of the UK, 'Social anthropology is what social anthropologists do' and he had the means of establishing their credentials. I am acutely aware that this trajectory is not readily available to others entering the discipline now. I just hope that each takes personal advantage of the historical opportunities and is not crushed by the constraints.

I have made a case in this Epilogue for research and writing in anthropology to be existentially motivated. The truth of social experience is always local, but we need to extend ourselves to grasp what kind of world society we live in. Such a global society is constituted by power relations, but the bridge to an understanding of our common humanity is moral. Morality is the ability to make personal judgements about the good and bad behaviour of people, including ourselves. Anthropology ought to be a means of helping us to do that more effectively. There is no guarantee that people in the future will want to employ experts on the human condition trading under a five-syllable word of Greek origin. But if they do, I hope they will ask anthropologists to make world society personally meaningful for their students and the public.

APPENDIX   TERMS OF ASSOCIATION

Associate	To connect or join together; combine
Society	The totality of social relationships linking a large group of human beings
Societas	(Latin) A league of allies committed to mutual support in the event of an attack on one of them (*sokw-yo* from root *sekw-* to follow)
Société	(Medieval French) a bounded unit with a single centre, i.e. a state
State	Society centralised as a single agency
Territory	The land and waters under the jurisdiction of a state
Nation	A people who share a state
Federation	A union in which power is divided between a central authority and the constituent political units

Corporation	A group of people combined into or acting as one body
Community	A sense of belonging to a group; people united by a common purpose
Social network	An open-ended, often informal set of interconnections
Market	A social network constituted by buying and selling
The Internet	The network of networks; the system of global communications
Civilisation	The ethical, rational and cultural standards by which a great people live
Humanity	A collective noun for all people, past, present and future; a quality of kindness
World	The earth with its inhabitants; universe; human society; people as a whole; all that relates to or affects the life of a person
World society	The totality of social relationships linking the inhabitants of earth

[Based loosely on *The American Heritage Dictionary of the English Language*, 1996]

REFERENCES

Barabasi, A.-L. 2002. *Linked: The New Science of Networks*. Cambridge: Perseus.

Beck, U. 1992. *Risk Society: Towards a New Modernity*. London: Sage.

Berger, J. 1992. *Success and Failure of Picasso*. London: Granta.

Bott, E. 1954. *Family and Social Network*. London: Tavistock.

Castells, M. 2001. *The Internet Galaxy*. Oxford: Oxford University Press.

Durkheim, E. 1965/1912. *The Elementary Forms of the Religious Life*. Glencoe, IL: Free Press.

Engels, F. 1968/1884. *The Origin of the Family, Private Property and the State*. London: Lawrence & Wishart.

Fanon, F. 1970/1959. *The Wretched of the Earth*. Harmondsworth: Penguin.

Grimshaw, A. (ed.) 1992. *The C.L.R. James Reader*. Oxford: Blackwell.

Hardt, M. and A. Negri 2000. *Empire*. Cambridge, MA: Harvard University Press.

Hart, K. 2001. *Money in an Unequal World*. New York and London: Texere.

—— 2002. World society as an old regime. In C. Shore and S. Nugent (eds) *Elite Cultures: Anthropological Approaches*. London: Routledge.

—— 2003. Agrarian civilization and modern world society. In J. Cole and D. Olson (eds) *Festschrift for Jack Goody*. Cambridge: Cambridge University Press.

Kant, I. 1795. *Perpetual Peace: A Philosophical Sketch*. Various editions.

—— 1977/1798. *Anthropology from a Pragmatic Point of View*. Carbondale: University of Southern Illinois Press.

Latour, B. 2002. *The War of the Worlds*. Chicago: Prickly Paradigm Press.

Mintz, S. 1960. *Worker in the Cane: A Puerto Rican Life History*. New Haven, CT: Yale University Press.

Morgan, L.H. 1964/1877. *Ancient Society*. Cambridge, MA: Bellknap Press.

Rappaport, R. 1999. *Ritual and Religion in the Making of Humanity*. Cambridge: Cambridge University Press.

Rousseau, J.J. 1984/1754. *Discourse on Inequality*. Harmondsworth: Penguin.

Wade, R. 2001. *Is Globalization Making World Income Distribution More Equal?* London: LSE Development Studies Institute Working Paper Series, No. 01–01.

Werbner, R. 1991. *Tears of the Dead: The Social Biography of an African Family*. Edinburgh: Edinburgh University Press.

CONTRIBUTORS

Simone Abram is Lecturer at the Department of Town and Regional Planning, University of Sheffield.

Thomas Hylland Eriksen is Professor of Social Anthropology, University of Oslo.

Ulf Hannerz is Professor of Social Anthropology, University of Stockholm.

Keith Hart is Senior Research Fellow at the Arkleton Centre for Rural Development Research, University of Aberdeen.

Signe Howell is Professor of Social Anthropology, University of Oslo.

Christian Krohn-Hansen is Senior Lecturer of Social Anthropology, University of Oslo.

Marianne Lien is Senior Lecturer of Social Anthropology, University of Oslo.

Sarah Lund is Professor of Social Anthropology, University of Oslo.

Marit Melhuus is Professor of Social Anthropology, University of Oslo.

Daniel Miller is Professor of Material Culture, University College London.

Knut Nustad is Senior Lecturer of Social Anthropology, University of Oslo.

Karen Fog Olwig is Reader of Anthropology, University of Copenhagen.

Don Slater is Senior Lecturer of Sociology at Goldsmiths College, University of London.

INDEX

Compiled by Sue Carlton